The Secret Message of
JULES VERNE

DECODING HIS MASONIC, ROSICRUCIAN, AND OCCULT WRITINGS

MICHEL LAMY

Translated by Jon E. Graham

Destiny Books
Rochester, Vermont

Destiny Books
One Park Street
Rochester, Vermont 05767
www.DestinyBooks.com

Destiny Books is a division of Inner Traditions International

Originally published in French under the title *Jules Verne, Initié et initiateur* by Éditions Payot, 106, bd Saint-Germain, 75006 Paris
First U.S. edition published in 2007 by Destiny Books

Library of Congress Cataloging-in-Publication Data
Lamy, Michel, 1948–
[Jules Verne, initié et initiateur. English]
   The secret message of Jules Verne : decoding his Masonic, Rosicrucian, and occult writings / Michel Lamy ; translated by Jon E. Graham.
      p. cm.
   Includes bibliographical references and index.
   ISBN-13: 978-1-59477-161-3 (pbk.)
   ISBN-10: 1-59477-161-8 (pbk.)
   1. Verne, Jules, 1828–1905—Knowledge—Occultism. 2. Occultism—France—Rennes-le-Château. 3. Treasure-trove—France—Rennes-le-Château. 4. Rennes-le-Château (France)—History—Miscellanea. 5. Occultism in literature. 6. Free-masons—In literature. 7. Rosicrucians in literature. 8. Illuminati in literature. 9. Voyages, Imaginary—History and criticism. I. Graham, Jon. II. Title.
   PQ2469.Z5L3413 2007
   843'.8—dc22
                                                                    2007019202

Printed and bound in the United States of America by Lake Book Manufacturing

10 9 8 7 6 5 4 3 2 1

Text design by and layout by Jon Desautels
This book was typeset in Sabon with Schneidler Initials as the display typeface

CONTENTS

Part 3
JULES VERNE AND THE SECRETS OF
THE ROSICRUCIANS

Part 4
ONCE WAS A KING OF THULE

Part 5
FROM SABLE TO THE GOLDEN N

INTRODUCTION

A radiant sun crowned the autumn morning of 1968 when I first laid eyes on the town of Rennes-le-Château standing out against the Aude sky. Shortly before my visit there, I had read a very curious book, *Le Trésor Maudit de Rennes-le-Château* [The Cursed Treasure of Rennes-le-Château], wonderfully written by Gérard de Sède. Both enthusiastic and amazed by the story he told, I was then quite incapable of sifting what was true from what was false in it, but I did feel a vague call to adventure and mystery after reading it. Accompanied by several friends, I had been drawn to see for myself the place around which this story revolved. A fabulous treasure found by a parish priest, falsified tombs, mysterious deaths, a church transformed into a rebus, paintings filled with symbolic clues, books based on actual individuals—all these elements combined to give the Rennes affair a fantastic frame. If we add to this the fact that this little town in the Aude region is alleged to hold the secret of the French royal family, connected to the return of the Great Monarch as predicted by Nostradamus, it is easy to sense the scent of mystery I caught as I climbed up one steep turn after another on the little road leading to the Rhedae of antiquity, former capital of the Visigoth kingdom and now reduced to a handful of inhabitants.

I was far from suspecting what would happen to me here. Fascinated by this mystery and the personal quest it represented and having fallen in love with this land, I returned each year to this small, lost corner of the

Aude region, and each time I came, my stay would extend a little longer. I have to admit that this enchanting land is a kind of microcosm in which everyone can discover himself, which is another kind of journey with its own risks and perils. It is a land of sharp contrasts: red hills under a beating sun, adorned with gold broom, and cool green and shady valleys where streams flow with water almost fresh from the Pyrenees. This is the land of the Oc language[1] and the Cathar faith, a land of peaks and winds, a land of caves and precious stones, a land of salt and ochre.

Over a span of years, I patiently collected documents from near and far that dealt with the Rennes affair and with the history of that region. I studied the texts and the monuments, cross-checking and learning to separate the good seeds from the weeds (for "fakes" are plentiful in this affair), and gradually I gained a more exact idea about this enigma.

Several hypotheses had germinated and grown stronger inside me. I sensed a certain number of connections among the region of the Razès and the doctrines offered by the most hermetic of the secret societies. One of these hypotheses concerned the kingdom of the Agarttha. Still missing, however, were several elements I needed to be sure I was on the right road. One day, the Marquis Philippe de Cherisey,[2] one of the top Rennes-le-Château specialists, told me of a possible link between this affair and Jules Verne, who had named one of his fictional characters after one of the mountains in the area. What an idea! Jules Verne's name alone awoke childhood memories in me. Parading through my mind were sweet Nell the heroine of *Indes Noires* [The Underground City], Captain Nemo and the *Nautilus,* and the invisible man William Storitz, and I could also see Michael Strogoff wandering through the night against the castle of the Carpathians outlined against a reddening sky.

That Jules Verne was mixed up with the Rennes-le-Château business was something I could hardly bring myself to believe. Unfortunately, Philippe de Cherisey did not know the name of the novel related to this adventure; thus this partial tidbit of information served only to frustrate

---

1. [That is, Languedoc. —*Trans.*]
2. Philippe de Cherisey is the author of a very curious work entitled *Circuit.*

me. As chance or providence would have it, though, shortly thereafter I found an original edition of *Clovis Dardentor* in a library, and in it I discovered the character that Philippe de Cherisey had told me about. I borrowed the book and photocopied it—then I began my work.

I quickly became convinced that the clue was indeed serious and that Jules Verne held the keys to the mystery of Rennes-le-Château and the treasure of the French kings. For several years I studied Jules Verne's life in appropriate detail and rediscovered the links connecting him to initiatory societies. For me, as the mystery of Rennes shed light on Jules Verne, so Jules Verne would shed light on the Rennes's enigma.

The revelation of this two-fold mystery is what follows in this book on the life and work of Jules Verne.

Part 1

JULES VERNE, INITIATE AND INITIATOR: AN OPUS IN SERVICE OF FREEMASONRY

THE CODED LANGUAGE OF JULES VERNE, OR THE CARNIVAL OF MYSTERIES

THE JULES VERNE MYSTERY

Yes! A Jules Verne mystery really does exist—or, to be more exact, several exist. The first, the one that will occur to everyone, concerns his gift for seeing the future. Jules Verne was the predictor of modern science (some have even called him a prophet) and was the father of science fiction. These ascriptions are true, of course, but this futuristic aspect of his work should not be exaggerated and, most important, it should not be used to hide the essential. In fact, if we consider his novels as a whole, the ones that describe futuristic machines are fairly rare. Furthermore, with a few rare exceptions, these do not owe a great deal to his imagination. For example, the submarine of *Twenty Thousand Leagues under the Sea* was preceded seventy-four years earlier by the one constructed by Fulton; the helicopter in *Robur the Conqueror* had actually existed for some twenty-three years (even if its flying results were not as spectacular); and the television of *The Castle of the Carpathians* owes everything to similar devices that had come before: Edison's phonograph and the cinetoscope. In addition, several centuries earlier, Leonardo da Vinci and Cyrano de Bergerac supplied the principles behind the majority of these machines. Jules Verne generally made use of inventions that already existed, at least as prototypes. The difference was that he had the intellect to expand upon their effects and imagine what they might offer after several decades of improvements and fine-tuning. All of this involved projection more than invention, meaning that it was undoubtedly not in Jules Verne's futuristic imagining that we should concentrate our search for his great secret. Nor should we look for it in the numerous themes he touched upon, for he quite often borrowed them from others, some of whom, incidentally, protested his habit.

While there is no visionary mystery in Jules Verne's work, however, it all the same contains a certain inexpressible quality that inspires passion. Michel Butor described it this way: "Everyone has read Jules Verne and experienced his prodigious power to make us dream, which was the gift of his scholarly and naïve genius. The myths that Jules Verne revealed in his precise language still dwell inside us." For his part, Rudyard Kipling wrote: "Give an English boy the first half of *Twenty Thousand Leagues under the Sea* in his native tongue. When he is properly intoxicated, withdraw it and present to him the second half in the original." Kipling maintained the child would find a way to understand it. There is an endless supply of quotes in this vein.

From where does this fascination come? Is it from the art of the writer? Of course, but I do not believe that is enough by itself. A good novel with well-described characters and a well-contrived plot is interesting and offers food for thought, but does not prompt fascination. To achieve this, the author must draw the reader into the world of dream; the world of fantasy; or the world of deep, inner archetypal awareness even (and perhaps especially) if the reader is not aware of it. This dreamy awareness is something Jules Verne has inspired and even imposed. What do the machines matter? They are merely paraphernalia suitable for breaking the daily rhythm, for dragging the mind off the beaten path and away from its common concerns. Rather than acting as a means for connecting to the tangible, to reality, these serve to help the mind teeter into the fantastic. We are no longer certain if the castle in the Carpathians is animated by machinery or inhabited by the devil, if the *Nautilus* belongs to the world of ships or the world of sea monsters, if the Albatross is a flying machine or a fabulous bird worthy of the thousand and one nights. (I will, however, be happy to refrain from discussing the steam elephant.) The machine offers reassurance when confronted by the irrational, but it bears within itself the seed of that irrationality. This sensation had to have been even more potent at a time when the existence of such machines was known only to a small number of people.

With this artifice, Jules Verne disorients the reader, dispels his suspicion, and leads him unknowingly, step-by-step, to the very bottom of himself. When the last page has been turned, the reader emerges from the dream with a nostalgic aftertaste and the impression of having glimpsed, for the space of an instant, at a profound truth briefly unearthed.

Before elucidating his work, let us return to the mystery of Jules Verne.

THE SECRET JULES VERNE COULD NOT REVEAL

The end of the author's life seems to have been marked by a deep moral solitude and a very odd melancholy, which we will explore more later, and his entire life up to that time was inscribed beneath the sign of the unknown. His wife, Honorine, felt he was haunted by some incomprehensible mystery that he refused to share with anyone and which sometimes appeared to be suffocating him. Why, for example, did Jules Verne burn hundreds of letters, personal papers, unpublished manuscripts, and account books before he died? Was this to forget some hidden facet of his private life and to ensure that no one would discover its existence after his death?

What became of the three thousand to four thousand crossword puzzles and logogriphs that he wrote in 1866 and bequeathed to his son Michel? Who destroyed them? Are they truly lost? Could they hold the essential keys to his work? Jules Verne's desire before his death to destroy his papers can only hide an important secret. As Malraux asks and answers: "What is a man? He is what he is hiding."

Some have sought to find in Verne's private life the key to this enigma and have attributed this desire for secrecy to an inadmissible passion:

Jules Verne was a homosexual. Stuff and nonsense! This Freudian interpretation is dangerous in that it has made numerous biographers feel they can no longer explain anyone's personality without relating it to sexual matters and an individual's deviations regarding them. For the fanatics of psychopathology, every word, every writing, inevitably becomes the extension of the repressed unconscious. According to this kind of system, such scholars conclude that what an author writes is precisely what he did not want to write. It is true that the pun, like a dream, sometimes serves as a safety valve for the subconscious. As Marc Soriano[1] points out: "On analysis, apparently gratuitous puns are revealed to be aggressive, in other words reasserting the rights of the impulse censored by the social superego and forming a return of the repressed relatively socialized by its complicity in the suddenness of the attack." And as a bonus, you will get the age of the captain.[2] While there can be, perhaps, legitimate reason to psychoanalyze an author; that is not my intent. Moreover, while an author's work is the property of all his readers, it is not so certain that his unconscious is any of their business. Finally, the psychoanalytical approach is generally sterile, making the author of a book only a portion of an individual rather than a total person.

I therefore don't share the perversion of this moral voyeurism. It is not without some scruples, however, that I undertake my own analysis because it will lead me into violating a taboo, at least relatively speaking. Several times Jules Verne stated that he should be read, not interrogated. On May 25, 1902, Verne responded with a categorical refusal to the young Italian Mario Turriello's request that the author write his autobiography. "A writer is of interest to his country or the world only as a

---

1. His book *Jules Verne: le cas Verne* [The Verne Case] is worth reading.
2. [The "age of the captain" refers to a mathematical riddle posed by the author Flaubert to his sister and is centered on deducing a captain's age from unrelated data: "Because you are now studying geometry and trigonometry, I will give you a problem. A ship is sailing across the ocean. It departed Boston with a cargo of wool, and with that cargo, it weighed a total of two hundred tons. It is bound for Le Havre. The mainmast is broken, the cabin boy is on deck, and there are twelve passengers on board. The wind is blowing east-northeast, the clock says it is 3:15 in the afternoon, and it is the month of May. How old is the captain?" —*Trans.*]

writer," Verne said. Likewise, the Italian De Amicis, a friend of Verdi, who met Verne in 1895, told how the author, at the slightest allusion to his life or his work, would change the subject of the conversation and would respond most evasively to questions posed more directly.

In order, then, to give the maximum respect to Jules Verne's desire in this regard, it is only on his work and his public life that I will seek to shed light. As readers, such seeking is totally within our rights and is even our duty. But how far are we permitted to go? If this interrogation should unearth a portion of the secret of Jules Verne, is it legitimate to reveal it? I hesitated for a long time before sitting down to write this book, but now the step has been taken. May his shade forgive me if I overstep the role that his readers may rightfully assume.

To unearth the secrets of extraordinary journeys, however, it is still necessary to find the key.

THE LANGUAGE OF THE BIRDS

There does exist a skeleton key that opens the doors to mysterious knowledge. It is contained in the very works and most particularly in the language Verne uses: initiatory language—a language of the birds worthy of the thirteenth-century troubadours.

It is in large part within numerical combinations and the associations of sounds that the key to the Verne strongbox is held. By intentionally veiling a secret teaching beneath the folding screens of language, he gives all his readers the opportunity to discover it, just as his heroes may pierce their own mystery by examining the elements that they sow behind them.[3]

It is not his unconscious that Verne is seeking to conceal behind words. His writing style—like his research—is far too meticulous for

---

3. The mystery of Jules Verne lies in the mystery of each character. Indeed, mystery is so much like a second skin for Verne that at times others have added to it for their own pleasure. For example, a rumor was spread that Jules Verne did not exist; his name was the corporate name for a group of black men working for the publisher Hetzel. Doubt has also been cast on his ancestry—although it is clearly established—by those claiming Verne's forebears were Jews, Poles, or members of some other group.

him to indulge himself in such a way. No, he is not betraying anything about himself; he writes exactly what he means to write, and that's that. But behind the text, for those who know how to read it, another text appears and allows to filter through something far more fascinating.

But to allow everyone to undertake the task of decrypting Jules Verne's novels without assistance, I first must make a slight digression to discuss methods of cryptographic writing that are fairly simple in this instance, for we all employ them from time to time without even being aware of it, a little like Monsieur Jourdain writes prose without knowing it.[4]

A TASTE FOR FARCE AND WITTY EXPRESSIONS

Jules Verne always had a taste for farce and the pun. His family tradition is quite definite about this; as an adolescent he was a comedian who always made jokes. One of his first plays on words was based on his own name: The suitor of his cousin who was the object of Verne's own amorous fantasies happened to be amused by the fact that both the man wooing her, Cormier, and Verne bore the name of a tree.[5] Verne expressed feeling sorry for himself by saying, "From what kind of wood is this poor young man named Jules Verne made?" On another occasion he praised the ineffable perfections of Miss Lucie Laënnec: "There is one with no superior."[6]

The puns and anagrams that fill his work were therefore an extension of his everyday life. In addition to amusing games he played with his own name,[7] one episode from Verne's youth left a marked impression: The young Jules lived in Nantes and daydreamed constantly about the large ships filled with fabulous beings, animals, and plants that left there for faraway islands. One day, no longer able to stand it, he decided to sail off, and without a word to his parents he made arrangements to take a cabin

---

4. [Monsieur Jourdain is the lead character in Molière's comedy *A Bourgeois Gentleman*, which pokes fun at middle-class aspirations to climb higher on the social ladder. —*Trans.*]

5. *Cormier* means "whitebeam" and *verne* is the Celtic word for "alder."

6. [*"La est l'nec plus ultra."* —*Trans.*]

7. Verne, cavern, averne [Avernus], and so forth.

boy's place on a boat about to set sail. Once his disappearance was discovered, however, his father had just enough time to get him back before the ship reached the open sea. According to a family source, the matter ended with the young Jules promising not to travel again except in dream. The oddest detail of this affair is that the child declared he had embarked on the *Coralie* to look faraway for a coral necklace for his cousin Caroline. In *Coralie,* coral, and Caroline, we hear the magic of sounds, their identical natures, and the incorporation of dreams.

Similarly, the letters he wrote his parents and his publisher are studded with witty expressions. Overloaded with work during the time he was living in Amiens, he wrote his publisher and signed himself "Your Beast of Burden"[8] Another time, as a penniless young man living in Paris, he wrote his mother to thank her for the new handkerchiefs she had sent him. In the letter, his nose expressed its gratitude for such fine treatment, and he signed it Nabuco.[9] Jokes and facetious remarks leap off every page of his family correspondence.

Likewise, he displayed this spirit in his earliest novels. We can find traces of such wordplay in a work of his youth: The plot of this novel centering on hermeticism takes place near a basilica and in the setting there are streets named Clavurie and Emeri.[10] Following the path of the Scholars (if not the adepts), the characters manage to decode a satanic message with the help of the witch Abraxia (Abraxis is a gnostic pentacle). Equally notable in this vein is a killer named Mordhomme.[11]

This is a typical example of what can be found in the entire Verne opus, as is the equally representative pseudonym he used for his book *Le*

---

8. [*"Votre bête de Somme." Bête de Somme* is the French for "beast of burden" and Somme refers to the department of Somme, where Amiens is located. —*Trans.*]

9. [This is a pun on buccal (near the cheek) and Nabuco, as in the opera *Nabucco* by Verdi. —*Trans.*]

10. This "roman à clef" is not made for those who are "thick as a brick." [*Clavé* means "key" and Emeri is reminiscent of Hermes or hermeticism. A Novel with a Key is a novel whose characters are real individuals loosely described. The French term for "thick as a brick" is *bouché à l'émerie,* as in the novel's street name Emeri, which can be translated literally as "clogged with emery." —*Trans.*]

11. [Manbiter or Mankiller. —*Trans.*]

Chemin de France [The Path of France]. This name, Natalis Delpierre, is one in which we can discern "born from Peter's bed" or "born of Peter,"[12] with Peter being the name of Jules Verne's father.

THE PROVEN RECIPE OF A SLANG LANGUAGE

It should be said that Jules Verne was not the only one of his time to amuse himself with puns and wordplay. Perhaps he might have been inspired by a seventeenth-century work attributed to Swift or Sheridan, *The Art of Word Play: The Flower of Language in Sixty-Nine Rules for the Limitless Perfection of Conversation and the Support of Memory, Fruit of the Labor and Industry of Tom-Pun-Sibi*.[13] The rules defined in this treatise demonstrate the vast degree of freedom tolerated by the art of the pun. There is nothing forbidding someone, for example, from using foreign languages for their approximate sonorities. Thus the English phrase "Tom, where are you?" could phonetically represent the word *temeraria*.[14] These almost identical relations are often quite difficult to detect. Fortunately, Jules Verne is generally much more precise. Thus in *Bourses de Voyages* [Travel Scholarships], one character suggests phonetically translating the Latin phrase *Rosam angelum letorum* into the simple phrase *Rose a mange l'omelette à rhum*.[15] We can detect games of this kind in the works of Balzac, George Sand, and even Victor Hugo, who composed the following distich out of phonetically similar sentences:

> *Dans ces meubles laqués, rideaux et dais moroses*
> *Danse, aime, bleu laquais, ris d'oser mots rose.*[16]

---

12. [*Né du lit de Pierre* and *né de Pierre*, respectively. —*Trans.*]
13. Originally titled *Ars Punica sive flos linguarum.*
14. [From *témeraire*, French for "reckless" or "foolhardy." —*Trans.*]
15. ["Rose has eaten a rum omelet." —*Trans.*]
16. [Among these lacquered furnishings, curtains, and morose daises / Dance, love, blue lackeys, laugh from daring rose words. —*Trans.*]

In fact, these idle amusements, which we now find surprising, were quite common during the time, and almanacs [17] crammed full of puns enjoyed enormous success. Since that time, authors such as Alphonse Allais have bestowed on this style pure and simple entertainment. Nonetheless, this game was sometimes much more serious than we might think. During the Middle Ages, games of wit formed part of the fundamental knowledge of the troubadours and trouvères. Wordplay permitted the use of an allegorical language that masked declarations that might earn their authors a quick trip to the stake. The art of *trobar clus* used by the troubadours [18] consisted specifically of uncovering the double meaning of these encrypted texts. Hence the name *troubadour* and *trouvère:* those who "found" [19] and uncovered the hidden treasure of language. In this sense, Rabelais was a true troubadour, and the entire Renaissance witnessed a huge flowering of books filled with wit and wordplay. The first proper anthology of enigmas was the hermetic work by Alexandre Sylvain, whose name conceals membership in a most discreet secret society.

The style especially flourished in the seventeenth century to the extent that a very renowned expert in heraldry, the Jesuit father Claude-François Menestrier (1631–1705) published a book in 1694 entitled *La philosophie des images énigmatiques* [The Philosophy of Mysterious Images] in which, following a few relatively brief and general remarks on the enigmatic wordplay, he explains its use in all its forms: anagram, rebus, and so forth in the allusive or canting and punning arms that were then highly in favor among not only the nobility, but also the bourgeoisie. [20] Earlier, in 1659, he wrote a book dedicated to the chancellor Séguier entitled *Devises, emblèmes et anagrammes* [Devices, Emblems, and Anagrams].

---

17. The most famous of these is *The Vermot Almanac,* founded by the Freemasons.

18. This was particularly true of the troubadours of the Languedoc region during and after the Albigensian crusade. The trobar clus is a closed form of poetry used by the troubadours for a more discerning audience.

19. [The French word for the verb "to find" is *trouver.* —*Trans.*]

20. See also Marcel Bernasconi, *Histoire des énigmes* [The History of Enigmas] (Paris: P.U.F., 1964).

No doubt, one of the methods of wordplay Jules Verne used most often was the anagram,[21] which makes it possible to form one word out of another, but can also play with an entire phrase. Some anagrams are particularly famous: *Révolution française* can be transposed into *Un veto corse la finira.*[22] This interesting example shows that the anagram is not gratuitous; the result should have some connection with the original subject. In fact, before such wordplay became merely a game of wit, it was considered a sacred game whose invention was attributed to the Greek Lycophron of Chalcis (a poet who lived in the third century BCE), but really seemed to be a derivative of the very ancient art of *onomatomancy,* a method of divination using names.

The ancients firmly believed that the fate of men was indissolubly tied to their names not because a name influenced a man despite himself, but because there was an obligatory correspondence between the two. This is why an individual would change his or her name when initiated, something that is still true for religious orders. In times since, particular virtues have been attributed to numerous saints according to references to their names: St. Clair, for example, heals eyes (hearkening to "clear"). The kaballah that permits an interpretation of the individual based on his or her name should not really be cause for surprise, at least since the time the Catholics were able to see the fifty-fifth (LV) Cain in Calvin. Janus words[23] are one variety of anagrams that consists of words that read the same forward as they do backward, such as the word *radar.* We can find other examples of the anagram in Spoonerisms and in *verlan,* a kind of French slang that involves inverting the syllables of a word and then saying it backward. A number of the names Jules Verne used for his characters were born from these methods. For example, in Michel Ardan is hidden the name of his friend Nadar[24] and the name Hector Servadac contains the reverse word of *cadavres* and an anagram of the word *torche.*[25] These are not just

---

21. From the Greek *ana* (overturning, reversal) and *gramma* (letter).

22. [French Revolution and "a Corsican veto will finish it," respectively. —*Trans.*]

23. The Roman god Janus had two faces.

24. [The French photographer Felix Nadar. —*Trans.*]

25. ["Cadavers" and "torch," respectively. —*Trans.*]

chance creations, as everyone who knows how to read between the lines of these novels will understand.

A close relative to the anagram is the metagram in which one letter of a word is changed to produce another word (such as *tent* changed to *tint*). Another is the logograph, which offers even more word possibilities because it permits the formation of many words out of the base word that contains their letters. Thus, with a word like *orange* we can make *gore, grange, groan, ogre, organ, rang, range,* and so on.

We have lingered over this subject for good reason: Such word games were part of Verne's daily life and played a role in his writing, where, most important, they mask important secrets.

THE JULES VERNE METHOD

Jules Verne is a veritable master of this kind of wordplay. In his work, the game often pivots on the names of his characters.[26] Moreover, there are constants that can be found in these proper names. For example, we can point to the theme of the axis recalled in the characters of Axel in *Journey to the Center of the Earth* and Aronax in *Twenty Thousand Leagues under the Sea*. In fact, the symbol of the axis forms one of Verne's obsessions.[27] Sometimes the name of a character has a connection to his or her function in the story, such as Tom Turner, who causes the engine of the *Albatross* to "turn." In addition, this *Albatross,* Robur the Conqueror's spaceship, is described by its master as a bird-ship, a play on the Latin word *avis* (bird), to which we can add an *n* to produce the word for "boat," *navis*. As to the name Robur, it can be turned around and read in palindrome as *rubor*.[28]

---

26. This is particularly true in *La famille raton* [The Adventures of the Rat Family]. [The characters in this book include the father, Raton; the mother, Ratonne; their daughter, Ratine; her cousin, Rate; the cook, Rata; and the maid, Ratane. —*Ed.*]

27. See also *Sans dessus dessous*. [This is a play on the French expression *sens dessus dessous,* meaning "topsy-turvy." With *sans* replacing *sens,* the meaning becomes "without top or bottom." —*Trans*]. Also curious is the frequency of the fragments *car* or *sacr* in the names of Verne's bandits: Scarpante, Carcante, Carpena, Sarcany, Sacratif. Was this meant to show that they were *sacripants?* [*Sacripants* are "scallywags." —*Trans*.]

28. [The red of the rose. —*Trans*.].

Sometimes these plays on words are merely jokes. Robert Pourvoyeur reminds us of the odd names of certain characters: T. Artelett, Ox et Ygène, Parazard,[29] Gil Bralter, and Jovita Folley, a girl who is both mad and jovial. In other instances, the language grows more complicated. For example, in *Journey to the Center of the Earth,* the heroes are faced with a Latin text written backward. Along with its more overt meaning, Axel discovers English, Hebrew, and French words in the text. "There are four different idioms in this absurd phrase! What connection could possibly exist between the words *ice, monsieur, anger, cruel, sacred grove, changing, sea, ark,* and *mother?*" This is a wink from Jules Verne, for these words in fact announce the unfolding of the voyage that follows: Axel makes his way to an icy land with his uncle, an angry gentleman who sometimes seems cruel because of the ordeals he imposes on Axel. On this journey, Axel discovers an inner sea and a sacred grove. From his journey to the heart of the earth he returns transformed into a loving individual and, like a child of the race of the ark, it is to the sea where the earth will deliver him before he marries his cousin. Coincidence? In fact, we can find further confirmation in the book. By rereading the Latin text backward, we can discover other words that Axel did not mention: *wall, greenhouse, lake,* and *jitters* all herald important episodes in the story: the block that stops the travelers, the tertiary forest, the underground sea, and Axel's vertigo. Thus a word game, a cryptogram, reproduces the novel in miniature. Giving it an analogy to heraldry, the author André Gide has dubbed this procedure a *mise en abyme.*[30]

We should recall the essential keys to Jules Verne's novels are often supplied by the characters, such as Orfanik, who, in *The Castle of the Carpathians,* brings us back to the myth of Orpheus. We should also cite the scientific novel based on the axis and the circle, *Without Top or*

---

29. [*Par hazard* in French means "by chance." —*Trans.*]

30. [*Mise en abyme,* literally meaning, "place into the abyss," is a heraldric term used to describe the circumstance of one quadrant of a coat of arms containing an image of the entire coat of arms. The expression is also used in art and literature to denote the idea of a dream within a dream. —*Trans.*]

Bottom, in which the French mathematician is named Alcide Pierdeux, an appropriate name for giving us the area of the circle (πr^2).[31]

WARNING: ONE PLAY ON WORDS CAN HIDE ANOTHER

Jules Verne is a veritable goldsmith when it comes to words with double meanings, the very essence of puns, "those mental droppings that soar," as Victor Hugo defined them. There is a good reason for this: These words paint a picture and strike the mind or intrude on memory.[32]

We should note that Jules Verne took advantage of his skill with wordplay to make a good number of jokes that were rather daring for the time, with some, frankly, in very poor taste. One day he wrote his mother to say, "I will marry the woman you find for me. I will marry with eyes closed and purse opened."[33] The innuendos and underlying meanings are not to be left out, for his jokes, while they ignore propriety, are perfectly open to the scatological, as Jean-Jules Verne has noted. Similarly, although the subject seems completely unambiguous, we can raise questions about the title of his text *Dix heures en chasse* [Ten Hours Hunting or Ten Hours in Heat]. And in *Château en Californie* [Castle in California], doesn't the maid Catherine, a specialist in approximations and other slips of the tongue, say, *"la queue sur la main,"* when she means to say *"le coeur sur la main"*?[34]

But look out! One play on words might be hiding another. Some

---

31. [Pierdeux can be translated as "pi R squared." —*Trans.*]

32. Like Christ's famous words "You are Peter and on this rock I will build my church." [The pun is not as obvious to English readers, but *Pierre*, the French version of Peter, also means "stone." The name Peter is itself a derivative of the Latin *petra*, meaning "stone." —*Trans.*]

33. [The open purse on one level refers to the stereotypically male image of existing as a constant source of money for the women in his family, but purse also has sexual connotations, both as a metaphor for male and female genitalia. Iago in Shakespeare's Othello admonishes Rodrigo to "put money in his purse," meaning "to get some balls" and the purse has appeared as a symbol of the vagina in many cultures. —*Trans.*]

34. ["The prick in the hand" instead of "the heart on one's sleeve." —*Trans.*]

of Jules Verne's puns have not only a double but also a triple meaning. Marc Soriano thinks this is a case of compensation for guilt, but rather than the risqué meaning being masked by another, the exact opposite is the case. The reader is often brought to a halt by the bawdy meaning when he discovers the pun and he doesn't think to investigate it further, to keep searching precisely there, where its true meaning is located. Thus this true meaning has been doubly concealed. This is particularly the case with *Clovis Dardentor,* in which we can discover the true meaning hidden behind the lewd joke that plays on *dard en l'or* (Dardentor) and *désirant d'elle* (Désirandelle).[35]

In fact, the word treasures in Jules Verne lead not only to vulgar jokes, but to many treasures.

---

35. [*Dard en l'or* refers to "gold stinger" or "gold penis" and *désirant d'elle* means "desiring her." —*Trans.*]

THE TREASURE
IS IN THE CIRCLE

LA JAGANDA, PROTOTYPE OF JULES VERNE'S CRYPTOGRAPHIC NOVELS

The essential characteristic of Jules Verne's initiatory language resides in his use of the cryptogram. His novels often begin with the chance discovery of an indecipherable message perhaps found in a bottle cast into the sea by the victim of a shipwreck or transported by a wounded pigeon. This message, always incomprehensible at first, is the key to the novel—enlightenment will come as a result of its decryption and quite often the plot of the story is structured around it. Jules Verne thereby dictates to us the attitude we, as his readers, should assume: We are not dealing with common books, but with enormous cryptograms that it is our task to decode. It is the heroic role of one on a quest for the Grail that Jules Verne reserves for us.

This is the case for *La Jaganda,*[1] which opens with the text of an incomprehensible message on which depends the life of one of the heroes as well as the conditions of the other characters. It is only at the end that this logogriph is deciphered, and the entire plot unfolds within the context of a labyrinth.

---

1. [The title is translated as *Eight Hundred Leagues on the Amazon* and sometimes appears as two separate volumes, *The Giant Raft* and *The Cryptogram.* —*Trans.*]

In the story, Joam Garral, who is actually the hiding Joam Dacosta, a man condemned to death, decides to turn himself in to the legal authorities in order to prove his innocence so that his family, who are completely ignorant of his accusation, will never have cause to be ashamed of him. Married to Yaquita, he has two children, Benito and Minha. His daughter Minha later marries a friend of her brother, Manuel Valdez. Complicating matters is that Joam is the victim of a blackmailer to whom he refuses to surrender. He dismisses the swindler although he possesses the proof of Joam's innocence. Eventually, this proof is recovered from the corpse of the bandit, but it is in the form of a cryptogram. Judge Jarriquez, convinced of Joam's good faith, seeks to learn its secret. He vainly resorts to the methods advocated by Poe,[2] but does not succeed in decoding it. The solution is found by the barber Fragoso,[3] who alludes to a famous wigmaker named Leonard, a choice of name that is not at all gratuitous, for it brings us to the famous Leonardo da Vinci, whose method the judge applies in trying to read the cryptogram in the opposite direction.[4] In the story, there is a constant shifting from one trail of clues to another, the following of Ariadne's thread in this labyrinth. At the very beginning of the book, Fragoso, who becomes the final savior, is himself saved by a young girl. This girl, whose name is Lina, follows a liana (woody vine) and finds the barber hanging from its end on the point of expiring. The story ends with Fragoso saying, "With the difference of only a letter, aren't Lina and liana the same thing?" Following this logic, with only the difference of a letter separating them, are not Garral and Graal[5] the same thing? As Judge Jarriquez notes at one point concerning the cryptogram, the most important detail is often found in the final paragraph, and here Fragoso, using analogy, allows us to find one of the keys to the novel.

The book revolves around the cryptogram, and because of this, Verne

---

2. Jules Verne writes: "The Magistrate who had often read and reread *The Gold Beetle* was fully familiar with the analytical procedures meticulously employed by Edgar Allen Poe."

3. The name Fragoso is reminiscent of another very famous barber: Figaro.

4. Leonardo da Vinci wrote his treatises in such a way that it required a mirror to read them.

5. [Grail. —*Trans.*]

makes Judge Jarriquez—"he, the seeker after numerical combinations, the amusing problem solver, the decoder of charades, rebuses, logographs, and other such things"—an expert on the subject: "Here before his very eyes was a cryptogram! So from that moment he thought of nothing but how to discover its meaning, and it is scarcely necessary to say that he made up his mind to work at it continuously, even if he forgot to eat or to drink." Is this a portrait of Judge Jarriquez or a self-portrait of the author? The fact remains that Jules Verne took advantage of the judge to present in detail the most common methods in which secret messages are formed.

The publisher Hetzel was particularly alarmed by the importance the cryptogram took on in this book, and Jules Verne had to promise his editor that he would try to limit the place devoted to figures in the work. Nevertheless, he still insisted on its importance: "For me the interesting thing, the book's originality should be in all the attempts made to read the document. In *The Gold Beetle,* a novella of about thirty pages, the figures took up ten of them and Edgar Allan Poe felt that all the interest of the story lay in these, even though a man's life was not at stake." Jules Verne was proud of his cryptogram in *La Jaganda* and believed it capable of resisting any attempt at elucidation by anyone who did not have the key to it beforehand. Yet because the novel appeared as a serial, one reader found the solution long before it was provided by the author. Verne initially believed this resulted from an indiscretion originating with his publisher. This was not the case, though, and Verne made arrangements to meet the perspicacious reader so he could explain to the author how he had found the solution. At the end of their conversation, full of admiration, Verne could only repeat over and over: "What powers of analysis! It has me literally dumbfounded!"

THE WORK OF JULES VERNE IS A GIGANTIC CODED MESSAGE

Cryptograms abound in the entire Verne opus. For example, in *Les Enfants du Capitaine Grant* [In Search of the Castaways or The Children of Captain Grant], there is a triple text written in three different languages, which takes the form of a coded message. The manuscripts in which it is contained have deteriorated from exposure to seawater. The interpretation of this text is like the construction of a puzzle, and successive mistakes drag the heroes from one end of the world to the other, with the lone immutable piece of information being the latitude at which the shipwreck of the *Britannia* occurred. Further, only chance permits them to find Captain Grant, leader of the shipwrecked vessel. This is noteworthy because it is always chance, or rather providence, and not the labor of man, that permits the coded message to be deciphered. Providence nonetheless steps in as reward for the persistence of the Vernian heroes on their quest. Contrary to what some have written, the hand of God soars over extraordinary journeys.

In *Mathias Sandorf,* at the center of the entire story is a cryptogram that can be decoded with the aid of a grid. In the book, Jules Verne extends himself at length on the use of grids in the coding of texts. In *The Eternal Adam,* it is a scientist from the future who deciphers the message written by the last survivors of a planet-wide catastrophe. The book containing this indecipherable rebus is a little like the spiritual testament of Jules Verne, and the scientist protagonist, Zartog Sofr-Ai-Sr, requires several years to understand it. I wager it would take as many years of assiduous study to decode all cryptograms in Verne's "extraordinary journeys."

Cryptograms similarly come into the picture in the *Mirifiques Aventures du Capitaine Antifer* [The Fabulous Adventures of Captain Antifer], *Journey to the Center of the Earth,* and other Verne novels. The fact is, however, that all of Jules Verne's language is a code, and, when necessary, the entire novel becomes a ciphered message full of winks and signs of the author's complicity. A word game at the beginning will sometimes serve to set things off and to summarize the entire plot. The purpose of all this is of course entertainment, but could also be said that the entertainment is not the essential point.

THE OUROBOROS AND THE OBSESSION
WITH THE CIRCLE

The peculiar author Raymond Roussel was the odd character who applied the same systems and narrative structures used by Jules Verne and on whom the father of *Around the World in Eighty Days* exercised a profound influence. Roussel lived from 1877 to 1933 and was a multi-millionaire. He spent his time writing lengthy poems, encrypted novels, and plays, some of which caused scandals. He admired Jules Verne to such an extent that he once wrote in a letter to Eugénie Leiris: "Ask me for my life, but don't ask me to lend you a Jules Verne." Roussel tells us in *Comment j'ai écrit certains de mes livres:*[6] "I once had the good fortune to be received by him [Verne] at Amiens, where I was doing my military service, and there shake the hand which had penned so many immortal works. . . . He raised himself to the highest peaks that can be attained by human language. . . . O incomparable master, may you be blessed for the sublime hours which I have spent endlessly reading and rereading your works throughout my life."

It is not by chance that this vibrant homage finds itself in Raymond Roussel's book with the intention of explaining how Roussel composed the majority of his works. It is a good idea, in fact, to take a moment to linger over the Rousselian procedures. François Rivière[7] writes: "When entering the world of *Locus Solus* and Roussel's long poems, we are struck by the particularly suffocating nature of a premeditated delirium, a truncated landscape filled with metaphorical 'circular' snares, Vernian in short for its scientific theatricality taken to delirious heights." And this is what Roussel himself has to say of his method: "I chose almost two identical words (reminiscent of metagrams)—for example, *billiard* and *pillard*.[8] To these I added similar words that each had two different meanings, thus obtaining two almost identical phrases. In the case of *billiard* and *pillard*, the two phrases I obtained were:

---

6. [Raymond Roussel, *How I Wrote Certain of My Books,* translated by Trevor Wink-field (New York: Sun, 1977.) —*Trans.*]

7. François Rivière, "L'un commence, l'autre continue," in *Europe* (Nov–Dec 1978).

8. ["Billiard table" and "plunderer," respectively. —*Trans.*]

1. Les letters du blanc sur les bandes de vieux billiard . . .
2. Les letters du blanc sur les bandes de vieux pillard . . ."⁹

Raymond Roussel also made use of the multiple meanings that one word could have, such as the circle that means "round" and the circle that refers to a gaming circle. As another example, one of his novellas begins with *La peau de la raie sous la pointe du rayon vert miroitait en plein soleil du mois d'août,* and the entire plot unfolds to end with *la peau de la raie sous la pointe du crayon vert.*¹⁰

The man who transformed *J'ai de bon tabac en ma tabatière* into *jade tube onde aubade en mat a basse tierce*¹¹ could not help but admire Jules Verne and his methods in which we can find the use of these Rousselian procedures. In fact, in *Castles in California,* we begin with *pierre qui roule n'amasse pas mousse* and end with *père qui roule n'amasse pas de mousse.*¹² But an important distinction separates the two authors. For Raymond Roussel, the play with words and the construction of the text following a distinct process seems to be an end in itself; for Jules Verne it is a method for signifying a second meaning in the story. There is a world of difference between these two points of view, even if the stories by Roussel and Verne are both sometimes constructed on the circle, like serpents biting their own tails.

The circle appears to be a true obsession for Verne. It is omnipresent in his "extraordinary voyages," with every meaning that can be connected to the word circle. It sometimes takes the appearance of the historical cycle, a traditional explanation for the history of the world based on the law of analogy. For Verne, every cycle ends with a cataclysm, and one day another deluge of water or fire will come to put an end to

---

9. [The first translates as "The white letters on the cushions of the old billiard table," and the second translates as "The white man's letters on the hordes of the old plunderer." —*Trans.*]

10. ["The ray's skin beneath the tip of a green ray shimmering in the August sunlight" and "the skin of the scratch under the tip of the green crayon," respectively. —*Trans.*]

11. ["I have good tobacco in my snuffbox" and "jade tube water lecture in mat (mat object) third bass," respectively. —*Trans.*]

12. ["A rolling stone gathers no moss" and "the father who roams collects no cabin boy." —*Trans.*]

the age in which we are currently living. A few survivors will then start over and relaunch a new cycle and a new life. With all of civilization destroyed, through the centuries they will build a new world that will not fail to offer numerous analogies to our own. It is this theory that serves as the basis for *Le Nouvel Adam*,[13] which takes place between the year 2000 and the year 3000. As pointed out by René Pillorget, this theory is quite close to the themes defended by Nietzsche,[14] and there is a comparison to be made between the names Zarathustra and Zartig Sofr-Ai-Sr, scientist in *The Eternal Adam*.

This cyclical theory does leave humans their free will, however. They can design the world during the cycle and accelerate or delay its duration. The purpose is the purification of matter in order to reach spirituality, which inspired Mireille Coutrix-Gonaux and Pierre Souffrin to write:

> Verne seems to be saying throughout the length of his opus that from the time of his advent, the human being can decide to emerge from the earthly "spheroid," accelerate the "transmutation," and prepare for the coming of a new realm, that of pure Spirit. This, at least, is the end that Verne assigns the efforts of men, most particularly the scientific revolution experienced at the end of the nineteenth century, with science becoming the instrument of this transformation. Humanity, however, seems to have taken another path, which, far from leading to the ultimate metamorphosis, seems to be leading into a dead end or to a murderous catastrophe.

The work of Jules Verne is a cycle of cycles, and all the roads in it are curved. Verne himself seems to be unaware of the straight line. He climbs back up the spiral of time in an incessant quest for its origin. Because Jules Verne's novels are geographic, the circle is ceaselessly manifested in the journeys taken by the characters. The hero or explorer

---

13. [New Adam. —*Trans.*]
14. René Pillorget, "Optimisme ou pessimisme de Jules Verne," in *Europe*.

leaves only in order to return, whether they are undertaking a world tour, as in the case of Phileas Fogg;[15] whether they throw themselves into the Sacred Goose Game in the American territory;[16] or whether they make a detour to the middle of the earth before returning home. The story cannot end if the discoverer of lands cannot return to recount his discovery. To pursue his quest, the hero cannot remain static; he must depart and return like the pilgrims of an older time who made their way to the sepulchre of Saint James of Compostela. He has to "circulate," like blood, and what's more, circulate "circularly." It little matters what the purpose of the journey is; the essential in Jules Verne's work is the voyage itself because this state of errantry is a destabilization and provokes a rupture with the daily routine, thereby creating a privileged state in which experience—most particularly of an initiatory nature—is possible. Do characters circulate ceaselessly in order to learn to be? Perhaps, for Jules Verne believes bad cities are the ones in which people do not circulate. He sees wandering as a way to gain access to the spiritual realm despite the risk it entails—for example, the wandering mind and madness that afflicts Captain Hatteras in *The Adventures of Captain Hatteras.*

THE TREASURE IS IN THE CIRCLE

The circle also appears as a veritable rite of appropriation. To encircle a place is to take possession of it. This aspect is perhaps the origin of the importance of the island in Jules Verne's stories: The mysterious island, the submerged island, the floating island is a world of its own, a microcosm encircled by water. Landing on it is to enter the circle, to penetrate, visit, and explore it. The purpose is always to find the region where the mystery will be solved. What mystery? That does not matter! They are all resolved in the supreme mystery: the meaning of life.

---

15. Jules Verne said of Fogg, "He is not traveling; he is describing a circumference." We can add that the entire adventure comes to life in the Reform Club, a "gambling circle."
16. [The Sacred Goose Game is the French name for the ancient game now known as Snakes and Ladders. —*Trans.*]

The island-ovum that is penetrated and fertilized by the traveler-spermatozoid is the seat of life, the mystery of mysteries. But be warned: the traveler there takes an enormous risk because no one has ever searched with impunity to discover the secret hidden within the supreme center of the circle of all circles. Michel Serres says: "The island is the first microcosm in the circle of the waters. Because it is closed, it takes a miracle to reach it—from above, by a balloon pushed by air currents; from below, through an underwater canyon; from the center, by a column of fire through a crater. A miracle of air, water, fire, and earth."

The search for the central point is also the hunt for a treasure. "The circle is more hole than center, the treasure is hidden within," Michel Serres tells us. This quest for gold is rarely material; it bears much more resemblance to an initiatory, alchemical itinerary. In *L'Étoile du Sud* [The Star of the South], the treasure takes the form of a fabulous diamond, a black diamond, the largest in the world. In *Le Testament d'un Excentrique* [The Will of an Eccentric], it is a legacy. In *Around the World in Eighty Days*, Phileas Fogg is led to cash in a treasure, the total sum of the bet that triggers the events of the story. At the end of *The Mysterious Island*, sequel to *Twenty Thousand Leagues under the Sea*, Captain Nemo entrusts a treasure to the heroes that permit them to set up a kind of phalanstery.[17] Here again it is necessary for money to circulate; the gold must be put back into circulation in order for it to be transmuted.

To find the center of the circle in order to discover the treasure, it is necessary to know how to plot a position. Jules Verne does not stint in indicating methods to follow,[18] and throughout his work, latitudes,

17. [A phalanstery is a utopian communal settlement based on the principles established by the philosopher Charles Fourier. —*Trans.*]

18. For example, in *The Mysterious Island,* characters obtain the latitude at night with the help of a crude homemade sextant: They take the angular sector from the height of a star above the horizon and are thereby able to measure the latitude with sufficient accuracy. To obtain the longitude the following day, they determine the local noon at the time when the sun passes over the zenith of their location, then note the time on Spilett's watch. The difference between the two times allows them to determine the island's longitude in relation to the Richmond Meridian. Knowing the Richmond Meridian's position relative to the Greenwich Meridian, simple addition gives them the island's longitude.

and longitudes play an important role. One of his novels even makes the measurement of a meridian axis part of the main plot outline,[19] and there are hardly any important locations in Jules Verne's books that aren't referenced by their distance from the Zero Meridian.[20]

The most interesting novel in this regard is the *Fabulous Adventures of Captain Antifer*, written in 1894. This book recounts the story of a Saint Malo native who has set off in search of a fabulous treasure. At the moment he is finally able to take possession of it, the island on which it is found vanishes beneath the waves. As is often the case, the novel's adventure starts with a manuscript to be decoded, and, as in *In Search of the Castaways*, false trails are followed in succession until the final resolution of the plot. Starting from the fact that a circle can be plotted from three positions,[21] the quest is constructed in the form of triangulation, though it is circles, not triangles, that are the subject of the search. Michel Serres writes:

> Just think: The position is a space in the middle of three straight lines within sight of seamarks. Two lines of a compass will give only a poor calculation. The ship is protected inside a triangular cradle. In deep sea navigation, it's the same: The hour, dead reckoning, and bearings close off the approaching zone three ways. Where am I? Between three lines, or better, between three circles, and each circle in turn is issued from a position. My position . . . is vibrating inside a spherical triangle. Now deduce the triangle, the circumference, the position, and you have Antifer's plan and its key.

In any event, Captain Antifer's quest is certainly an odd one. The impetus for this adventure is provided by a pasha, or honorary Ottoman official, who decides to give to all the men who have helped him at

---

19. *Aventures de trois russes et trois anglais en Afrique australe* [Adventures of Three Russians and Three Englishmen in Southern Africa] includes a chapter with the very strange title "Triangulate or Die."
20. At this time, the Zero Meridian was the Paris Meridian, not the Greenwich Meridian.
21. See Jules Verne's letter to Mario Turiello, April 10, 1896.

crucial times a means of discovering his treasure. Captain Antifer holds the latitude of the sought-for location, but he must discover who knows the longitude. Once the location is discovered, no treasure is found, only an enigmatic clue giving a new latitude. This results in a new walk-on character, a new longitude, and a new location—which also turns out to be a disappointment. Three successive points are finally determined in this way, but no treasure is found until the fiancée of one of the heroes, Enogate, suddenly notices on a planisphere that the three determined points successively form a triangle and that a circle joins them together. Wouldn't the center of this circle be the place they were looking for, the fabulous center where the gold is stashed? They race to the spot and find . . . another disappointment. A treasure island did in fact once exist at the indicated position. It surfaced one day following a volcanic eruption, but since that time, another eruption restored it to its abyssal kingdom. The mystery therefore remains intact about what might sit at the center of the circle of circles.

IT IS ENOUGH TO KNOW THE RULES OF THE GAME

In Verne's novels, the challenge imposed is first to decipher the message and then to find the circle, the center, and the treasure—and to accomplish this, what is required is intimate knowledge of the rules of the game. Games, in fact, often play a role in Verne's novels. Indeed, many of his characters are passionate about them: Nicholl, Keraban, Doctor Schwarzencrona, and Bredeford, for example. The greatest player, however, is undoubtedly Phileas Fogg: His tour of the world begins with a game of whist during which the fabulous wager is made, and another match plays a role during his crossing of America. He is an absolute gambler because he stakes his entire fortune on the adventure. Other games in the work of Jules Verne include the croquet match in *The Green Ray* and the drawing in *The Lottery Ticket*. The descriptions of the stories' locations themselves use ludic elements: For example, Salt Lake City, the city of the Mormons, is "a checkerboard about which it can be said that there are more checkers than squares," and the Sherman Hotel in Chicago is "similar to a large die."

The most extraordinary game reference can be found in *The Will of an Eccentric*. The main character, W. J. Hypperbone, a member of the Club of Eccentrics, has decided to write his will leaving his fortune to one of six Chicago inhabitants who wins a match of the Goose Game.[22] But this is no ordinary Goose Game; it uses the entire United States for its board, with each state corresponding to one square and the state of Illinois recurring fourteen times and playing the role of the squares holding a goose. Dice are used to send the player from one state to another until one finally reaches the sixty-third square.

This novel provides the perfect example of Jules Verne's use of the game as a method for writing his books. I should say at the start that anyone seeking to decipher this book thoroughly will encounter numerous surprises (among them, intentional mistakes by the author) and will have to untangle plays on letters and numbers.

Why did Jules Verne use the Goose Game in this way in the novel? Is it merely an amusing diversion, as his biographers have generally believed? I propose that Jules Verne was perfectly aware of the sacred meaning of the Goose Game. As we have seen elsewhere,[23] the goose is significant in ancient myth. The game perhaps has come down from the ancient Egyptians, or even the Trojans, keepers of the Pelasgique tradition. Let's briefly examine the rules.

Every nine squares, a goose is encountered on the spiral path of the game,[24] and the entire journey consists of seven times nine squares. All the resources of the numerical kabbalah can be applied to the game, and some squares possess noteworthy distinctions: For instance, in

---

22. [Again, this game is known in English as Snakes and Ladders or, more currently, Chutes and Ladders. I have opted to leave the literal translation in the text, however, to support the author's argument regarding the traditional role of the goose in ancient and hermetic traditions. —*Trans.*]

23. Michel Lamy, *Histoire secrète de Pays Basque* [The Secret History of the Basque Country] (Paris: Albin Michel, 2000).

24. In compagnonnage, or the system of fraternities of journeyman, the division of a circle by nine is known as a goosefoot.

addition to the hostelry welcoming the pilgrim; the bridge, symbol of passage; the prison formed by our material desires; and the labyrinth;[25] we should give special attention to the well and the death's head on this course that is the journey of life and the after-life. The well is located at the midpoint of the course because it connects with the interior of the earth and, at the same time, the truth that can gush from it can lead to awareness and to the godhead. Its axis extends in ideal fashion toward the heavens, but also plunges straight to the heart of the earth. As for death, it occupies the fifty-eighth square $(5 + 8 = 13)$[26] and the person who lands on this square has to go back to the beginning and start the course over. Thus, he who has not been capable of "being born in spirit" before death will have to reincarnate and begin a new earthly life. In contrast, someone who has been able to marry his or her soul will pass beyond death so that only five squares separate him from the final goal of immortality. It so happens that the number five is that of human realization and fulfillment, dear to the Pythagorians and the Cathars alike, as well as to Leonardo da Vinci. With respect to the total number of geese in the game, fourteen, this number, too, represents a sign of immortality and passage into the beyond (it is one more than the fateful thirteen).

We should refrain from regarding such games as simple diversions, for they have come to be viewed as sources of amusement only because we no longer have eyes with which to see or ears with which to hear. The goose, like the Milky Way, leads to death, but death is overcome by spiritual resurrection. It is clearly this meaning that guided Jules Verne through the entire novel. Indeed, this is the reason he chose the "noble game more or less renewed by the Greeks." Further, if we recall the Trojan origin claimed by the Merovingian kings, we can see why one of the heroes of *The Will of an Eccentric* is named Max Real (meaning "true royal axis"). In a certain sense, he is the winner in this adventure because during it he finds love. With respect to the state that serves as "goose,"

---

25. Labyrinths are sometimes called Trojan walls or walls of Troy.
26. [The card of Death in the Major Arcana of the Tarot is 13. —*Trans.*]

Illinois, not only can we find the consonance of *oi* in its name,[27] but it is the anagram of Ilion-Lis, meaning Lis (royal lily) of Troy (Ilion). Is this a gratuitous hypothesis? Not at all, as we shall see in the upcoming material concerning Rennes-le-Château.

Jules Verne created a large number of plays on words in *The Will of an Eccentric*,[28] but he also made wide use of symbolism It is worth noting that the fifty-eighth square, connected to death, is represented by California, the westernmost of the American states, and in antiquity, the West was considered the land of the dead. The fact remains that the six heroes of this strange story are beaten in the game by a seventh, surprise competitor: XKZ (or 6 + 1 = 7, which is the base number that, multiplied by nine, results in sixty-three squares and is the constant sum of the two opposing faces of a die). The winner is none other than the person who is responsible for the game in the first place. He is not dead, as everybody believes. Simply, W. J. Hypperbone, "like a new Lazarus broken out of the tomb," had decided to follow through on a wildly eccentric whim: to entrust his fortune to chance, and chance gives it back to him His tomb in the Oakswood Cemetery (whose name, oak wood, also has a sacred significance) is empty and Hypperbone (we may as easily say Hyperos) is not a skeleton. In contrast, the other contestants in the game certainly came across nothing but snags along the way.[29] Having accepted being stripped of everything by providence, the winner gains immortality.

AND NOW, TO WORK!

Though there is certainly much more to *The Will of an Eccentric;* the elements discussed here may give readers the means to conduct their own research on the work of Jules Verne. Any such study must take into

---

27. ["Goose" is *oie* in French. —*Trans.*]

28. For example, the chief of a tribe of Seminoles is named Oisela, indicating that *l'Oie c'est là*. [This means "the Goose is there." —*Trans.*]

29. [The French expression for "hit a snag" is *tomber sur un os*, literally "fall upon a bone." —*Trans.*]

account anomalies, "mistakes," plays on words, and cryptograms and the meanings of all these as we follow Ariadne's thread that Verne never fails to give us. Additional interpretive assistance is sometimes provided by the illustrations. Interestingly, Jules Verne gave precise instructions to the illustrators, providing them with extremely detailed descriptions and insisting, when necessary, that they redo certain plates. It is worth noting that Hetzel did not choose his regular illustrators to illustrate Jules Verne's work. Neither Garvani nor Gustave Dore did the work; instead, Riou, Férat, Neuville, Montant, Philippoteaux, Benett, Bayard, and others were engaged as if a more discreet and submissive team had to be organized. As we will see, with respect to the novel *Clovis Dardentor,* this was essential.

Illustrations aside, having a cryptographic linguistic arsenal makes sense only if a writer has something hidden to say—that is, if he has secrets to reveal only to those who can understand them. This was clearly the purpose pursued by Jules Verne.

JULES VERNE, FREEMASON

JULES VERNE AND MONSIEUR JOURDAIN

This is not the first time it has been claimed that Jules Verne was the author of initiatory novels. Simone Vierne has devoted a thick tome to this theory, citing as evidence the immutable scenario of initiatory ceremonies that always present three sequences: preparation, voyage into the beyond, and rebirth. Vierne has no difficulty in demonstrating that the majority of Jules Verne's novels follow this outline. She even shows that the "extraordinary voyages" can be classified according to the initiatory degree to which they correspond: initiation of puberty, heroic initiation, and higher initiation. The journeys of exploration and quest form part of the first category. This includes *Journey to the Center of the Earth, Eight Hundred Leagues on the Amazon, The Green Ray,* and a good many others. The second degree consists of the battles against monsters (*Twenty Thousand Leagues under the Sea, Michel Strogoff, Begum's Millions, Robur the Conqueror, the Castle of the Carpathians,* and so on). Finally, higher initiation has its corresponding works in those that place their heroes in direct contact with the sacred, such as *The Mysterious Island, Hector Servadac, The Underground City, Mathias Sandorf, The Survivors of the Jonathan,* and others.

I have no intention of denying the value of this classification or underestimating the valuable labor performed by Simone Vierne. It is regrettable, however, that Vierne does not have a better understanding of initiatory rituals; because she is an anthropologist, her analysis is that of an academic studying a primitive people. Jules Verne would be a kind of Monsieur Jourdain (see chapter 1, note 4) who practiced esotericism without knowing it. In short, the "extraordinary voyages" follow an initiatory model only by virtue of the laws of chance and as a result of a bizarre aspect in Jules Verne's psychological structure, and he, of course, was totally unaware of what he had written.

> Jules Verne did not intend to transmit within the covers of a book intended for children a specific initiatory message in the same manner in which Mozart, for example, used a theater piece devoid of interest to exhibit his faith in Freemasonry. Nonetheless, impelled by the strength of a dynamic model whose seed can be found in the genre itself, Jules Verne was brought to pose the same questions that religious initiation strives to solve: How can we overcome the mortal destiny of humankind with a radical transformation of being obtained by the direct and mystical revelation of the sacred?

I claim the opposite of these suppositions is true. As we will see here, not only did Jules Verne intentionally follow the model of initiatory rituals, but what's more, he very precisely followed Masonic rituals. Not only did he, like Mozart, write a Masonic work, but also he quite closely followed *The Magic Flute* to express his own involvement in Freemasonry.

AN INITIATORY JOURNEY TO THE CENTER OF THE EARTH

Michel Brion has best described *Journey to the Center of the Earth* as follows:[1]

---

1. Marcel Brion, *L'Allemagne romantique: Le voyage initiatique* [The Romantics' Germany: The Initiatory Voyage] (Paris: Albin Michel, 1977–1978).

All the themes of and links to the imaginary voyage are to be found here: the illegible message of *Treasure Island* and *The Gold Beetle;* the peril-filled adventures that lead to winning the Lady, with love therefore becoming one of the motivations if not the major motivation of the adventure, as in *Perceval* and *Lancelot* . . . Axel, the "knight" of Jules Verne, must wed the pretty Grauben, who is not the cause of courage and audacity displayed in the underground world, but who is their reward. It matters that a woman be associated, externally and in a supporting role, with the adventure, stimulation, temptation, coronation, and success, but she should not take part in these.

Many critics have attributed this sublime role devolved upon a woman to misogyny on Jules Verne's part, but would do better to follow Michel Brion's lead.

Axel is the poor metal that must be forged in the fires of the earth (the volcano), washed and hardened in the waters of the subterranean inner sea, and hammered into shape by the dangers he meets. He is formless and will take shape only through violent contact with ordeals. Until that time, however, he is malleable, without any clear profile or consistency. Adventure gives him his face, his meaning, his true being.

The journey to the center of the earth appears like a kind of descent into hell worthy of Orpheus, a quest for the center at the heart of all the mystery religions. According to the ancient myths, this will enable the hero to acquire a new life after a veritable rebirth. It is symbolic of this to see Axel, Jules Verne's hero, descend into the earth through the crater of an extinct volcano and reemerge into the light during the eruption of an active volcano. In addition, we have the priest initiator of the hero, who is his uncle, the strange savant Lidenbrock, whose name means "he who opens the eyes" (*lid* in his name refers to the eyelid, and *brocken* "to break").

Daniel Compère[2] demonstrates the principal initiatory elements of the novel:

> The discovery of the site takes place during a sacred time, the summer solstice, just as initiations take place at certain set times for religious reasons. Early on, the novice is rudely separated from his world and undergoes several preparatory ordeals: lessons of the abyss, meeting with the lepers, encountering the figure of death, and ascending a mountain (Sneffels). The initiatory journey begins with the descent into the crater. The entry into the realm of the dead is accompanied by purifying rites: lack of water, the crossing of the diamond, and becoming lost in the labyrinth. The novice loses consciousness and comes to in a sacred space. Axel bathes in the primordial waters before undertaking the crossing. He is then sent back to the origins of the world in a dream. He contemplates the "source of life," the geyser that spurts up from the islet that receives his name. . . . In the middle of the storm, Axel receives a baptism of fire. Finally, the return to the profane world takes place. The expulsion is accomplished by fire, the image of a violent rebirth.
>
> In this way Axel has absorbed his lessons of the abyss: He has become fit for contemplating higher things.

Quite a few of Jules Verne's other novels follow a similar initiatory diagram. In *The Adventures of Captain Hatteras*, the entire plot involves the quest for a sacred place, which entails the risk of going mad. The young hero of *In Search of the Castaways* sets off in search of his father, guided by another father who is an "initiator." The elements of an initiation also figure in *Michael Strogoff*: a battle against a monster; ritual blackouts; complete dispossession; a plunge into total darkness; and ordeals of fire, water, earth, and air. In addition the "cave of the

---

2. Daniel Compère, *Un voyage imaginaire de Jules Verne: Voyage au center de la terre* [An Imaginary Voyage of Jules Verne: *Voyage to the Center of the Earth*] (Paris: Archives des Lettres Modernes, 1977).

dragon" in *Begum's Millions* is connected to a labyrinthine city.[3] Nonetheless, simply stating that Jules Verne used an initiatory template for the structure of his books is not enough. We must have further proof of his conscious initiatory intent, and we can find it in closer examination of one of his most beautiful and fascinating books, *The Underground City.*

THE UNDERGROUND CITY

For a full understanding of the author's motives, let's begin by reviewing the plot of the novel.

Engineer James Starr receives a secret invitation to go to the Dochart Pit in Aberfoyle, Scotland, which he is strongly urged to accept. A miner who has refused to leave the mine has invited Starr to return there, where Starr had long worked until, with a heavy heart, he was forced to quit when its seams ran out. This upstanding miner, Simon Ford, lives with his wife and son in a house built at the very base of the mine, in a subterranean cavern. After receiving the invitation, however, Starr received another letter, even more mysterious than the first one, which tries to dissuade him from returning to Aberfoyle. James Starr, however, remains firm in his initial intention to go and makes his way there, where he is welcomed by Simon Ford's son, Harry, who guides the engineer to the mine. As they begin their journey, they meet Jack Ryan, a friend of Harry, who has come to invite him to a party set to take place soon. They enter the maze of galleries when an enormous stone falls at their feet—which does not seem to have happened by accident.

We learn that Simon Ford never wished to accept the notion that the mine was exhausted. He has continued a tireless search for new seams and has found something he wants to show James Starr. But he has also found something of a mystery in the mines: On several occasions, Harry has heard noises and seen a gleam that seemed to flee as he drew near.

---

3. The labyrinth, in one form or another, figures in more than twenty of Jules Verne's novels.

Could there be a spirit in the mine? More concretely, explosions have sometimes taken place, causing support columns to collapse. Leaving all suggestions of haunting and trouble aside, however, Harry, Simon, Madge, and Starr visit a gallery in the old mine at the end of which Simon believes he has discovered a new deposit. James Starr makes a strong effort to relaunch the exploitation of the seam. With dynamite our hero opens a "door" to the new deposit, the New Aberfoyle. There the group finds an immense underground cavern with a lake and high vaults. The only element missing is an interior sun. This cellar could serve as a dwelling place for an entire population. Above the spot, on the earth's surface, lies Loch Katrine. Suddenly, they hear the noise of beating of wings and the lamp is knocked over and broken. The explorers of New Aberfoyle are condemned to find their path in complete darkness—but it is impossible to get out; the passage has been blocked. What could be the mysterious being that protects this domain with such ferocity?

After a week, James Starr's absence begins to alarm his friends. For his part, Jack Ryan is surprised at not having seen Harry at the party and decides to go back to the mine, but it is impossible to descend into it. The ladders have been broken. Jack asks for help, equips himself, and the search begins. A strange bobbing light guides the rescuers to the place where Harry and the others are lying. Imprisoned for ten days, they would not be alive were it not for the help of a mysterious individual who sometimes brought them food and drink but was never seen.

After the rescue, all these incidents are forgotten as the New Aberfoyle begins operating and a town named Coal City is established in the cavern. Harry, however, remains obsessed with the thought of the unknown individual who saved them, and Jack Ryan is convinced it was some sort of sprite or fire maiden. One day, Harry detects a natural pit plunging even deeper into the mine. There he seems to hear sighing and the beating of wings. He decides to explore it, and at the very bottom he finds a young woman—but when he pulls on the rope, the signal to be pulled up from the pit, a bird attacks him. While defending himself, he damages the rope that holds him. Catastrophe is barely averted only because his companions grab him just as the rope breaks.

The young woman, Nell, pulled up from the abyss with Harry, is cared for by the Fords, but the mystery continues: It clearly seems that someone else is hiding in the mine. Nonetheless, little by little, Nell, who has never seen daylight, learns to live a normal life. She and Harry fall in love, but he does not wish her to become accustomed to loving him before she understands what the surface world can offer, and he plans to settle once and for all at the bottom of New Aberfoyle.

One day it is decided that Nell is ready to surface, and the great adventure begins for her. She emerges to see the daylight, the sun, and the outside world—a kind of birth. For two days she visits the area and then, only then, does she choose her life. This is a touching excursion that gives the author the opportunity to make numerous allusions to the work of Sir Walter Scott. Harry asks Nell if she really wishes to marry him and she has barely accepted him when, all at once, Loch Katrine appears to empty, its water disappearing into the ground. What consequences will this have on New Aberfoyle? Is this another misdeed to be attributed to the spirit of the coal mine? Fortunately, the flood does not have overly tragic consequences.

Several days before Harry and Nell's marriage, new threats are made signed "Silfax," the name of a "penitent" who has the extremely dangerous job of detecting firedamp emanations in the mine. To help him in this endeavor, Silfax has reared an owl, a kind of night bird. Having grown mad over time, Silfax has decided that the mine is his kingdom and that none should be allowed to enter it. It was he who raised Nell, his granddaughter, and it was Nell who had saved Harry, Simon, Madge, and James Starr by bringing them the food and water they needed to survive and by guiding their rescuers to them. As for the bird that attacked Harry as he brought Nell up from the pit, it was Silfax's owl.

On the day that the marriage of Nell and Harry was to occur, Silfax releases a pocket of firedamp and tries to ignite it, but the gas is too high. He then gives his torch to the owl and sends the bird to set fire to the gas. The bird, however, obeys Nell, and the torch falls into the water and expires. As for Silfax, he disappears forever in the black waters of the subterranean lake.

Six months later the wedding takes place.

ABERFOYLE AND THE NOVEL OF THE ABBOT

Upon examining this story closely, we can see that it perfectly follows the pattern of every initiatory quest. Here is what Marcel Brion has to say on this subject:[4]

> The route that leads to the mine: Thus begins every journey, and the man who does not first inhale the breath of the earth spirit will not rejoin later, at the end of the race, the spirit of the celestial spheres. The earth must hold him fast, enthrall him with her mineral mysteries and deliver him to the omnipotence of the queen who holds captive the Elïs Fröbom of E. T. A. Hoffmann and Hugo von Hofmannsthal. He is the man returned from the sea and is now symbolically fastened to the land by the death of his Mother. At the center of his underground palace, he takes back in his breast the Mother of the Elements.

The mine is the happy abode that recalls the prenatal period. Without hesitation, Simon Ford describes this world as secure and reassuring. It is a perfectly clean environment subject to a consistently average temperature that knows neither the heat of summer nor the cold of winter, neither the Scottish rain nor the smoke from factories. There is no aggression there—not even tax collectors.

This mine presides over a new, spiritual birth. In this place where "all is silence and darkness," as in a crypt, in this "obscure maze of galleries" there is "a high gallery like the nave of a cathedral." On several occasions, Jules Verne emphasizes in this way the functions of the Temple assigned to the mine. "A labyrinth of galleries, some higher than the most lofty cathedrals, others like cloisters, narrow and winding—these following a horizontal line, those on an incline or running obliquely in all directions—connected the caverns and allowed free communication among them. No Egyptian hypogeum or catacomb of Roman times

---

4. Marcel Brion, *L'Allemagne romantique: Le voyage initiatique* [The Romantics' Germany: The Initiatory Voyage] (Paris: Albin Michel, 1977–1978).

could compare to it. . . . The New Aberfoyle was not the work of men, but the work of the Creator."

This mine-cathedral is also a hive: "This excavation was composed of several hundred divisions of all sizes and shapes. It might be called a hive, with numberless ranges of cells capriciously arranged, but a hive on a vast scale." It so happens that the bee, producer of the edible gold known as honey, has always been considered by the ancients to be a symbol of the soul escaping from matter.[5] Did Jules Verne seek to reinforce this aspect by choosing to situate the plot near Aberfoyle in Scotland and to name his mine the New Aberfoyle?[6] The choice can be viewed as an odd one in any case, for Aberfoyle is one of the only places in that entire region that does not actually have a mine. In fact, this site was the setting for one of Sir Walter Scott's most famous novels, *Rob Roy*, which Jules Verne liked very much. It is also the setting of a story by Charles Nodier, *Trilby ou le lutin d'Argaïl* [Trilby or the Goblin of Argyle]. Nodier alludes to the phantom of Aberfoyle, who may have partially inspired the character of Silfax. All the locations of *The Underground City*—Loch Katrine, Ben Lomond, and so forth, also appear in Nodier's story.[7]

What is more, Aberfoyle is a place where strange things have occurred.

> At the end of the seventeenth century, Reverend Kirk, an adept of the diabolical sciences, adopted this concept for the return to godhood. His interactions with the "thunder bearers" took place on the Hill of the Fairies, near Aberfoyle, bordering the Scottish moors. His mysterious death has the character of all the Luciferian

---

5. See the Greek legend of Aristeus.

6. Aberfoyle could be read as Abe-rfo-yle, meaning *abeille* [French for "bee." —*Trans.*], with *rfo* being similar to Ford, the name of the hero's family. Aberfoyle could also be interpreted as Aberfowl, from *aber* [meaning "deep estuary" in both French and English. —*Trans.*] and *hollow*, by extension, womb of the earth, or fowl or owl. Aberfoyle then becomes the refuge of the owl Harfang and the madman Silfax.

7. See also another story by Nodier: *La légende de Saint-Oran* [The Legend of Saint Oran].

destinies: It corresponds to a particular instant at which the adept is confronted by his final earthly test.[8]

Reverend Kirk's tomb still exists today in the Aberfoyle cemetery. This ecclesiastic has left a curious testimony of his thought, *The Secret Organization,* the first edition of which appeared in 1815 (one hundred twenty-three years after his death) and was translated into French. We might ask if the "book of the priest" Jules Verne alludes to isn't the work of Reverend Kirk rather than the novel *The Abbot* by Sir Walter Scott.

The story is told that one evening in 1688, Reverend Kirk made his way up to the Hill of the Fairies, located in the middle of a small valley bordering Aberfoyle. On his return, what he confided to a Mrs. J. MacGregor, the cemetery guardian, scared her out of her wits. She later recounted how the reverend had the power to disappear on the day and time he wished and that he was assured of never experiencing death or old age. It seems that the rites followed by Kirk fell into the domain of Red Magic. The fact remains that one day, in 1692, he met his end on the Hill of Fairies. Mrs. MacGregor always maintained, however, that his coffin contained only stones and that the reverend had gone to rejoin the spirits of the Hill of Fairies. Did Jules Verne know this strange story?

VISITA INTERIORA RECTIFICANDO INVENIES OCCULTUM LAPIDEM, OR THE MYSTERIOUS QUEST FOR THE UNDERGROUND CITY

Jules Verne's novel is, in fact, the story of a man in search of his soul, that divine element that each of us must find within our deepest heart by means of successfully overcoming ordeals. It is necessary to free from its material straitjacket the hidden pearl, the *anima,* the Lady of the troubadours that was the object of a quest they called the *minne.* Com-

---

8. Jean-Paul Bourre, *Les secrets luciferiennes aujourd'hui* [The Luciferian Secrets Today] (Paris: Belfond, 1978).

plete determination is required to undertake this quest. "Let's dig to the center of the earth, if we have to, in order to tear out the last piece of the coal," Simon Ford says. Harry feels profoundly the appeal of his anima: "He felt irresistibly animated by the hope of finding the mysterious being whose intervention, strictly speaking, had saved himself and his friends." The internalization and the inner quest must occur: "Harry . . . became increasingly introspective and reserved." Despite his infectious good humor, Jack Ryan cannot succeed in drawing him out. Just what is Harry searching for within himself? Melancholy overtakes him; he cannot stop dreaming of his anima, personified by Nell in this adventure. "'By the lady, I don't know.' 'Creatures that live in these holes, Harry, don't you see? They can't be made like us, eh?' 'But they are just like us, Jack.'"

Nell is the personification of the anima that Harry tries to reawaken within himself. Furthermore, Nell is the one who is denied the sun, denied the light until Harry brings her to the surface. Her very name is a composite of the negative *n* and *hel,* the word for "sun" in the Celtic language just as *helios* means "sun" in Greek. But *hel* is also connected to the Celtic hell and the *hel* of the Icelandic *Eddas,* in which it designates the home of the dead. Deprived of light, Harry brings Nell back to life with a spiral progression in the form of a helix. She bears within the ambiguity surrounding the transition of death: She is the daughter of the night and the kingdom of darkness (hell), but she is also a promise of luminosity (the Celtic *hel*). As Jules Verne wrote: "However that might be, there was, under the Scottish subsoil, what might be called a subterranean county, which to be habitable, needed only the rays of the sun or, for want of that, the light of a special planet."

Harry must cross the infernal river like a modern Orpheus setting off in search of his Eurydice.[9] This quest is not without difficulties, for it violates taboos and was often presented by ancient writers as a rape of the earth mother because it involves escaping from the natural cycle and the wheel of reincarnation to come closer to godhood. The name Harry

---

9. Harry's last name, Ford, is significant here in the sense of "to ford a river."

might be seen to be synonymous with "ravaging" or "harassing." This quest triggers catastrophes because the individual places himself outside the law of matter, and true to this, a catastrophe punctuates every confession of love between Nell and Harry for as long as the quest remains unfulfilled. In addition, this rape of the earth mother takes place at the site of the underground city. Harry uses dynamite to carve a path to the new deposit, a veritable promised land for a miner. Thus, the doorway is created by a violent act of penetration, and "Harry, lamp in hand, entered unhesitatingly, and disappeared in the darkness."

Because he is the son of Simon and Madge (names in which we can recognize Simon Magus), Harry is invested with powers and is something of a magician[10] (see figure 1, p. 112a). His mother Madge is also the "good woman" or "good wife," terms often used to describe witches who specialized in the use of herbs. She also always hails tourists with her best "wishes," which closely resembles *witches*.[11]

With a lamp hanging from his left hand and a long staff in his right, like the hermit of the tarot,[12] Harry thus sets off in pursuit of his quest, distancing himself from the material and abandoning superficial laughter[13] in order to approach the divine fullness offered only by love. But he who seeks his anima will also encounter the old man pride, the dark principle that is also the light bearer, Lucifer. It is as necessary to divest of the old man, as it is to state all the traditional doctrines. In this instance, the old man is Silfax, Nell's foster father. Silfax is the other name of Lucifer (*fax* is "torch" and *sileo* means "to remain silent"); he is the light

---

10. Simon holds one key to the adventure, as can be seen in the engraving from the story (see figure 2, p. 112a).

11. We can also note that Simon and Harry have the coal man's faith [the French term for blind and simple faith is *foi de charbonnier.* —*Trans.*], which is an allusion not only to their vocation as miners, but to Carbonari as well. [In nineteenth-century Italy, the Carbonari was a secret society responsible for fomenting revolution. It possibly descended from and was organized similar to the Freemasons. —*Trans.*]

12. *The Underground City* consists of twenty-two chapters, one for each of the Major Arcana.

13. Jack Ryan, or laughing Ryan, as he could be called, says to Harry, "While you are rising into infinity, I will be descending into the abyss."

bearer. Furthermore, his former job, that of penitent, consisted of carrying a flaming brand to detect firedamp. Michel Serres writes:

> Silfax is the other name of Lucifer, the light bearer, the other name of the moment that does not speak, that has no speech and carries into all places the explosive power of the flame , , , He is the Other, but he is God, the other God, all powerful and deceiving, the omnipotent one of this inverted theology . . . He appears standing in a dinghy in the very middle of the lake in the flickering light of his torch.

The old man is inside each of us, and it is not hard to grasp why Simon Ford says, "Who could have penetrated so deeply into the secrets of my thought?" Yes, who if not the old man? And Silfax is old—he is ageless, the one whose interests are opposed to the awakening of the divine soul.[14] The quest will therefore not be easy. Harry must carry out his descent into hell, his plunge to the bottom of the mine, which means to the innermost depth of himself. This can be likened to the *miniere* of the alchemists and the poorly understood *minne* of the troubadours. Only after this can he be born a second time, and this time it will be a birth in Spirit.[15] Nell is still the small light guiding him through the darkness, the one who props him up despite her own weakness. For a long time, she vanishes every time he tries to grab hold of her like a neophyte who senses fleeting impressions of clarity of mind, a summons that cannot be retained as long as he remains the plaything of his sense and passions.[16]

Harry perceived the manifestation of his anima only because he was available, "in expectation," having preferred to internalize (remain at

---

14. One of the heroes says in the book, "I see in this affair an interest running counter to ours."

15. The children who are born in New Aberfoyle will all have to undergo a second birth: "Here it has been eighteen months since they stopped nursing and they have yet to see the light of day."

16. Harry is struck by certain phenomena, the explanations for which eluded him.

the bottom) rather than live in a superficial fashion (on the surface). The desire aroused by these visions is enough to incite Harry to pursue a veritable quest next to which nothing else exists: "I will know, when it should cost me my life!" he says. He will go to the very end of his strength: "'Tomorrow I will go down into the abyss!' 'Harry, that is tempting God, that is!' 'No, Jack, for I will beseech his aid to go down there.'"[17] Harry is at the bottom of the mine, but to find the hidden pearl—his soul—and free it from matter, he must go even farther and find a pit that descends even deeper into the entrails of the world. There he meets himself, but woe to him if he is not the pure and crazy individual to whom the promise of the Grail is reserved. Jules Verne underscores this danger, "[i]f some enemy threatened Harry, if he was to be found at the bottom of the pit where the young miner went looking for him." He descends to the end of the rope,[18] but he is aided by his friends, and his comrades will pull him back up as soon as he yanks on the rope. Here we can look at the text crafted by Jules Verne, one of the most beautiful passages ever written concerning a descent into hell:

> Then his friends began to let him down and he slowly sank into the pit. As the rope caused him to swing gently round and round, the light of his lamp fell in turns on all points of the sidewalls, so that he was able to examine them carefully. . . . No lateral gallery opened from the sidewall of the pit, which was gradually narrowing into the shape of a funnel. But Harry began to feel a fresher air rising from beneath, whence he concluded that the bottom of the pit communicated with a gallery of some description in the lowest part of the mine. The cord continued to unwind. Darkness and silence were complete. . . . One of the fears he entertained had been that, during his descent, the cord might be cut above him, but he had seen no projection from the walls behind which anyone could

---

17. Divine aid appears to be a necessity. This idea can be seen again in another passage: "Without a helpful being such as God had sent them, an angel perhaps . . . a mysterious guide, they would never have escaped from their tomb."

18. The rope is comparable to the silver cord of the Tibetans.

have been concealed. The bottom of the abyss was quite narrow. Harry, taking the lamp from his belt, walked round the place and perceived he had been right in his conjectures. An extremely narrow passage led aside out of the pit. He had to stoop to look into it, and only by creeping could it be followed; but as he wanted to see in which direction it led and whether another abyss opened from it, he lay down on the ground and began to enter it on his hands and knees. And there he found a body in which, although icy cold at the extremities, there was some vital heat remaining. In less time than it takes to tell it, Harry had drawn the body from the recess to the bottom of the shaft, and seizing his lamp, he cast his light on what he had found, exclaiming immediately, "Why, it's a child!"[19]

Yes, this anima is still just a child, for it must be allowed to develop. The passage goes on: "The child found at the bottom of this abyss was still breathing, but her breath was so weak that Harry felt it might cease at any moment. There was not a moment to lose. He must carry this poor little creature out of the pit and take her to his cottage, where Madge could care for her." Harry climbs back up the rope, but it breaks under the attack of the owl, Harfang. Harry's companions catch hold of him at the very moment when it seems to be the end of him; Harry would have remained at the base of the miniere with his anima. In this passage Jules Verne clearly warns us against attempting mystical experiences without help: If the silver cord breaks, it would be madness, to say the least.

Harry brings from the pit Nell, daughter of the night.[20] When questioned, she cries, "I'm hungry. I have not eaten since . . . since . . ." She is unable to provide a date and reveals that she has no notion of time; she doesn't know her age or what a day or a year represents.[21] Thus the anima still must be educated and time has no hold over her, for she is eternal. Below, she was only asleep, like Sleeping Beauty. It is necessary

---

19. "She appeared to only half belong to humanity."
20. Nell can also be an abbreviation of Selene or Helena, personifications of the moon.
21. "It could be seen that she was not accustomed to dividing time either by hours or days, and that the very words were unknown to her."

for Nell to abandon the kingdom of darkness and accept the solar world so that the mystic wedding may be celebrated: Harry says, "I long, Nell, to hear you say, 'Come Harry, my eyes can bear daylight, and I want to see the sun! I want to look upon the works of God!'" But Nell, night's daughter, is distraught and replies: "That darkness is equally beautiful. If you but knew what eyes accustomed to the deep darkness can see! Shadows fly past, and one longs to follow them in their flight. . . . You need to have lived down there to understand what I feel." Finally, the day comes when Nell is ready to see the sun. For the first time she looks on the sky, clouds, moon, and stars. It is James Starr who guides, he who has played the role of initiator throughout the course of the story.

The first water Nell encounters is salted, the sign of a baptism, which follows the same symbolism as the Christian ceremony. The anima abandons the world of the night and receives divine light. She renounces Satan-Silfax-Lucifer, and his pomp and works. Nell's eyes easily tolerate the moonlight, which the ancients viewed as a psychopomp. She does feel a kind of vertigo, though, because until this time she has never known anything but what might be called the reverse world, the subterranean-infernal world. "It seems that the firmament may be like a deep abyss into which one is tempted to throw oneself," says James Starr. At dawn, Nell sees the luminous star of the sun for the first time. It is almost too much for her, and she feels that it is sapping her strength. She then faints, unconscious, into the arms of Harry, which are open to catch her. She still needs more education; it is too early to expose her to the full light of the golden star. In the Masonic initiation, this episode corresponds precisely with the placing of the blindfold over the eyes of the neophyte after he has been exposed to a dazzling light.

This first victory, this first step on the way leading to the mystic wedding, provokes a reaction from the old man, and Loch Katrine subsequently empties into the New Aberfoyle:

It is clear, though, that an implacable foe has sworn the ruin of New Aberfoyle, and that some interest compels him to seek every possible way to satisfy his hatred of us. No doubt too weak to act openly, he hides in the shadows to lay his snares, but the intelligence he exhibits makes him a formidable enemy. My friends, he must know better than we the secrets of our domain, as he has eluded our searches for all this time.

Who would have such an interest if it were not the old man? Jules Verne emphasizes: "Think hard. There are monomaniacs of hatred that time does not soften. Think back to your earliest days, if need be. Everything that has happened is the work of a kind of cold and patient madness, which requires you to summon up even your oldest memories to shed light on this point."

Silfax knows all; he is the "king of fire and shadow" with the egoism of a madman. It seems Nell is destined to be his sacrifice, she who could have "experienced happiness in this world," which is not the lot of every soul. Harry and James Starr do not allow this sleeping beauty to be carried back into the darkness. Nevertheless, when Harry and Nell are on the verge of being married, Silfax arrives in a boat with his head covered by a hood, accompanied by Harfang with its black and white plumage. The affair is of course brought to a happy ending after the death of the old man. It is only then that Nell is completely free from matter and able to unite with Harry. The mystic wedding is celebrated in the underground chapel of Saint Giles, a detail that esotericists can appreciate.

JULES VERNE'S *THE UNDERGROUND CITY* AND MOZART'S *THE MAGIC FLUTE*: TWO MASONIC WORKS

All this evidence sufficiently shows that Jules Verne wrote *The Underground City* as an initiatory and mystical work, but it follows a precise framework provided by one of the most beautiful Masonic works ever realized: Mozart's famous opera *The Magic Flute*. We know that Jules Verne greatly loved this musician. In his novel *In Search of the Castaways*, the character Paganel hears in the desert Mozart's aria "Il mio tesoro tanto" from *Don Juan*, "that sublime inspiration of the master of masters." Indeed, the name Paganel is reminiscent of Papageno in *The Magic Flute*. The relation becomes quite obvious when Paganel is surrounded by all kinds of birds, as if by enchantment, and goes so far as to believe he is one himself.

In any event, it is worth noting how the framework of each of the two works can be superimposed on each other, as illustrated in the following chart.

THE MAGIC FLUTE	THE UNDERGROUND CITY
Act 1, scene 1	
The curtain rises on a wild site in the mountains, the chaotic symbol of nature that is still virgin and brutal, with a few trees here and there to suggest hope in life's rebirth. A round temple sits in the midst of enormous mountains.	The beginning of the novel opens on the site of the Aberfoyle region of Scotland, a desolate area. The coal mines have been abandoned. The pits are neglected, the galleries deserted, and the effect of the whole is of chaos, with the world subjugated by the elements. Jules Verne reminds the reader of the dangers of the mine: cave-ins (earth), fires (fire), floods (water), and methane explosions (air) that strike like lightning. Life seems to be in suspended animation.
Prince Tamino is pursued by a serpent. Weaponless, he faints before this dragon. This fainting appears as a symbolic image of death.	Harry Ford, the equivalent of Tamino, explores a new gallery with his friends. The hope of restoring life to the mine elates Harry. When they try to return, they find the passage blocked. Harry and his companions swoon from lack of food.
Three veiled women, messengers for the Queen of the Night, slay the monster and gaze at the beauty of the fainted prince.	Harry and his companions are saved by Nell, daughter of Silfax, the man who has never left the mine and its eternal night. Nell is touched by Harry.

THE MAGIC FLUTE	THE UNDERGROUND CITY
Enter Papageno (the popinjay-parrot), the bird catcher who lets Tamino believe that it was he who saved him. The three messengers punish Papageno for this lie.	Led by a mysterious glow (carried by Nell), Jack Ryan brings help and pulls Harry out of his rough spot. Jack Ryan, like Papageno, is connected to the element air: He is a piper (bagpipes). Like Papageno, he is superstitious, loves the good life, is a drinker, and is not very deep-minded. His name, Jack, brings to mind that of the popinjay: Jacquot the Parrot. In one of the engravings (see figure 3, p. 112a) depicting him, Jack seems to be accompanied by birds soaring through the sky. He is merry, like his totem bird.
The night messengers give Tamino the portrait of Pamina, the daughter of the queen, whom the wicked genie Sarastro holds prisoner. Pamina was kidnapped on a May night (connected to Walpurgis Night), when she was sitting in her favorite place, a cypress grove (the abode of the dead). Tamino becomes infatuated with this beauty and promises to free her. The messengers give him a magic flute and they give Papageno a set of magic bells.	Harry falls in love with the being who saved him without knowing who it is. He is ready to brave all to discover the mysterious glow perceived in the cavern. In both the Verne story and *The Magic Flute*, this first phase of initiation consists of discovering the path of love and the anima. Does Harry sense that the unknown is a prisoner, just like Pamina?

Act 1, scene 2

The next scene takes place in a room of an Egyptian palace. Three slaves are rejoicing over the escape of Pamina, but she is brought back by the Moor Monostatos, who lusts for her and wants to clap her in irons.	Nell is punished by Silfax and imprisoned in a deep gallery. She is guarded by Harfang, a night bird who loves her passionately.
Papageno informs Pamina of the imminent arrival of her liberator.	Jack helps Harry when he goes to save Nell.

THE MAGIC FLUTE	THE UNDERGROUND CITY
Pamina fears that her mother, the Queen of the Night, is worried.	Nell cannot stop worrying about Silfax.
Pamina faints.	Nell faints.

Act 1, scene 3

The next scene depicts three temples in a sacred grove: the Temple of Wisdom, the Temple of Reason, and the Temple of Nature. Three children guide Tamino toward the temples, where they look for Sarastro, the enemy of the Queen of the Night. Tamino is welcomed by an old priest and learns that Sarastro is not the malefic being described to him. Sarastro is connected to solar symbolism, but it is a "black sun" (Sar = "black, night" and Astro = "star"), the mysterious star dear to Dürer and Nerval. We can recall that the Templars consecrated churches to Our Lady the Real de Sar ("queen of the night"). Jacques Chailley says of Sarastro: "This character is a static figure, almost an abstraction. He experiences neither passions nor adventures. A solar symbol, he is never married and rules over his world of initiates."	Harry has an equivalent of Sarastro in his friend and teacher, James Starr, who bears the name of a star that burns in the night. Chailley's words might apply to Starr as well as Sarastro.
Tamino interrogates the stars. Voices give him encouragement. An answer to his flute comes from the penny whistle of Papageno, who arrives accompanied by Pamina.	With the help of Jack the piper, Harry pulls Nell from the hole in which she has been held prisoner.
Monostatos pursues them, but Papageno's magic bells charm the Moor and force him to flee.	The nocturnal raptor Harfang attacks Harry and tries to prevent him from carrying away Nell. This bird that has been reared by Silfax (like Monostatos, who is in the service of the Queen of the Night) feels a powerful love for Nell.

THE MAGIC FLUTE	THE UNDERGROUND CITY
Sarastro punishes Monostatos for his jealousy. He joins Tamino and Pamina but then separates the two to subject them to trials over which they must triumph.	James Starr decides to guard Nell and places her under the protection of Harry and his parents, thus uniting the two young people. But several circumstances still keep them apart and only the trials they experience together or separately will permit their union.

Act 2

This second act consists of the initiatory ordeals traced along the journeys of the Masonic ritual to the grade of apprentice. The four elements—earth, air, water, and fire—appear in succession.

Act 2, scene 1

THE MAGIC FLUTE	THE UNDERGROUND CITY
The first scene takes place in a palm grove near Egyptian pyramids, recalling the rites of Egyptian Freemasonry. Eighteen thrones crafted from leaves evoke the grade of Rosicrucian.	Jules Verne describes the New Aberfoyle, mentioning the Egyptian hypogeums.
Sarastro asks the gods to grant wisdom to the couple of Tamino and Pamina, and the initiates gathered there decide to admit them into the trials. Osiris and Isis are invoked and Tamino and Papageno are led into the underground reaches of the temple where they undergo various temptations that they must overcome by silence. Tamino passes the test successfully, but Papageno has great difficulty keeping quiet.	The idea of a union between Harry and Nell is encouraged by James Starr. Certain trials are necessary, however. Nell must know life outside the mine before making her choice. Will she have the strength to resist the temptation of the sun and a normal life for the benefit of an "inner life?" Harry takes the risk of introducing the outside world to Nell.

THE MAGIC FLUTE	THE UNDERGROUND CITY
Act 2, scene 2	

The next scene takes place in a garden. Monostatos attempts to seduce Pamina. The Queen of the Night gives her daughter a dagger to kill Sarastro. The Moor gets hold of the dagger and threatens Pamina, but Sarastro stops him and drives him away.	The emergence into the open air takes place at night. Nell suffers the attack of the forces of the earth, but like Pamina, she refuses to believe the Queen of the Night. Nell does not allow herself to be tempted by the common world. Also like Pamina, despite the attempts by Silfax to take her back, she remains with Harry.
Papageno remains bound to earthly pleasures and Sarastro gives him a companion worthy of him: Papagena. Papageno fails the water test. He drinks a little too much and the earth opens and swallows him up.	Jack remains bound to earthly pleasures. He remains a man of the surface, a hearty drinker and a jolly fellow. He fails his water test by misinterpreting the reason for the collapse of Loch Katrine (as if the ground had opened up).
Tamino and Pamina undergo the water test.	The water test for Harry and Nell is the collapse of Loch Katrine and the flooding of a part of the mine.
Tamino, bound by the test of silence, cannot speak to Pamina, who despairs.	It is Nell who cannot speak and refuses to reveal her secret to Harry. She dreads Silfax. In a certain way, Harry is also undergoing a trial of silence: It requires a great deal of patience and love for him to keep his silence and not to ask ceaselessly the questions burning on his lips.

Act 2, scene 3	
The next scene takes place in the caverns of the Temple.	The scene takes place in the caverns of the mine.

THE MAGIC FLUTE	THE UNDERGROUND CITY
Led underground by Monostatos, the Queen of the Night and her ladies prepare to wage battle against Sarastro. All are carrying black torches. (Monostatos, rejected by Pamina, has offered his services to the Queen of the Night).	Aided by Harfang, Silfax tries to set fire to the mine and explode the entire place by carrying a torch into a huge pocket of firedamp. After Harry saved Nell, the owl returned to Silfax. Just like Monostatos, Harfang is in some way the symbol of degraded, vulgar love.
The Queen of Night curses her daughter. Jacques Chailley writes: "The day on which her own daughter will rejoice for sharing with the chosen man his ascension and forming with him the perfect couple, her fury will know no bounds."	Silfax curses Nell, whom he raised as if she were his daughter. Jacques Chailley's observations about the Queen of Night could equally apply to Silfax.
With a crack of thunder, the Queen of Night is swallowed up with her retinue. She disappears beneath the earth: the feminine (the queen) sinks into the masculine (earth).	The brilliant explosion is avoided because Harfang obeys Nell rather than Silfax, who falls from his boat into the depths of the lake: the masculine (Silfax) sinks into the feminine (water) and drowns.
Having triumphed over the trials of fire and water, Tamino and Pamina are worthy of each other. The powers of the night have been vanquished and Tamino and Pamina are consecrated at Sarastro's side. Their union is a culmination.	Having triumphed over the trials of fire and water, Harry and Nell are worthy of each other. Silfax has vanished and the inhabitants of New Aberfoyle are no longer in danger. Harry and Nell are veritable heroes at James Starr's side. Their marriage is celebrated.

Concerning *The Magic Flute,* Jacques Chailley writes:[22] "*Die Zauberflöte* is centered on the drama of Pamina's passage from one universe to the other as much as upon Tamino's initiation, and perhaps more. It is a sorrowful passage, which at first requires that she be kidnapped against her will and which causes tears and sufferings, but one that will

---

22. Jacques Chailley, *The Magic Flute Unveiled* (Rochester, Vt.: Inner Traditions, 1992).

end in the final apotheosis of the Couple." It seems Chailley could also be writing about Nell.

JULES VERNE AND SCOTTISH FREEMASONRY

The majority of authors who have concerned themselves with the initiatory aspect of Jules Verne's work have recalled as evidence the initiatory structure of his work, but have hastened to take a step backward by attributing this to the author's unconscious. In the same way, some might no doubt be tempted to say that the relationship between *The Magic Flute* and *The Underground City* does not prove that Jules Verne was aware of the Masonic aspect of Mozart's opera. Simone Vierne has written:

> It is possible to think that Verne knew about Freemasonry. From 1864 he was directing alongside Jean Macé[23] Hetzel's *Magasin d'Education et de Récréation,* and in a letter to Macé, Verne writes: "I like Hetzel and I owe him more than I do you. . . . He is my special [spiritual] director." His friend the musician Hignard, with whom he made his first journey to Scotland and his journey to Denmark and Norway, was also a Freemason. Indeed, Freemasons must have been numerous in the entourage of the republican and agnostic Hetzel, but all that can be said is that Verne must have heard of these doctrines, though, based on my information, he was not initiated himself.

Yet if Jules Verne wasn't a Freemason, would he have known the rituals as well as he seems to know them? Would he have felt the need to scrupulously mention every Masonic temple he encountered on his travels in the unpublished recounting of his trip to England and Scotland? Would he have alluded to Freemason lodges in his book *In Search of the Castaways* as "signs of civilization"? Would he have mentioned a Masonic temple in *Robur the Conqueror* or the signs of recognition in

---

23. Jean Macé was a very influential Mason.

Begum's Millions, along with numerous other allusions? Would he have included the invocation of the Great Architect in *The Journey to the Center of the Earth,* where nature proceeds with square, compass, and plumb line, or included the wordplay on Aronnax[24] or the play on the true snails?[25] We can also consider *The Green Ray,* in which Jules Verne says of a young imbecile named Aristobulus Ursiclos that he did not listen, saw nothing, and never shut up: The opposite maxim—*Audi, Vide, Tace*—was the Freemason's expression for wisdom. In addition, there is Mr. Dubourg in *Castles in California,* who appeals to God by pressing over his heart his work tools—a square, a compass, and a plumb line.

We could go on citing such examples forever. To return to *The Underground City,* it seems this novel is sufficient on its own to prove Jules Verne's membership in Freemasonry and, more specifically, in its Scottish branch. James Starr, one of the main characters of this story (which, as we now know, takes place in Scotland), serves as an initiator. It is he who will bring the mine back to life after it has been closed for many years. We have already seen that his name is evocative of that of Sarastro, but with him Jules Verne created a double play on words: James Starr is also reminiscent of James Stuart,[26] the king who reawakened Freemasonry, which had gone into slumber following the Templar trial (if we put credence in the legend). Starr, too, brings the mine back from its sleep. Interestingly, James Starr lives in Edinburgh, in the Canongate, where the houses of the Scottish nobility were once located and at the end of which stands the royal palace of Scotland, Holyrood.

The analogies continue. We are told by Jules Verne that James Starr belongs to an old family of Edinburgh and is part of an association of Scottish antiquarians of which he has been named president. The allusion to Freemasonry becomes fairly obvious when Verne stresses: "He held a high rank in this old capital of Scotland." We might read this as: He was of high rank, of a high grade in Scottish Freemasonry. Furthermore, an

---

24. See *Twenty Thousand Leagues under the Sea.*
25. [This refers to *colimaçons* in French, with *maçons* being Masons. —*Trans.*]
26. In 1603, James VI of Scotland became king of England under the name of James I and became grand master of the English Operative Masons.

engraving from the book (see figure 4, p. 112a) shows us James Starr and places next to him a book (no doubt the Gospel of John) on which rests a T-square next to a compass. Additionally, Jules Verne tells us that James Starr belongs to the "Royal Institution." What could this be if not the Scottish Freemasonry instituted by James Stuart? Further, the institution's president is named Sir W. Elphiston, a very revealing name. Elphiston[27] is in fact el-phis-ton, or *el* (the) *fils* (son) stone: the son of the stone. What a fine name for a Mason and a wink on the part of Jules Verne, who is himself the son of stone, for Pierre is his father's first name. It is Elphiston whom James Starr will alert when he cannot attend a meeting, just as a Mason is obliged to alert the elder of his lodge if he will be unable to attend a meeting.

In *The Underground City* the mine itself appears as a lodge whose inhabitants are designated as the children of the widow: "The old coal mine will thus rejuvenate like a widow who remarries." There are many other equally significant Masonic details in the book. For example, at the beginning of the novel, James Starr brings up old memories with Harry. He does not respond to Harry's questions, however, because they are outside and might be overheard. As a Mason would indicate to a brother the danger of being surprised by indiscreet ears, he limits himself to saying: "Cover up Harry, it is raining." Likewise, later, Simon Ford says: "It is raining above. Here it never rains," for they are then in the mine. He could just as easily have said: The lodge is covered, for this "vast hall illuminated by several lamps" is a Masonic temple. When it comes time to initiate Nell to the light, being on the outside of the mine, they reverse the terms. The meeting will not be held from noon to midnight, as intended by the Freemason ritual, but during the exact opposite time: "from midnight to noon, she will undergo these successive phases of light and shadow so her eyes can gradually become accustomed."

All Masonic rituals mention purification by the four elements. Similarly, Nell, imprisoned underground as if in a cabinet of reflection, encounters the air when she emerges into the outside world, then boards a

---

27. Elphiston is also the name of a character in *From Earth to the Moon*.

boat that places her in contact with water before discovering the fire of the sun. Other allusions are made to the four elements throughout the novel, as we have seen.[28]

Finally, we turn to Harry, the hero of this adventure. Who is he? Jules Verne offers that he is Harry Ford, the "perfect type of Lowlander." The word *lowlander* here means just that: Harry is an inhabitant of these low lands. But Jules Verne no doubt had another specific reason for using this term: Because *low* is synonymous with *down,* the term *lowlands* can be easily transposed into *lands-down,* a term that designates the oldest Masonic constitutions, which date from the sixteenth century.[29] Harry "was at the same time, *a solid journeyman*[30] of brave and good nature" (my italics). He was himself the son of a Mason (Loveton), for:

> . . . [G]uided by his father, pushed by his own instincts, he had worked, he had improved his mind from an early age, and at an age when one is barely more than an apprentice, he had managed to make something of himself—one of the first in his position—in a country that has few uneducated people because it does everything to eliminate ignorance. While, during the first year of his adolescence, the pick never left Harry Ford's hand. Nevertheless, the young miner did not delay in picking up the knowledge sufficient to rise in the hierarchy of the coal mine, and he would certainly have succeeded his father as foreman of the Dochart Pit if the mine had not been abandoned.

This really speaks for itself: Harry, son of a higher Mason (a *foreman,* etymologically speaking, is one who is at the head of other men),

---

28. Among these, we can recall: the ongoing battle, the danger of cave-ins (earth), fires (fire), floods (water), and methane explosions (air).

29. See Jean Tourniac, *Principes et problèmes spirituals du rite ecossaise rectifié et de sa chevalerie templière* [Spiritual Principles and Problems of the Rectified Scottish Rite and its Templar Knighthood] (Paris: Dervy, 1969), 17.

30. [The word *compagnon* in French means companion and journeyman, as in the second of the symbolic grades of Freemasonry. —*Trans.*]

was able to receive Masonic training sooner than usual, a privilege reserved for the sons of Masons. As for the country that has done its all to eliminate ignorance, it is quite obvious that this designates Scottish Freemasonry, which has always openly displayed this intention.

I do not think it should be necessary to add anything more to demonstrate that Jules Verne belonged to Freemasonry, yet for the most skeptical, I will make one final observation: It would have been fairly simple for Jules Verne to procure information about the Masonic rituals for the apprentice, journeyman, and master, but not for the high grades, one of which is mentioned in *Michael Strogoff*. There, in fact, we see the hero fighting a bear, and much later, Michael Strogoff is tortured and becomes blind. We can see marked similarities in a passage from Charles Le Forestier's *La Franc-Maçonnerie Templière et Occultiste* [Templar and Occult Freemasonry] concerning the grades of Elect or Vengeance:

> The candidate presents himself to the Venerable with red-spattered gloves, declaring that the blood that stains his hands was that of the bear, the tiger, and the lion that criminals had raised to guard the entrance to their den. The newly initiated member consents to die in the worst torture, after which his eyes will be ripped from the light with a red-hot iron, if he ever violates his oath of discretion.

This is what happens to Michael Strogoff after he breaks his oath in order to rescue his mother.

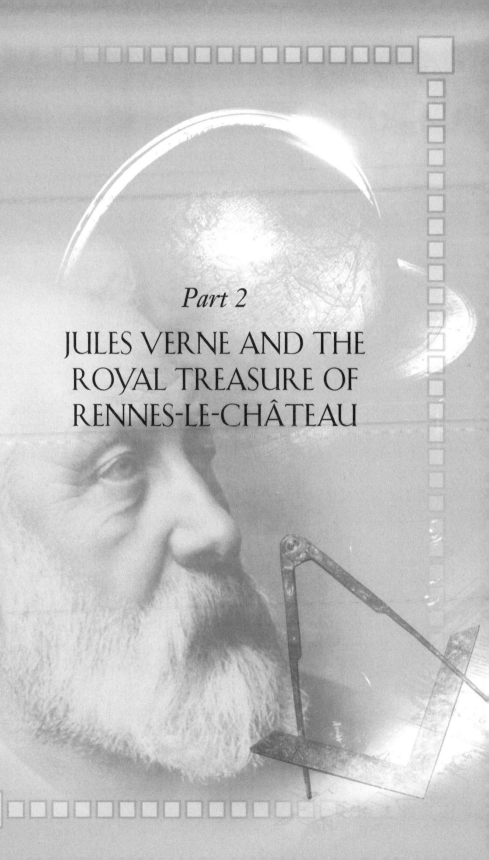

Part 2

JULES VERNE AND THE ROYAL TREASURE OF RENNES-LE-CHÂTEAU

THE TREASURE OF
FATHER SAUNIÈRE

BÉRENGER SAUNIÈRE

The story of the treasure of Rennes-le-Château is a curious tale to which Jules Verne holds the key.[1] First, however, we must look more closely at the setting in which this adventure took place.

Rennes-le-Château is a small village occupying the top of a hill overlooking the Aude Valley, south of Carcassonne. To reach the former capital of the Visigoth kingdom from the town of Couiza, you have to take a fairly narrow steep road through a landscape dominated by red soil and golden broom. This area known as the Razès, part of the Corbières region, is a strange and fascinating land of contrasts. Here, people have to deal everyday with the elements in a tangible fashion. The hills are crushed by the sun and the ever whistling wind, while the valleys, which are quite green and often cool, give shelter to somewhat fast-flowing rivers carving paths through banks riddled with caves. An alchemical land, the Razès is one of the most tellurically charged regions of France.

It was here in this land of fire and water that François-Bérenger Saunière was born on April 11, 1852, in Montazels. In 1885 he became the parish priest for the little village of Rennes-le-Château. At the age of

---

1. This affair began to be known publicly only starting in January 1956, when the first articles on the subject began appearing in *Dépeche du Midi*.

thirty-three, this man with the build of a rugby player and a keen and somewhat disturbing gaze in a strong-willed face, started a new life without knowing it. The church he headed, dedicated to St. Mary Magdalene, was not one to give the priest any consolation. It was practically falling into ruin, and Saunière was sometimes obliged to celebrate Mass in the rain that fell through the holes in the roof. It was wretchedly miserable, and the priest suffered particularly from being unable to buy the books he needed to perfect his knowledge of Greek, Latin, and Hebrew.

Seduced by this fellow, a young girl of eighteen, Marie Denarnaud, abandoned the hat-making workshop where she was employed to become his servant. It seems clear that she quickly became the mistress of Saunière, who had a reputation in the area for being hot-blooded. She shared his secrets and right up to the time of her death, always refused to divulge them to those who attempted to make her reveal them.

Bérenger Saunière was not a man to back down from adversity of any kind. Because the church was in poor shape, there was nothing that could be done but to restore it. One of his predecessors, Father Pons, had bequeathed a small sum to the parish, though unfortunately it was too small to cover all the necessary repairs. Yet it would at least allow the most pressing work to be undertaken, and some repairs started to be made in 1888.

THE DISCOVERY OF THE FIRST TREASURE

To get the repairs underway, Bérenger Saunière succeeded in convincing the municipality of Rennes-le-Château to agree to a loan, though at this time the priest had no idea of how he was going to pay it back. The most important work began in 1891. Because the altar table was damaged, the decision was made to move it and—surprise! —It was found that the Visigoth column on which it had rested was hollow. Inside it the priest found three wooden tubes sealed with wax, which contained parchments packed in dried ferns.

Saunière alerted the municipality and together they decided to sell the parchments as a way to reimburse the town for all or part of the loan they had given him. This was not something that could be done in the space of a few days, and in 1893, the bishop of Carcassonne, Felix-Arsène Billard, convinced Saunière of the significance of the parchments. Whatever the bishop discovered in their contents, it was a sufficiently important clue for him to give Saunière enough from the bishopric to pay back the loan granted by the municipality without having to sell the documents. What's more, he sent Bérenger Saunière to Paris with an introduction to Father Bieil, director of Saint Sulpice. At this time, a number of occultists, experts in ancient history and religion, and members of secret societies were gravitating around the parish of Saint Sulpice. There Saunière also found men well versed in ancient tongues and secret languages, who took on the responsibility of decoding the mysterious parchments. This task would have been made all the easier for them because Saint Sulpice Church itself contained a number of elements connected to the same mystery, as we shall see.

While in Paris, Saunière began frequenting a strange cenacle for whom the occult sciences offered few secrets. The little priest from a poor village in the Aude thus entered high society and experienced Parisian salon life. There he also met a famous and very beautiful soprano who was well-known in esoteric circles, Emma Calvè, who would become his mistress for a time, most likely on the orders of a secret society.

After three weeks, Bérenger Saunière returned to Rennes-le-Château without the parchments (though he had copies), but he was supplied with valuable information. Without wasting any time, he resumed construction work in the church and had workers move a paving stone that was placed at the foot of the high altar. There was carving on the other side of the stone facing the ground.[2] It depicted a hunting scene and a knight who seemed to be holding a child on the neck of his horse. At the exact location of this paving stone, Bérenger Saunière had a hole dug about three feet deep, then he discharged the workers. Before leaving the church, however, these men had enough time to see two skeletons as well as a pot filled with shiny objects. To the questions that inevitably arose about this matter,

---

2. It can be seen today in the small souvenir shop adjoining the church.

Saunière responded by claiming that they were only worthless medals. In the weeks that followed, he made other excavations in various locations in the church and dug up several objects about which we know very little.

THE MYSTERIOUS TOMB

Saunière curiously spent some of his nights in the church's cemetery. The village eventually became very worked up about this activity of the priest, which far exceeded the normal parameters of his profession. What gave him the right to excavate a grave and then erase the inscriptions from its tombstone? This sepulcher he tended belonged to Marie de Negri d'Ables, wife of François d'Hautpoul, marquis of Blanchefort and lord of Rennes, who died shortly before the French Revolution.

What was the motive for the priest's strange labor? The answer can no doubt be found in the text that appeared on the tombstone. Ancient grave rubbings, of which Saunière knew nothing, have told us what it was. Very quickly a number of anomalies were detected in it: spelling mistakes in the name of the deceased, errors in the date of death, groups of characters without apparent meaning, words arbitrarily chopped off, some letters that are smaller than the others, and so forth. So many mistakes would be unacceptable on a tombstone. If we apply a decoding method to the text formed by these anomalies (the Vigenère Method well-known to decryption experts and connected to a key contained in the text itself)[3] and if we duplicate this key with the "knight's move," another decoding method requiring a chessboard, a clear albeit sibylline text will emerge:

Shepherdess no temptation that Poussin Teniers hold the key, peace 1631—by the cross and horse of God I finish[4] this demon guardian at noon. Blue apples.

---

3. The name comes from Blaise de Vigenère, the person charged by the Medicis to set up the Academy of Arcadia.

4. [Or finish off. —*Trans.*]

The text resulting from the decoding of the parchments that Saunière is supposed to have found is reportedly the same.

SUDDEN WEALTH

The fact remains that after these episodes, Saunière began traveling a good deal. The humble parish priest who did not have two pennies to rub together, who was starving, was opening bank accounts in several places, including those abroad.[5] He carefully concealed the purpose of these trips just as he kept his silence about the numerous checks that he received from almost all over Europe, addressed to his servant Marie Denarnaud.

Now this modest country priest who began with no money embarked on a series of wild expenditures. First, in 1896, he undertook the renovation of his church at his own expense. These were not simple repairs but large-scale construction projects: On the priest's instructions, the windows were relocated, a secret room was added to the sacristy, a wall was breached to fit in a staircase leading to the rostrum, and a mosaic floor of alternating black and white paving stones was laid. For several months after the construction, Saunière incurred the expense of the artists and workers he hired to decorate his church. To this end, he gave very precise instructions concerning the placement of the Stations of the Cross as well as the Calvary and the painting of the Sermon on the Mount. He had several details redone and took up the paintbrush himself to paint St. Mary Magdalene beneath the altar.[6] In 1897, he invited his bishop to inaugurate the now finished church. What could Monsignor Billard's thoughts have been when he read the inscriptions on the porch?[7] It seems that he was in a very great hurry to take his leave and get away from this excessively odd church where a sense of malaise

---

5. Traces of an account he may have opened have been found in a Budapest bank.

6. Contrary to what has often been written, the only interesting element in this sculpture in the round is the painting, for the relief is connected to a very common image of Mary Magdalene and owes nothing to Bérenger Saunière.

7. [*Terribilis est locus iste* (This place is terrible). —*Ed.*]

seemed to hover. It should be noted that the alarming demon holding up the holy water stoup had a decided influence in the creation of this ambiance.

One question occurred to everyone who saw the renovations: Where did Bérenger Sanière get the money enabling him to finance all this construction? Did he find it in the "medals" discovered in the church? Even if these were ancient coins, the modest quantity he found would surely not have been enough to cover the expense or the work. The question was still unresolved in 1900, when the priest bought the land that sat at the top of the village. Here, on a site from which could be seen the snow-topped peaks of the Pyrenees as well as the gentle valleys below, Sanière had built a neo-Gothic tower that he called the Magdala Tower. It was constructed with a circular terrace standing over a cistern and several fine halls. To the tower he added a small greenhouse to serve as space for a winter garden. After this, he had built the Villa Bethany, a spacious bourgeois mansion consisting of a dozen rooms. There he had built a pool and laid out gardens—in short, he put together an entire domain costing a veritable fortune. Where did the money come from? As if the construction was not enough, the priest also enjoyed a high and costly lifestyle that included a collection of one hundred thousand rare stamps, ten thousand postcards, and rare books. He also had the entire region photographed at his expense and received a number of important figures at his villa, among whom were the state secretary of fine arts Dujardin-Baumets and a Hapsburg archduke, a cousin of the Austro-Hungarian emperor.

It is easy to imagine the astonishment of the inhabitants of this small village before such munificence. Tongues wagged, imaginations ran wild, conjectures were made, but this fabulous wealth of a poor little parish priest exceeded imagining and talk began of . . . treasure. In any case, the jealous were soon appeased and the rumors never strayed beyond the borders of the village because Sanière was extremely generous to everyone.

As for the ecclesiastical authorities, they closed their eyes, at least during the tenure of Monsignor Billard, who may well have known much about what was going on. A subsequent bishop upon whom Saunière was dependent demanded explanations from the priest about his revenues, but Saunière did everything he could to stall for time and avoided responding. Summoned on May 27, 1910, to appear before the ecclesiastical court of the diocese, the priest did not appear and was convicted in absentia for selling Masses and was declared *suspens à divinis,* which in plain English means that he no longer had the right to say Mass or administer the sacraments. He appealed to the Vatican, and without skimping on fees; he hired a lawyer in Rome to argue his case. Eventually, the Holy Congregation of the Council lifted the sanctions and reduced to nothing the accusation that he trafficked in Masses.

Shortly after this time, World War I started and Bérenger Saunière began to hurt for money. He had difficulty settling certain bills and even had to solicit a mortgage loan from the Credit Foncier of France. After a certain time had elapsed, however, it seems he returned to his plans: He was thinking of having a road built between Rennes-le-Château and Couiza, installing running water in the entire village, and building a new chapel and a tower some two hundred twenty feet high that would serve as a huge library. At the beginning of 1917, he may well have been capable of financially carrying out his projects, but on January 17, he suffered a stroke at the door of the Magdala Tower. He died five days later, on January 22, at the age of sixty-five.

WHAT WAS THE SOURCE OF SAUNIÈRE'S MONEY?

The death of the priest set everyone's tongue wagging. Gossip was rampant and people tried to glean information from Marie Denarnaud, his servant, but her lips were sealed. Soon people recalled the set of bizarre events at the church in this region that was quite rich in legends of treasures. If Bérenger Saunière had in fact discovered some fabulous loot, that would explain all, and what's more, if he had planned projects just before his death, it meant that his trove was far from exhausted.

Many people have hunted for this treasure in Rennes-le-Château, including a good many of those who will swear to you, if you ask, that the treasure never existed. Some did not hesitate to use dynamite, and the local authorities were forced to ban all excavations to prevent the transformation of their village into a pile of ruins.

Behind the folklore, however, we can ask: Is the existence of a fabulous treasure in Rennes-le-Château plausible? Yes, there is no doubt this possibility exists, and a quick glance at the region's history should convince us. First of all, this would not be the first time that valuable objects were discovered in this remote corner of France. Long ago, there was the discovery of a gold ingot weighing about forty-five pounds and made from amalgamated Arabian coins. Then, in 1860, another ingot, this one weighing one hundred ten pounds, was discovered coated in a tarlike substance. Saunière himself offered one of his colleagues a very ancient chalice whose provenance is not known. From where came the wealth of Cayron, parish priest of St. Lawrence of the Caberisse, if not from treasure, as some of his parishioners believed?

In fact, the existence of objects made from precious metals is not greatly surprising in this region because it is a land of springs and mines that encouraged habitation in ancient times. During the Roman era, hot springs existed in places such as Alet, Campagne, and Rennes-les-Bains, and everywhere mines can be found that contain gold, silver, copper, jet, iron, and other precious substances that were exploited in the remote past. Various hypotheses have been constructed to explain the tenacious legends concerning a buried treasure in this area. There are even claims that no less than twelve different troves are hidden in the Rennes neighborhood. Among those that are subject of speculation is the treasure of Henri de Tastamare, not to mention the Grail that the Cathers are said to have had in their keeping. What we do know for certain is that the Templars, who were solidly established in this area, had invited German foundry workers, whom they settled near Rennes. These foreigners allegedly worked in a gold mine located just next to Blanchefort, but what purpose do foundry workers serve in the exploitation of a gold mine? They would need primarily miners to extract the gold—unless the mine contained a deposit of gold objects rather than gold in mineral form, and a decision had been made to melt them down. It would then be very easy to understand why foundry workers had been "imported" from abroad, for foreigners were much less likely to talk with the natives.

Perhaps this is the secret Bérenger Saunière sought to reveal in the first station of the Stations of the Cross he had constructed for the church of Mary Magdalene. In this depiction, we can see Pontius Pilate sitting on a gold throne, which brings to mind Solomon as painted by Nicholas Poussin. Pilate is washing his hands in front of a white platter held by a small black child whose pose is reminiscent of certain ancient chess pieces that replaced the castle and also bore the name of rook. At the very bottom of the station, the cloth covering the throne's dais is folded in an odd way as if to depict the entrance to a mine.

We can read this rebus thus: The gold is enthroned in the mine located at the foot of Roco Negro (black rock), which supports the plateau of Blanchefort (white plateau). In fact, the mine that was exploited by the Templars is located quite close to Blanchefort, beneath the plateau, next to Roco Negro. Surely this is not a coincidence. But where did this gold come from, and is it still there? As we will see, several clues indicate that the trove was transported to a new location still in this region.

GOLD FROM THE TEMPLE OF SOLOMON

As for where the gold came from, the most fantastic but still quite plausible explanation says that it was the gold of the biblical King Solomon. In the year 70 CE, Emperor Titus took possession of Jerusalem and his soldiers pillaged the city. The Romans devoted particular attention to the Temple of Solomon, which they stripped of its wealth. This event was commemorated by the Arch of Triumph in Rome on which is depicted a seven-armed candelabra, among other images. The riches of Solomon's Temple are the stuff of legend: It is said that more than five hundred tons of gold and a great many precious objects were seized. The roof of the temple alone is said to have been studded with a large number of gold-plated spikes to keep birds from alighting upon it. Piles of offerings, all quite valuable, were stacked everywhere. When Titus returned to Rome, he sold some of the gold ingots and plate he had stolen, which was enough to cause a crash in the gold market at the time. But the majority of objects, such as the candelabra, were kept and stored in the Temple of Peace located in the imperial palace.

On August 24, 410, these objects were undoubtedly still there when the Visigoth king Alaric attacked and captured Rome. For a period of six days his troops pillaged the city and took from it, among other things, the loot from the Temple of Solomon. After the sack, Alaric returned to Languedoc and the treasure was housed in Carcassonne. In 507, however, following Clovis's capture of Toulouse, the Frankish king besieged Carcassonne and only the intervention of the Goth king of Italy, Theodoric, permitted the city to be saved. Nevertheless, Alaric II had been slain and Carcassonne, now a border city, was no longer safe. Some—but not all—of the treasure was carried away to Toledo. At this time, the capital of the Visigoth kingdom north of the Pyrenees was no longer Carcassonne but Rhedae, now known as Rennes-le-Château. It is hard for us in the present day to imagine that this modest village was at one time the capital of a kingdom that numbered, according to some, around thirty thousand inhabitants, who were of course living on the entire plateau. It is not impossible, therefore, that the gold from Solomon's temple would have been hidden near Rhedae, and why couldn't its location have been in the Blanchefort mine?

We might ask what remains of it today. That is another story. What seems certain is that the Templars did not take it all, for Louis IV ordered searches to be carried out at this same site, and it seems these searches achieved success.

The majority of people who have taken an interest in the Rennes-le-Château affair have followed Gérard de Sède's lead and accepted the hypothesis of Solomon's treasure. I have to admit that for my part I find the evidence rather thin. My research has gradually brought me to consider this hypothesis as plausible, however, not only because the Seal of Solomon can be seen on many of the monuments in this area, not only because it seems that the Israeli Secret Service has taken an interest in the region, not only because the high rabbi of Jerusalem has taken a particular interest in the area, but also because there are quite a few similarities shared by this region and Jerusalem.

For example, in Arques, near Rennes, we might find an anagram of the lower city of Jerusalem known as the Heights of Acra. Facing the Antonia Fortress in Jerusalem is Bizita Hill, and facing Rennes (with its legends connected to St. Anthony) is the Bézu and its mountain that holds the ruins of a former Templar fortress. It is also perhaps worth noting some other distinctive features of Jerusalem such as the pool of Siloe. (Hezekiah, 716–687 BCE, brought water into the city by damming the upper flow of the waters of the Gehon and directing them down toward the west of David's city). Near Jerusalem in 1880, some children were playing on the banks of a pond when one of them fell in and tried to swim to the other side, where there was a rocky outcropping. He suddenly found himself in total darkness and saw he had entered a narrow passageway. This was how a tunnel about 40 inches wide, 5 feet high, and 1,640 feet long was discovered. After two main detours, the tunnel ended at the fountain of the Virgin Mary (formerly Gehon Spring) that had provided Jerusalem with water. A text in ancient Hebrew was carved on the wall of the gallery, explaining how it was hollowed out. Oddly enough, for no apparent reason the canal was formed in the shape of a large S, which more than doubled the length of the tunnel. An old legend states that these curves were motivated by the intention to go around the tombs of David and Solomon. This is reminiscent of the place near Rennes known as Aram, the same name of one of David and Solomon's ancestors, which is located quite close to Pech Auriol (gold peak).

It is said that Solomon's treasures had a powerful effect on dreams, and it is curious that this subject inspired Jacques Cazotte to write the novel *Le Chevalier!* [The Knight!]. In it a Muslim by the name of Habib (Beloved) makes a long journey underground during which he visits the chambers housing the treasures of Solomon. There he must open and close forty doors in succession. In the first chamber he must disarm a black slave of gigantic height and take away from him the sword of the great Solomon by speaking the word written on the blade: *power.* Then the hero must descend 1,490 stairs, which correspond to the word *ADTZ* or *ADSIZ*, meaning "nameless" in Turkish.[8] We should take note of the relation among ADSIZ = 1 + 4 + 9 = 14; the word *nameless;* and one of Jules Verne's essential heroes, Nemo, the nameless, whose initial is the fourteenth letter of the alphabet.

THE MYSTERY OF THE CRÉQUIER AND THE SEVEN-BRANCHED CANDELABRA

All of these similarities may be seen simply as signs lacking any consistency and they do not offer any proof for the presence of Solomon's treasure in Rennes. Another clue can be found, though, in the Créqui family. What was the Créqui family doing in this region? From where did the house of Créqui acquire their fabulous riches? How could Lord Créqui de Blanchefort, prince of Foix, duke of Equières, peer and marshal of France, advisor to the king in both his state and private councils, a knight of his orders, first gentleman of his royal chamber, lieutenant general for His Majesty the Dauphin, and ambassador to Venice have accumulated so many titles? As for his arrival in Venice on July 16, 1634, he was sparkling with diamonds and other precious stones, and when he went to pay homage to the duke of Tuscany, he received "the most signal honors and the most affectionate greetings that appeared suitable to His Highness, not only due to the grandeur of he whom he represented, but also to the particular merit of such a great lord."

Just what was this "particular merit" of Sir Charles de Créqui de Blanchefort that he would receive more due than the king of France? For whom was he really the permanent ambassador? Wasn't a Créqui at Rennes-les-Bains in 1662 while Colbert was carrying out searches in Blanchefort?

The mystery does not stop there, for the Créqui family bore allusive

---

8. See Jean Richer, *Aspects ésotériques dans l'oeuvre littéraire* [Esoteric Aspects in Literary Work] (Paris: Dervy, 1980).

arms: gold with a créquier in gules.[9] Father Ménestrier describes the cré-quier as a kind of wild plum tree in Picardy whose fruit is called *créque* in the local dialect. According to Dom Plessis,[10] the word *créquier* comes from the Teutonic *kerk,* meaning "church" or "temple." It is easy to see a bit of Solomon's Temple beginning to poke through here. Let's now follow the lead of F. Cadet de Grassicourt and Baron de Roure de Pau-lin,[11] for whom the créquier is nothing other than the seven-branched candelabra. This might be viewed as an additional confirmation of the possible presence of the treasure from Solomon's Temple in the region of Rennes. Furthermore, in Rennes-le-Château, in the church of Mary Magdalene, there is an extremely rare depiction of a créquier, which Bérenger Saunière ordered to be included in the interior decoration. It is gold with a créquier in gules: the gold and the candelabra in règnes.[12]

THE SON OF MEROVEUS

The other great mystery of this region concerns the survival of the Merovingian dynasty. Though this subject has been raised in several books, unfortunately readers are advised to approach most of them with caution. One of the best known of these books specializing in the Rennes affair is *Généalogie des rois mérovingiens et origins des diverses familles françaises et étrangères de souche mérovingienne d'après l'abbé Pichon, le docteur Hervé et les parchemins de l'abbé Saunière, de Rennes-le-Château* [Genealogy of the Merovingian Kings and Origins of various French and foreign familes of Merovingian stock based on Abbé Pichou, Dr. Hervé, and the parchments of Abbé Saunière of Rennes-le-Château]

---

9. [The créquier is a heraldic tree that appears on coats of arms. It is often defined as either a wild plum or wild cherry tree (with thorns), and is sometimes referred to as "the seven-branched candle holder of the Temple." —*Trans.*]
Device on the arms: *Nul ne s'y frotte* [Don't get too close].
10. Dom Plessis, *Description géographique et historique de la haute-Normandie.* [Geo-graphical and Historical Description of Upper Normandy] (Paris: Giffard, 1740).
11. F. Cadet de Grassicourt and Baron de Roure de Paulin, *L'Hermétism dans l'art héraldique* [Hermeticism in the Heraldic Art] (Paris, 1907).
12. Règnes, like gules, is a designation for the color red in heraldry.

by Henri Lobineau. Also of note is the work of Madeleine Blancasall,[13] *Les descendants mérovigiens ou l'énigme du Razès Wisigoth* [The Merovingian descendants or the Mystery of Visigoth Razès].

According to these authors, the Merovingian line was not extinguished with the murder of Dagobert II in the forest of Woevres,[14] near Stenay on December 23, 679. His son, Sigebert IV, allegedly slain at the same time, is said to have escaped the attack. He is supposed to have been saved by a loyal follower and found refuge in Rhedae, where he took the title of count of Rhedae. At his death in 758, he was supposedly interred in the church of Rennes-le-Château, beneath the famous paving stone known as the Knight's Stone, with a depiction on it that is said to commemorate the event. Several years ago, in this location, there was actually found a skull bearing a ritual groove identical to the one on the skull of St. Dagobert II, which has been preserved in Mons, Belgium.

From this perspective, the treasure of Rennes-le-Château takes on the appearance of a dynastic treasure amassed over the years for the purpose of one day restoring the Merovingian royal family. I should point out that while this hypothesis deserves some attention and involves, in fact, one of the most mysterious episodes of French history, we should nevertheless approach with caution these genealogies, for they are not strictly based on any known document and come in the form of peremptory but absolutely gratuitous assertions. We will return to this analysis later.

IF SION WAS TOLD TO ME

One of the manuscripts allegedly found by Saunière seems to confirm the hypothesis of the survival of a Merovingian offshoot. In fact, it does not require much perspicacity to perceive that a certain number of the letters in the manuscript are raised over the others. When read in the order of

---

13. Her name is a pseudonym formed from the names of the Magdalene Springs and the Blanque and Sals Rivers.
14. See also Gérard de Sède, *La Race fabuleuse*. [The Fabulous Race] (Paris: J'ai Lu, 1973).

their occurrence, these letters produce: *To Dagobert II king and in Zion is this treasure and it is death.* The letters at the end of the last word in the four lines of the document can be read vertically to spell *Sion* (Zion). Other specific arrangements make it possible to read *teke* (chest) and *olene* (forearm) or even *rex mundi* (king of the world), and so forth.

We might wonder why *Sion* is so insistently emphasized. To some researchers, it is possible to see in this the signature of the Priory of Sion. This secret society was allegedly founded in Jerusalem by Godefroy de Bouillon in 1099. Its alleged mission was to keep watch over the destiny of the descendants of Meroveus and to prepare their eventual return to the French throne. In 1188, the Brothers of Ormus, sympathizers of the Priory of Sion, are said to have prompted the creation of the Order of the Temple for the purpose of serving the Priory. Apparently, in 1187 or 1188, however, a rupture occurred in Gisors between the Templars and the Priory of Sion at the field of the ironbound elm. The Priory then appointed as its grand master Jean de Gisors. The order claims among the leaders that would have succeeded him in this position, such figures as Blanche d'Evreux, Nicholas Flamel, Leonardo da Vinci, Robert Fludd, Johan Valentin Andreas, Charles de Lorraine, Charles Nodier, Victor Hugo, Claude Debussy, and, closer to the present day, Jean Cocteau. In the 1960s an odd monthly review called *Circuit* appeared in Paris with the subtitle "A publication of cultural, philosophical, and social studies." *Circuit* had its headquarters in Seine et Oise, in Aulnay-sous-Bois on the rue Pierre-Jouhet. Frequently appearing in its columns were articles signed "Chyren"[15] whom Anne-Léa Hisler[16] identified as a friend of figures as diverse as Count Israel Monti; one of the brothers of St. Vehme; Gabriel Trarieux d'Egmont; one of the thirteen members of the Rosicrucians; Paul Le Cour, the philosopher of *Atlantis;* M. Lecomte-Marcharville, delegate of the Agarttha; Father Hoffet from the Vatican's department of documents; Th. Moreux, the director of the Bourges Observatory; and so forth.

---

15. Pseudonym of Pierre Plantard de St. Clair.
16. Wife of Pierre Plantard de St. Clair who died in 1971.

We are therefore presented with a secret society founded in 1099 on Mount Zion by Godefroy de Bouillon, who was himself a Merovingian descendant, as well as the later presence of a legitimate descendant of the line, Pierre Plantard de St. Clair, alias Chyren (which designates the Great Monarch in the prophecies of Nostradamus), descendant of both the famous Norman duke Rollo and the Merovingian kings through the marriage of Jean XIV of Plantard with Marie de St. Clair in 1540.

FAKES AND THE USE OF FAKES

Unfortunately, there is nothing that has come along to corroborate these assertions. Godefroy de Bouillon did indeed found an order in 1099, but it was an order of the regular canons of the Holy Sepulchre. In 1114 it was placed under the rule of St. Augustine following a reform later confirmed by Pope Calixtus II in 1122 and was ultimately charged with keeping watch over the tomb of Christ.

So what are we to think about the alleged Priory of Sion? Whatever we conclude, we must accept that fakes are common currency in this affair. From the articles by Jean-Luc Chaumeil in *Charivari* regarding the Visigoth column visible in Rennes to the copies of the parchments, many of the clues in the mystery are fakes constructed from whole cloth. Concerning the known texts of the parchments in a typewritten form dated July 25, 1977; Philippe de Cherisey states that he manufactured them himself in 1961. Similarly, there is good reason to be suspicious of the text of one of the tombstones of Marquise de Blanchefort. All of this trickery can be explained only by the importance of the secret at stake in Rennes-le-Château.

THE MYSTERY OF THE FAKE TOMBS

So what firm ground can we stand on when deception awaits us at every stage? How can we get our bearings? How can we know where to find the truth? There is but one solution: Follow step-by-step the clues that can be found on site, decode the mysteries, and explain the anomalies while subjecting every text and every element to critical vigilance. The first subject of investigation should be the tomb of Marquise de Blanchefort, with its text loaded with intentional errors. We may also use as a base the stone of Coumesourde, on which an enigmatic phrase is inscribed between the lines and the patty crosses.[17] In additon, we should investigate the collection of mysterious tombs in the cemetery of Rennes-les-Bains, in particular the two sepulchres assigned to one man: Paul Urbain de Fleury, whose birth and death dates on the monuments contain major errors. And regarding odd tombs, there is another one that is equally enigmatic. It sits on the right-hand side of a bend in the road from Couiza to Arques, near Peyrolles.[18] This funerary monument, as well as the landscape, bears a resemblance to those that figure in Nicholas Poussin's painting *The Shepherds of Arcadia*. The painter depicts his shepherds deciphering an inscription that reads: "Et in Arcadia Ego." This same inscription is supposed to have appeared on one of the two tombstones of Marquise de Blanchefort. Is this merely coincidence? If so, it would also be necessary to regard as coincidence the fact that Saunière brought back with him from Paris a reproduction of the painting *The Shepherds of Arcadia* and to regard as coincidence the presence of Poussin's name in the cryptogram on the Blanchefort tomb: "that Poussin Teniers hold the key."

Nicholas Poussin was an incredible character.[19] In 1656, Nicholas Fouquet, lord high treasurer for Louis XIV, had charged his younger brother, the abbot Louis Fouquet, to contact Poussin, then sixty-two, in

---

17. For the full report on these details, readers should refer to Franck Marie's book, *Rennes-le-Château, etude critique* [Rennes-le Château, a Critical Study, Sres-Verités Anciennes, 1978] as well as Gérard de Sède's *Signé Rose+Croix* [Signed Rose Cross] (Paris: Plon, 1977).

18. In old argot, the word *arque* designated one playing die. The name Peyrolles, meanwhile, comes from *peira ola*, "stone urn." Arques is also evocative of the arch, the celestial portal. Is it truly by chance that this village would be located at the foot of Paradise Pass? [The tomb described here is no longer there. It was destroyed by the landowner several years ago to discourage treasure seekers and trespassers. —*Trans.*]

19. Nicholas Poussin chose a very curious seal for himself that depicted a man holding a ship or an ark, and the motto *Tenet confidentiam,* translated as "he has trust" or "he is trusted" or "he holds the secret."

Rome. In April, the abbot reported on his mission, indicating that Poussin had planned something he does not seem to have dared speak about in a letter:

> Things that I shall with ease be able to explain to you in detail soon—things that will give you, through Monsieur Poussin, advantages that even kings would have great pains to draw from him, and which, according to him, it is possible that nobody else will discover in the centuries to come. What is more, it would not occasion much expense and could even be turned to a profit, and these are things that are so keenly sought after that all who exists on earth could not have greater fortune and perhaps not even equal it.

What could this mysterious and incredible secret have been? Perhaps it was connected to a dynastic mystery whose key was located in Rennes-le-Château, all the more probable given that Colbert and Louis XIV seem to have devoted more interest than usual to this region. After the arrest of high treasurer Fouquet,[20] Louis XIV attempted to take away the seized documents. We should further note that several of Fouquet's friends seem to have been aware of the secret of Rennes: La Fontaine, who remained loyal to him until the end; Claude Perrault, who was the architect of the Paris Observatory; and Charles Perrault, author of the famous fairy tales, who dissuaded Colbert from making excavations in the hunt for metals.

We certainly cannot pass over in silence the other curiosities in the Rennes-le-Château region, such as the painting *Christ with the Hare* in the church of Rennes-les-Bains or the monument to the dead of Couiza. These may have many things to teach us. First and foremost is the church of St. Magdalene, which Father Saunière transformed into a gigantic cryptogram. There we find the devil that holds up the holy water stoup and the angels above it; the statues of the saints; the odd

---

20. Several days before, Fouquet had been warned of the risks he was running by his friend Marquis de Créqui.

baptistery; the painting commonly known as "The Flowering Ground"; the confessional; the stained-glass windows; the Stations of the Cross; the wall decorations; the painting Saunière created himself beneath the altar, depicting Mary Magdalene praying in a cave—in everything there is a symbol and signal to us. Beneath the altar painting the priest placed a plaque, that has long since disappeared, which consisted of a Latin text:

JESU . MEDELA .VULNERUM + SPES . UNA . POENITENTIUM PER . MAGDALENAE . LACRYMAS + PECCATA . NOSTRA . DILUAS

If we treat this like certain cryptograms in Jules Verne's books and read it phonetically we get:

JESUS M'AIDEZ, LA, VU LE NÉ, ROMPEZ MA DALE, (IL) N'EST LÀ CRIME, ASPECT QU'A TEMPS OTERA, DIT, LU, ASPECT EU N'A PENITENT DE SION.[21]

This is rule rather than the exception for everything is in this odd church.

THE *ARS PUNICA* OF FATHER BOUDET AND THE CELTIC CROMLECH OF RENNES-LES-BAINS

Finally, in this list of the principal oddities that can serve as a guide in the hunt for the treasure of Rennes-le-Château, there is also and especially the extraordinary and extravagant book by Father Boudet, *The True Celtic Language and the Cromlech of Rennes-les-Bains*. This book was considered by his contemporaries to be the work of a gentle luna-

---

21. [Jesus help me, given the personality of he who is there. When time has passed it will no longer be a crime to break the tombstone. The penitent of Sion has not respected this precept. —*Trans.*]

tic, and it was soon forgotten after its publication, given that Father Boudet's linguistic lessons are highly contestable. In fact, it is a book encrypted in accordance with the *ars punica,* as hinted at by the author, who speaks constantly of the Punic language. Boudet used veiled words to reveal intentions in his preliminary observations: "Penetrating the secret of a local history through the interpretation of a name composed in an unknown language." He stated even more specifically a little later: "Dialects, proper names, and place names seem to me like almost intact mines from which it is possible to withdraw vast historical and philosophical wealth."

Perhaps the secret of the mines containing vast historical wealth is the true subject of this book composed from the language of the birds. What mastery the author reveals in his construction of cryptograms and puns! The language used by Boudet is that of trobar clus. He tells us, moreover: "The ancients used the language of Empedocles," knowing that the statue of Empedocles was always veiled. This is no doubt how we must undertake a search for the cromlech of Rennes-les-Bains. Strangely echoing this is a curious Greek manuscript cited by Saint-Hilaire,[22] which speaks of a labyrinth whose blueprint Solomon formed in his mind and had built with rocks arranged in a circle—in other words—a cromlech. Neither Jules Verne nor Raymond Roussel, the theoretician of writing in a closed circle, would have denied Boudet. Jean Ferry says of Raymond Roussel, "The greatest part of Raymond Roussel's imagination, folded or not by the necessity he created to employ certain phonetic combinations, revolves around this idea: how to hide something in a way that will later make its finding difficult but not impossible." These lines could just as easily apply to most of Jules Verne's books—and to the master book of Henri Boudet.

---

22. Paul de Saint-Hilaire, *Le mystère des labyrinths* [The Mystery of the Labyrinths] (Paris: Rossel, 1977).

CLOVIS DARDENTOR
AND THE SECRET OF
RENNES-LE-CHÂTEAU

WE LEARN HOW TO RECOGNIZE AN
ODD SAILOR WITH THE NAME OF A MOUNTAIN

Of all the mysteries connected with the Rennes-le-Château affair, not least of them is the role played by Jules Verne. His novel *Clovis Dardentor* is in fact an encrypted work revolving entirely around this mystery, and Verne set enough store by this novel to dedicate it specifically to his grandsons, Michel, Georges, and Jean Verne.

When I read *Clovis Dardentor* for the first time, I felt a curious impression of shock mingled with malaise. Something was not right in this insipid story of no great interest in which even humor failed to hold the reader's attention. It was enough to make me believe that the author had intentionally botched the novel, as if he wanted to weary the reader. In it, however, was a name that I found astonishing and which fascinated me: Bugarach, the name of a ship captain. Why the devil did Jules Verne pick such a highly original name that could not help but bring to mind the Peak of Bugarach located near Rennes-le-Château? I wondered if it wasn't a coincidence. I wondered if I shouldn't study the novel to find out more. Didn't Jules Verne himself invite the reader to do so? He asked us to "listen" in a particular way to what Clovis Dardentor said if we wanted to learn a great deal (perhaps a bit too much) when the valet

Patrice says: "Monsieur had talked . . . talked . . . and of things better left unsaid, in my opinion, when one does not know the people in front of whom one is speaking. . . . It is not only a question of prudence, but also a question of dignity."[1]

All those who have dedicated several years of their life to solving a mystery, all those who have searched for rare objects to collect have felt, in the presence of an object they never hoped to own or a primordial clue, a painfully exquisite sensation before they dared take hold of the object or imagined the reality of the clue. It is but a dream and will soon evaporate! Similarly, I shivered with expectation and anticipatory pleasure. I was convinced that the name Bugarach was not indicative of anything, and I did not dare search for proof of the opposite in the novel. I did not dare believe that Jules Verne was aware of this strange story, for fear of being disappointed. That the novel might hold clues seemed almost too much good fortune. I eventually drove all questioning from my mind, at least temporarily, and plunged into the plot, which was so thin that Jules Verne himself summed it up in these few sentences. It is the story

of two young penniless men, one of whom gets the notion to have himself adopted by the exuberant Clovis Dardentor, a wealthy bachelor of Perpignan, by saving Clovis's life at the risk of his own. Far from succeeding in this undertaking, it was this man who ended up being saved by his future adoptive father, as well as his more disinterested cousin. Finally, when this future father is actually saved, it is by a young girl whom he adopts. Everything ends with her marriage to the discreet cousin, who becomes the son-in-law of the rich Perpignan bachelor. As concluded, this story is only a burlesque. It is also a pretext for a visit to Majorca and a part of the Oran region in 1894.

Once I had turned the last page of the novel, I was again facing the question. What if it were not merely coincidence? In fact, when you

---

1. Of dignity, or of a dignitary?

take the road out of Rennes-les-Bains that goes to Bugarach in the Aude region, after you have traveled a few miles, you can see a ship below the road. It is the site of the ancient fortified castle of La Vialasse, which has the appearance of a ship with three bridges. Oddly enough, in the last several years an immense television antenna has been added that reinforces this resemblance by supplying the mast. There can scarcely be any doubt that it is this earth-bound boat that Jules Verne is thinking of when he writes: "It is certain that, on land, the boats don't give a damn about rolling and pitching. . . . That will come, that will come.[2]

Here, then, we have the boat, farther along the road is Bugarach, and if we continue in the direction of Camps-sur-l'Agly, we pass right by the farm of the captains. Everything in this area falls into place to give us a Captain Bugarach and his ship. It should be noted that a relationship to the Peak of Bugarach is reinforced by Jules Verne's description of the captain: He "appeared almost unapproachable" and some did not "have the strength to climb close to him." Just like this peak that dominates the entire landscape, the captain's head is also in the clouds: "The master after God, with a voice that rolled between his teeth like the lightning between the clouds of the storm."

Encouraged by these discoveries, I decided to continue my quest and immediately spotted something that should have leaped to my eyes from the very beginning: The proof I was looking for was clearly expressed in the title itself. Yes, Jules Verne was aware of the secrets of Rennes-le-Château; yes, he has revealed a portion of the mystery, perhaps even the whole of it, for those who know how to read him.

CLOVIS DARDENTOR AND THE GOLD OF THE MEROVINGIANS

Clovis Dardentor is a title that speaks volumes. First of all, the name Clovis obviously brings to mind the famous Merovingian king. As for

---

2. Jules Verne also writes later in the text: "Clovis Dardentor and the guide made landfall—a fairly accurate expression as the camel, in the words of the Arabs, is the ship of the desert," and the character Jean Taconnat immediately alludes to Captain Bugarach.

the name Dardentor, it can be deconstructed into *d'ardent or.*[3] The last word speaks for itself, and *d'ardent* refers to the title that was specifically given to the descendant of Dagobert II who allegedly found refuge in Rennes-le-Château, where his descendants, in turn, remained for a certain time. This title *rejeton ardent*[4] was most recently claimed by Pierre Plantard.[5] Therefore, the name of the main character and the very title of the book tell us that Jules Verne is going to speak to us in veiled terms about the gold of the descendants of the Merovingian kings! Further, the entire story consists of learning who will capture the inheritance of Clovis Dardentor. The very name of Captain Bugarach's ship clearly tells us where our trail is leading: *Argeles,* the way of argent.[6]

Once I discovered this, no doubt was any longer possible, in my view. I now had to read the book again while "working" it, page after page, flushing out the key words and the anomalies and seeking out the meaning for each character's name. The engraving on the frontispiece (see figure 5, p. 112b) further committed me by showing it was possible to read it like an open book for those who knew how to make the circular trip in the company of the author. Nothing should be overlooked. Indeed, one of the characters warns us: "Everything is interesting when traveling, even what is not."

The method to follow is in fact common to almost all the novels of Jules Verne: The reader must follow the laws of Gothic art to discover the hidden meaning behind the words. Here again the author spurs us on, saying of Clovis Dardentor: "In his colorful language, he said things as they came to him; in phrases sometimes abominably pompous, sometimes regrettably crude." This indicates that the words uttered by the characters are significant.[7] As might be expected, Clovis

---

3. ["Of burning" or "ardent gold." —*Trans.*]

4. ["Ardent offshoot." —*Trans.*]

5. [*Plant* = offshoot, *ard* = ardent. —*Trans.*]

6. [*Argent* refers to "silver" or "money." —*Trans.*]

7. Don't open your mouth like you do. Keep it closed as much as possible, or you will be tempting the devil," writes Jules Verne. And he goes on to say: "Clovis Dardentor had a mania for coining phrases."

Dardentor does not stint in the use of slang expressions that carry double meanings. Thus when he says the words *ça boulotte,* the mind first jumps to the gastronomic meaning,[8] but who will think of the word *boulotter,* "to roll like a ball,[9] with its argotic extension "to amass," "to save," "to make one's pile," as it is sometimes used? Jules Verne also resorts to slang when he indicates certain gaps that are usable in deciphering: "If I had let go of them at great price! One notch, okay, but two! As Patrice was not there, Mr. Dardentor had fine sport saying things as they came to him."

There can be no doubt about the language of the birds in this novel, and its protagonist Jean Taconnat confirms it, promising to be as "gay as the most finching of finches." This permits Clovis Dardentor to play on words (and writing) and to tell him: "Ah! Ah! Mr. Jean, you have therefore twigged your natural gaiety again?" How better to say something according to the methods of the gay (jay) knowledge dear to the troubadours of the Languedoc,[10] the great adepts of the language of the birds (magpie-jay). Periodically, Jules Verne uses this system to draw the reader's attention to important passages by pointing out, for example, a "nightingale sally" of the station master.[11] Other times, he warns us that we must "keep our eyes peeled." The reader must ceaselessly store the pieces of information he finds and keep them present in his mind, for they will be of use later. This is a painful form of gymnastics, but Jules Verne commits us to it: "Patrice was moving methodically along the streets, not believing himself obliged to see everything in one day, and enriching his memory with some precious souvenirs."

---

8. ["It will get gobbled right up." —*Trans.*]

9. This could be a possible allusion to the place names *les roulers* [the rollers] and *les pierre de pain* [stone bread] in Rennes-les-Bains.

10. [Or language of Oc. —*Trans.*]

11. The nightingale was a bird dear to the troubadours and often served as a "key" to introduce a hidden passage. This is why a skeleton key is called a "nightingale" in argot, for it opens doors that have been closed to the profane. It should also be noted that one of the characters, Agathocle, is the object of a play on words and is named Gagathocle. This G-jay, dear to Nerval, is also the bird of the G(j)ay knowledge, and it was appended to Agathocle precisely because of his lack of spirit.

Often as well, it is tiny errors that guide us. Sometimes all it takes is a misplaced accent, bringing to mind the methods used by Saunière and Boudet. Finally, Jules Verne alerts us that we must supply ourselves with guides and verify the clues concerning the regions traveled. He mentions the "traveler's guide" in Palma and, later on, when speaking of visiting that magnificent Tlemcen in depth, he describes "Dardentor, his *Joanne* in hand."[12] But he also refers on several occasions to the existence of a decoding grid[13] and the means of performing a triangulation to find where the hoard is stashed. This means we should be ever observant, like the character Eustache Oriental, who never appears without his telescope, which he is always pointing at the sun or the stars. Sometimes it is necessary to measure the shadows cast by the mountains, which appear regularly to remind us of the trees called *bella-ombra*. Indeed, this entire circular voyage that unfurls in the Oran region is a reminder of the Celtic cromlech of Rennes-les-Bains.

This journey on which we are following Jules Verne's heroes supposedly lasts fourteen days, which is to say one day for each Station of the Cross. The entire first part of the book is used to specify the scope of the riddle, but the more specific details regarding the sites of the hoard are encountered only beginning with the arrival in Oran. If we know how to grasp his meaning, Jules Verne leads us directly to the goal. "Here we are on the road," Marcel Lornans says, "on the road to . . ." Jean Taconnat replies, "The unknown, the unknown that we must search through to find the new, as Baudelaire says." And then he adds: "The unknown about which I hardly concern myself moreover, is the X of life. It is this secret of fate that during the times of antiquity men carved on the hide of the goat Amalthea." What an evocation! Amalthea is the mythological goat that furnishes the horn of plenty, the source of all the treasures of the earth.

---

12. The *Joanne* is the ancestor of the well-known *Guide Bleu* [Blue Guide].

13. "Patrice slightly turned his head away, because this vexing word *grillade* ["grilled meat" or "grill," but it also refers to *grille*, which means "grid." —*Trans.*] seemed to him to naturally evoke certain comparisons."

ON THE OTHER SIDE OF NAMES, OR THE POWERS OF THE VERB

We are now ready to follow Jules Verne's trail in *Clovis Dardentor,* but what are we looking for specifically? Verne himself has told us the answer: We are looking for a Merovingian treasure connected with a sacred tomb. The inheritance, the gold of Clovis is explicit—after all, the place we are going is called Oran *(en or).*[14]

As we have determined, the names of the characters in this story are significant. Let's start by looking at the ridiculous and self-serving Desirandelle family. Here, Jules Verne is amusing himself. Just as he has made a double wordplay on the name Clovis Dardentor (it can be read *clos vit dard en or),*[15] we can see the desire burning in the eyes of *desirant d'elle.*[16] As for Agathocle, the Desirandelle son, he brings to mind both a very wealthy courtesan (like Mary Magdalene) living in Alexandria and a tyrant of Syracuse born in Rhegium. But this also, and perhaps especially, emphasizes the importance of a key. Jean Tacconat is the postulant to be initiated, the patch, the little salmon, and the student of the druid.[17] This is confirmed by the expression "young escaped foal,"[18] which could lead us directly to the alleged Templar treasure of Gisors, but that is another story.

Marcel Lornans is the cousin of Jean Taconnat, and it should be clearly acknowledged that they have a family air about them. We could almost think we are dealing with the Templar twins.[19] The name Marcel Lornans is in fact a play on two meanings, one with a kind of

---

14. [*En or* = "in gold." —*Trans.*]
15. This childless man has his sex organ *(vit)* closed *(clos),* but his posterity *(dard,* or *dart,* also brings to mind a sex organ) will inherit a fabulous fortune.
16. [*Desirant d'elle* = "desiring her." —*Trans.*]
17. It is not at all surprising that he should have enlisted in the Seventh African Chasseurs, for the regimental hairstyle was known as a *taconnet.* [*Tacon* means both "patch" and "salmon fry." "Little patch" is also one of the French names for coltsfoot, which plays into the various mythical and esoteric meanings symbolized by the foal, as examined in a later chapter here. —*Trans.*]
18. [Or protégé. —*Trans.*]
19. [The Templar seal depicts two knights riding one horse. —*Trans.*]

risqué nature: We can imagine Marcel *lorgnant*[20] the beautiful Louise (whereas his cousin is ogling her inheritance), but we can also deconstruct his name as *mar cel lor nans*. In this way we learn that the gold is in the saltwater pond, which is a valuable piece of information. This deconstruction also recalls the name of the circular esplanade where David placed the Ark of the Covenant in Jerusalem. This area, beneath which lay a small cavern, like a silo, used occasionally for the storage of grain, bore the name of its owner: Ornan. Perhaps the implication is that the Razès region is carrying in its depths the Ark of Covenant that the Templars may have brought out of Palestine.[21] Or perhaps this is a simple allusion to Jerusalem and, therefore, to Solomon's Temple and its treasure.

We move on now to Doctor Bruno, the physician on board the *Argeles*. His name reflects a well-known spot in Rennes-les-Bains: the Fountain of the Circle (*brunn* is the German word for fountain and *o* designates the circle).[22] This is a veritable fountain of youth, if we can believe Jules Verne, for this "facetious doctor does not deserve the description of sawbones."

Patrice, Clovis Dardentor's domestic, provides more symbolism. On the one hand, he brings to mind a sheepfold (the *borde* of Patrice),[23] which was found in the Aude archives in 1807 and which was located in the territory of the commune or township of Rennes-les-Bains. On the other hand, the name can be connected to Paris, that shepherd of Is who discovered a treasure in Rennes-le-Château (a sinkhole on the plateau still bears his name) and paid for it with his life. "Go to the

---

20. [*Lorgnant* = "ogling." —*Trans.*]

21. See also Louis Charpentier, *Les Mystères templiers* [The Templar Mysteries] (Paris: J'ai Lu, 1979) and [*The Mysteries of the Cathedral of Chartres*. 2nd English ed. New York: Avon, 1975] According to this author, a chapiter at Chartres is the proof. It can also be noted that in one of the stained-glass windows there, Solomon is wearing the traditional garb of the kings of France.

22. The name is also related to the twenty-two paintings Eustache Lesueur devoted to the life of St. Bruno.

23. [*Borde* is an old term referring to what was once a typical rural dwelling unit. —*Trans.*]

devil," Clovis Dardentor often tells Patrice. This is exactly what the shepherd Paris did. We can still find a few traces of the cabin in which he once lived. A legend maintains that from this cabin, Paris was able to gaze out over the Valley of Isis, where lies gold.[24] Verne's Patrice stays in cabin 13 (13-IS),[25] where he unpacks his val-ise.

The surname of Louise and her mother, Elissane, is also quite interesting. Elissane is an anagram: E-Salines, meaning to the east of Les Salines. This is a valuable piece of information and it is easy to see why Jules Verne took more pains in concealing it because this Les Salines is located quite close as the crow flies from the farm of the Captains in Bugarach's shadow. Formerly, this place was devoted to the exploitation of the salt extracted from the nearby Sals River, which crosses through Rennes-les-Bains. Jules Verne would have been perfectly aware that he was increasing the difficulty of interpreting this by using an anagram that could be grasped only by those who held most of the keys to the affair. He also gives them additional confirmation of the meaning attributable to this name when he writes about Agathocle and Louise: "They got on together like sugar and salt."

A minor character in the novel, Pigorin, provides us with an extremely interesting detail. He refers us to St. Anthony, whether the holy hermit accompanied by a pig[26] or St. Anthony of Padua, to whom those in search of lost gold direct their prayers. Let's not overlook the fact that Bérenger Saunière brought back from Paris a painting by David Teniers called *The Temptation of St. Anthony.* It depicts a double cave and St. Anthony is on his knees, directing his gaze at a book resting on an enormous stone table. On this table there are a skull, a crucifix, an hourglass, and a vase. The devil is offering a cup to the monk marked with the tau. At the foot of the stone table are two books: One is open, a sign of the word given to all, and the other is closed near a wooden bowl, witness to that which remains to be uncovered, that which is still hidden, the

---

24. An effigy of Isis has been found in Rennes-les-Bains.

25. Isis, Bis.

26. Pig Goret [piglet], one could say, or a real piggy bank. Further, Dardentor describes him as "that animal Pigorin."

esoteric word. To the left of St. Anthony is an enormous *cheval* (horse) skull on which sits an owl.[27] We can note the existence of the hermitage of St. Anthony in the Galamus Gorge, not far from Bugarach, and, most important, we should note that a *Bulletin de la Société des Etudes Scientifiques de l'Aude* informs us that construction undertaken near Les Salines for the salt extraction starting in 1839 consisted of opening underground draining chambers that were designated by the names of Our Lady, St. Barbe, and St. Anthony (see figure 6, p. 112b).

We can also examine the case of the one who claims the title of president of the Astronomy Society of Montélimar: Eustache Oriental. Never without his telescope, he is often present to guide us in a very precise fashion, like a gnomon: "Eustache Oriental, always seated at the good end of the table . . . this chronometer in flesh and bones whose hands only mark meal times." It is all the more customary that he can be found at the table, for a *eustache,* in argot, is a "knife."[28] The name Eustache Oriental is also a fabulous anagram: sel-orient-château. In other words, go east when leaving from the château and take the salt *(sel)* as your guide. Here again we are reminded of Les Salines. Further, if we consider this name like a logograph, we can pull out the words *château, saline, or, trésor, roia,* Saunière, *reines,* and many other words that are significant.[29]

Finally, we might try to discover the significance of Commandant Beauregard, whom Jules Verne alludes to three times in two pages. Perhaps this could be Beauregard of the fifteenth century who claimed to be an issue of Solomon's line. From him came the second branch of the Blanchefort family.[30]

Some will not fail to claim that these significant details are coincidences, but if they are, then the entire book is a kind of coincidence.

---

27. From the perspective of the enigma at Rennes-le-Château, it is interesting to note that a copy of this famous painting exists in Canada, but with the subjects exactly reversed.
28. Jules Verne mentions sailor slang specifically with regard to Eustache Oriental.
29. [*Or* = "gold," *trésor* = "treasure," *roial* = "royal," and *reines* = "queens." —*Trans.*]
30. See the *Dictionnaire de la Noblesse,* [Dictionary of the Nobility] Paris: 1772 by La Chesnaie-Desbois.

THE SECRETS OF MAJORCA

The novel's adventure begins in Sète (which was written Cète at that time). As for why the vessel heading for Oran did not depart from Marseilles, Jules Verne's has entangled explanations for, but one of the engravings speaks quite plainly: It shows us Mount St. Clair, which holds a chapel "of the Salette" that overlooks Sète. It is also this mountain on which the *Joanna* guide, a famous nineteenth-century travel guide, extends itself, citing its ponds and "the vast salt marshes of the Midi border by a canal of circumvallation." Mount St. Clair gives us the name of the family that claims to have descended from the last Merovingian kings and to whom they believe the throne will legitimately return: Plantards de St. Clair.

Leaving this "first Frank port," we embark with Clovis Dardentor in the *Argelès* in the company of the Desirandelle family, the good cousins Marcel Lornan and Jean Taconnat, Eustache Oriental, Doctor Bruno, Patrice, and Captain Bugarach.

The first stage of the journey is to Palma in Majorca. Jules Vernes emphasizes the founding of the city:

[It] dated from the era when the Romans occupied the island, after long disputing its ownership with its inhabitants, who were already famous for their skill with slings. Clovis Dardentor was happy to accept that the name of Baleares was due to this exercise in which David was also illustrious, and even that their daily bread was given only to children after they had struck their targets with a shot from their slings.

This brings to mind that odd passage from Father Boudet's book on Rennes-les-Bains in which, speaking of David, he wrote: "He put his hand in his *panetière*,[31] took out a stone, and cast it with his sling—*davit* (from *devit*, "twisting") and whirling—and struck the Philistine in the

---

31. [*Panetière* = "shepherd's pouch." —*Trans.*]

forehead. The stone buried itself in the Philistine's forehead and he fell, face down on the earth—to dive *(daïve)*, to bury itself, to hit." There both cases incorporate David's sling and bread, just as in Rennes-les-Bains there is a "stone bread" that is round like sling shot. If this is mere coincidence, then why has Jules Verne included this clumsy paragraph and why does he give such a bizarre interpretation of the name of Baleares when its origin is known to be from the name of Hercules's companion Baleos or Balios. Elsewhere, Jules Verne confirms this interpretation by committing an error—intentionally—when he mentions the torrent of Palma's Riena; whereas this waterway's name is the Riera. I contend that this "mistake" shows Riena-Reina: the Reines of Aude.[32] Further on, Verne speaks of a statue decorating the Palais Royale without mentioning the name of the artist who sculpted it, Antonio Camprodon, who brings us back to the "camp of the Redons," which, according to Father Boudet, was once Rennes.[33]

Dardentor visits the cathedral of Palma, and we are given a description of the portal of the sea and the "finely drawn biblical scenes of a naïve and delicious composition." Here there are odd sculptures that represent quite interesting symbols of Mary and the Bible: sun, moon, stars, cypresses, lilies, rose bushes, palm trees, a temple, a well, a mirror, heaven's gate, spring, and a garden. Above the tympanum of the cathedral a significant inscription reads: "Nothing comparable has been made for any king." Here Verne alludes to the Valley of Jehosaphat and the Last Judgment, bringing to mind Laval-Dieu and its apocalyptic legend.[34] Clovis Dardentor enters the church, stops in front of the royal chapel, and admires a magnificent altar screen. Verne

---

32. [*Reines* = "queens." —*Trans.*]

33. Allusions to Rennes are quite numerous in this novel and sometimes appear in curious guises, for Jules Verne did amuse himself, although his motive was serious. For instance, he mentions names that have *gaster* as the root. These are few in number but one of them, "gastercanther," designates a kind of spider. Similarly, when he is dragged along by his pack mules, Dardentor notes the street is named after the architect Reynes, and so forth.

34. It is said that when the boulders of Laval-Dieu (located between Rennes-le-Château and Rennes-les-Bains) touch, it will herald the end of time.

says nothing more about it. Because we now know the methods of the author, this should arouse our suspicions. It so happens that at the edge of the choir there are two magnificent Renaissance pulpits which the travel guides of the time don't fail to mention —and each is the work of a sixteenth-century artist named Juan de Salas! As for the altar screen Clovis admires, it can only be the one that, gilded and painted, occupies the back of the chapel of Corpus Christi. On it can be seen the Last Supper, the presentation of the baby Jesus, the temptations of St. Anthony, Jesus and the men of the Law, the high priest, and Pilate. This work in a masterful Baroque style dates from around 1640—and is signed Jaime Blanquer!

Everything is perfectly clear. If these two important works seem to have eluded Verne's notice, it is all the better for drawing the attention of true seekers and putting them on the scent. The names of the forgotten artists, Jaime Blanquer and Juan de Salas, refer us back to Rennes-les-Bains: Right next to the Madaleine, or Magdalene, Springs, the two rivers that encircle Bugarach, the Blanque and the Sals, merge into one.

There is additional confirmation of this information in the allusion to the black marble tomb of King Don Jayme of Aragon. Verne goes on to say: "It is not in the Balearic Islands where you will encounter towns in which the rectilinear cord and the rectangular square trace out chessboard squares as in American cities." It so happens that it was the chessboard that permitted the decryption of the parchments in the church of Rennes-le-Château and which figures so prominently in the décor of the church there. And in case someone still hasn't grasped the allusion, Verne speaks of a church in Palma that is under the charge of the sisters of the Magdalene. In addition, in his description of the *ayuntamiento*, the city hall, he mentions a painting in the "sala" depicting the martyrdom of St. Sebastian, attributed to Van Dyck. Later, we will see the significance of this detail.

After visiting the cathedral in Palma, there is an excursion to the castle of Bellver (beautiful view). In order to get there, the travelers must go through the Terreno, a kind of suburb "considered a Balearic resort."

This pun, Terrano-balnéaire,[35] can be translated as "on the lands of Rennes-les-Bains." As for the castle-cistern of Bellver, it brings to mind the castle-cistern of Blanchefort. Further, because it is entirely black, it evokes the Roco Negro seated against Blanchefort (white fort). This comparison cannot be a coincidence, for Jules Verne underscores the resemblance to "the landscape in the French Midi."

After leaving Palma, the group tours the Carthusian monastery of Valdemosa and recalls George Sand, "that great novelist," and her novel *Spiridion.* Verne is definitely working with consummate skill here, for George Sand writes *a propos* of Vademosa and the surrounding area: "It is a veritable Poussin." We are thus in Arcadia, beside the tomb in Arques. As for *Spiridion,* its story revolves in part around a painting: "Our Saint-Benoit is a superb piece, of this we can be assured. Several art lovers have taken it for a Van Dyck, but Van Dyck was dead when this canvas was painted." Here we are once more taken back to Rennes-les-Bains and its church, where we find the famous rebus painting *Christ and the Hare.* This work offered by Paul-Urbain de Fleury is a somewhat altered (and reversed) copy of a canvas painted by Van Dyck in 1636 and displayed at the Museum of Fine Arts in Anvers.

ORAN: CLUES IN GOLD

We now follow Clovis Dardento to Oran, a name that brings to mind the precious metal gold. Here we find our heroes on the rue du Vieux Château in the quarter of La Blanca[36] (another coincidence?) in the home of Madame Elissane. We can stroll with them to the edge of the Rehhi Wadi (green ravine), a stream of color bordered by mills, and can see Oudinot Boulevard and its bastion of baths, not far from St. Roch Tower (also Rosas Cajas), the "new castle" whose fortifications are the work of the

---

35. [*Balnéaire* is French for seaside, while the name Terrano includes the French word for earth, *terre. —Trans.*]

36. [Rue du Vieux Château means Old Castle Street and *blanc* is "white" in French. —*Trans.*]

Knights Hospitaliers of St. John of Jerusalem. Jules Verne's visit to Oran is not lacking in interest, but why does he write "this city, the Gouharan of the Arabs," when the name Oran comes from Ouahran (the cutting)? Perhaps this is another coincidence, for a place near Rennes, located in the commune of Quillan, bears the name Gourg d'Auran.[37] We must also accompany the heroes on a visit to the suburb of St. Anthony.

Verne, describes and shows us Mers-el-Kebir, emphasizing this "*portus divinis* of the Ancients." Will this divine port open a divine door?[38] Generally, when Verne embellishes, it is not gratuitous. To my surprise, when I opened the *Joanna* guide of the era (dated 1885) and turned to page 182, under the heading "Mers-el-Kebir," I found several pages dedicated to the Bain de la Reine,[39] a thermal spring that is said to have healed leprosy and owes its name to the repeated sojourns that Jeanne, daughter of the monarch Isabelle, took there. The spring, buried beneath rocks that fell down when the Mers-el-Kebir road was opened, was restored to its former state and murmurs in a small cave. The *Joanna* says: "The waters of the Bain de la Reine are quite clear, quite limpid, and have no odor. Their flavor, which is quite salty and a little bitter, catches slightly in the throat. . . . When entering the cave, a visitor can perceive a slight smell of sulfur." The temperature of the water is about 113°F to 117°F. Here is a detail that is almost too good to be true: In Rennes-les-Bains there is a thermal spring called Bain de la Reine, which emerges from the ground at 113°F and has a very salty taste (0.285 grams of sodium chloride per liter). As for the sulfur, it can be found quite nearby in the Fountain of the Madeleine or the Fountain of the Gode.

Finally, in Bain de la Reine in Mers-el-Kebir we can note a ravine known by the name Salto del Cavallo (horse's leap), which precisely designates the method [the knight's move] permitting the decryption of the tomb of Marquise de Blanchefort.

---

37. It is listed on ordnance survey maps as Gourgaoura.
38. ["Door" is *porte* in French. —*Trans.*]
39. [Bath of the Queen. —*Trans.*]

CIRCULAR TRAVEL

Leaving Oran,

Clovis Dardentor had an idea—the kind of idea one might expect from such a man. The Algerian Railroad Company had just posted a round trip special at reduced price in the southern part of Oran Province. It was of a nature to tempt even the most domestic of individuals. One would leave by one line and return by another. Between the two, there were one hundred leagues of superb country to traverse. This would be the matter of about fifteen days curiously employed. The company's posters displayed a map of the region crossed by a fat red line in zigzags.

This could almost be the Roseline-Rouge line dear to Béranger Saunière.

Curiously, throughout the description of this journey, Jules Verne commits huge errors: He is wrong about the number of inhabitants, the capacity of reservoirs, and the altitudes—not to mention the countless spelling errors. None of this is accidental, however, and those who have an interest in cryptography will have no trouble convincing themselves that this is true.

Concerning travel in the Oran region, Jules Verne tells us of "a simple promenade that amateurs could execute from May to October, as they choose, which is to say during the months of the year that do not include great atmospheric disturbances." This bears strong resemblance to the advice Father Boudet gives under the pretext of speaking to us in the Basque language. Father Boudet wrote the book on the cromlech of Rennes-les-Bains and cites an allegedly Basque language related to Enblish/Cletic. [It's an inside joke for Rennes-le-Château buffs that would fizzle if a translator's note was added to explain it for the non-cognoscenti. —*Trans.*]

The first stop on this part of the journey is Sebgha (or Sebkha) and the great salt lake near the Rio Salado. The waters of the lake "were already quite low at this time and it did not take long to dry out completely in the burning heat of the hot season." Because this location is southeast out of Oran, it seems that Jules Verne is inviting us to leave Rennes-les-Bains by following the course of the Sals River, or, more exactly, to go southeast until we reach the Sals, then cross it and continue our journey due east.

Next we come to Tlélat and the road toward the east along a lake named the Salt Marshes of Arzeu, where a new and curious episode begins. "The train went back down toward Saint Denis after it crossed the river, which, under the name of Maeta, spills into a vast bay between Arzeu and Mostaganem." In reality, the name is not Maeta but Makta, but this error only causes us to concentrate our search here for a valuable clue. It requires only a little time to see that the area where the river flows into the bay has a specific name: It lies between Arzeu and Mostaganem, according to Verne, but the exact location is Port-aux-Poules. It is easy to see why Verne gave us this alert when we know that the sacred trove of Rennes-le-Château was long guarded by the Hautpoul family. Further, the author hits two birds with one stone: If we follow his directional clues, we travel due east until we cross the Sals again, then due south in the direction of "le Caoussé"—and Verne writes Maeta instead of Makta, leaving out either *k* or *e*.[40]

After this is when the journey really starts to get serious. (Verne writes: "This was the place where most of those traveling as tourists got off.") Clovis Dardentor has decided to continue the journey *transire vivendo,* which can be translated as either "traversing while seeing" or "going through where there is something to see." This part of the journey is made in traveler's wagons.[41]

The route, taken over the Razès region, leads us toward the peak of Bugarach, and Jules Verne again confirms our analysis. He commits another error by telling us the Jewish population of Saint Denis du Sig

---

40. [The French pronunciation of *k ou e* is almost a homonym of Caoussé. —*Trans.*]

41. This is precisely the ancient meaning of Rennes-le-Château: Rhedae, the traveler's wagon that also brings to mind the Big Dipper (or Chariot of David or Tomb of Lazarus). [One of the French names for the Big Dipper is the Grand Chariot, and chariot also refers to wagon in French. —*Trans.*]

is twelve hundred. In fact, the number is three hundred, which makes this a mistake of 300 percent. It so happens that on the ordinance survey map of the Rennes-les-Bains region, we find ourselves at an altitude of 1,200 meters, quite close to the summit of Bugarach (1,230 meters). In the event we still have not got it, Jules Verne provides us with confirmation a little later by speaking of Ben-Arrach. After this, he gives us even more precise clues: He discusses a dam that travelers encounter by following the river, though in fact, to reach this dam, you must follow an adjacent canal—and it so happens that there is such a canal (really, several) near Bugarach leading to the salt spring near Les Salines.

Jean Taconnat commits an error when he says: "It has been around for sixty-four years, perhaps since there was fighting in the bush to take possession of Oran Province." Given that the story takes place in 1885, this would take us back to 1821, but it was ten years later, in 1831, that French troops first entered Oran. What is the significance, then of this reference? Right next to salt springs, the Pass of Capela is at an altitude of 831 meters.[42] Meanwhile, the peak overlooking the spring is 844 meters, which explains the emphasis Jules Verne places on the founding date of the Union of the Sig: 1844. There are many more "mistakes" like these to be found throughout the novel.

DEFINITELY A SALTY STORY

On our journey, we are not far from Mascara—Mas-Arca—the house of the Ark, one of the quarters of which is called Baba-Ali, which brings to mind caverns filled with treasure.

The clues provided by Jules Verne have guided us to La Salines and the salt springs close by. But given that it is Louise Elissane who will become heiress to Clovis Dardentor's fortune at the end of the story, wouldn't it be near Les Salines that the heritage of the Merovingians is to be found? Returning for a moment to the church of Mary Magdalene as designed by Bérenger Saunière, the devil, the traditional guardian of

---

42. The name Pass of Capela reveals the former presence of a chapel.

treasure, holds up a holy water stoup bearing the cartouche "B.S.," designating the starting point of the "circuit:" the confluence of the Blanque and Sals Rivers, nicknamed the Benitier.[43] Deeper into the church, Christ is at the knees of John the Baptist and through the golden grain surrounding him, a river seems to be flowing. This river is *salée*,[44] having been used for baptism. Christ and John the Baptist are inviting us this way to follow the Sals back to its source in order to discover, perhaps, the silver of the shell and the gold of the grain.

With regard to the altar painting of Mary Magdalene in her cave, perhaps it is a chapel she is asking us to look for—perhaps the one that gave its name to the Pass of Capela? What is the Mount of the Eight Beatitudes telling us? Come to me[45] and I will ease your suffering! We can then take the direction indicated by the line of red crosses on Father Boudet's map: the direction of the Rose Line, and head toward Soulatgé— which harkens to the meaning behind the phrase in the painting "Come to me and I will ease your suffering."[46] We can follow the course of the Sals River by taking this road, but it would be a good idea to make a stop in Sougraigne, because a surprise awaits us near the church. A cross, allegedly given by Father Boudet to one of his colleagues, bears the word *confirmation* and seems to indicate a new direction. We can recall Verne's *Joanne* guide and deduce that it may well be the Jouanne guide.[47]

Once more the direction of Les Salines is indicated. But we should continue on our journey. Within a few miles, near Caoussé, the road ceases to follow the Sals. There, a bridge spanning the river (a depiction of which we can see above the Virgin placed on the Merovingian column in Rennes-le-Château, and we can also see in the church in Rennes-les-Bains) shows us the path that leads to the spring. But just before reaching the bridge, we should look just a bit upward. Facing us, on the top, a stone seems to be detached, like a monolith placed at an angle. Let

---

43. [*Benitier* = "font" or "stoup." —*Trans.*]
44. [*Salée* means both "salty" and "dirty" in French. —*Trans.*]
45. Repeated in the church of Rennes-les-Bains.
46. [The French for "to ease" is *soulage*. —*Trans.*]
47. The Jouanne is the name of a nearby farm.

not the courageous hesitate! Cross the bridge, then climb to the right up the side of the hill through the heather. It is a rough but not difficult climb, which prepares us for a nice surprise, for this is where the real "rollers" are. In fact, if it has ever been difficult to find the rocks thus named by Father Boudet at the location where he claimed they could be found—the Pla de la Coste—we can only marvel at finding them here, quite close to the sources of the Sal.

Now we can take the path that ascends beyond the bridge and that first leads us toward Les Salines. Before we reach this place, though, we see some scattered stones on the hill. Binoculars enable us to make out one of them, about seven feet high. We might guess that it is a little like a throne. Here's a surprise: If you want to see a model of this seat, you need only go to the display case in the Magdala Tower in Rennes-le-Château. There, next to the pierced skull with a sacred notch that was discovered under the floor of the church of Mary Magdalene, is a small throne carved in stone, about five inches tall, a miniature identical to the stone we can find in nature.

Next, we arrive at the salt spring and the ruins of the ancient Gabelous guard house. On the right, before reaching this spot, a boulder stands out in the middle of the foliage, and if you are lucky enough to see it in good light, you will recognize the head of the Savior. A little farther, between the farm and the salt spring, you will see the Mount of the Eight Beatitudes.[48]

Who will now dare say that Jules Verne is not a reliable guide? He has shown us the salt route that leads to gold. Incidentally, it is interesting to note the frequent relationship between salt and gold, both in alchemy and sacred geography.[49]

---

48. The owner of this property is convinced that this small prominence once held a temple of Isis.

49. The sites where gold mines are found are generally located near salt deposits. For example, the sole French mine that is still open is located in Salsignes. This cannot help but bring to mind the title of a treatise by Bernard Palissy: "The Nature of Waters and Fountains, Salts, and Salt Marshes, of Stones, of Earth, of Fire, of the Enamels and Veritable Recipe with which All Men Can Learn to Increase Their Treasures, with the Drawing of a Delectable and Useful Garden and that of an Impenetrable Fortress."

Salt is purely and simply one of the keys to what has come to be known as the Rennes-le-Château affair. Further, the name Magdala itself is derived from the Arab *magdal,* which means "salted fish." This definition is only confirmed by Mary Magdalene herself, whose tears are said to have redemptive powers. In fact, on an engraving dating from the sixteenth century, we can see the saint at Sainte Baume in Provence: The cavern hollowed into the cliff overlooks a small river named Salins. In the representation there is also a standard bearing a Templar cross. How could we doubt that the Magdalene of Rennes lodges in Les Salines?[50]

NICHOLAS POUSSIN AND THE GOLD MINE

To make sure the reader is grasping his message, Jules Verne repeatedly emphasizes details throughout this novel. Clovis Dardentor tells us: "When there is no water in a landscape, it seems to me that it is lacking a certain something. I own several works by the masters at my house at the Square of the Lodge, and water is always in the foreground—if it wasn't, I wouldn't have bought it." The allusion is obvious, and all those who know the paintings of Nicholas Poussin (namely one of the versions of *The Shepherds of Arcadia*) will understand. The river god is constantly returning in these paintings, the pitcher beneath his arm dispensing the fluid of life.

In this regard we can also note the works depicting Midas and the Pactole (or Gold Mine) River that transforms everything into gold. Add to this Marcel Lornans's words: "So we are off in search of places where there is water. Do you want them to be fresh water? It doesn't matter to

---

50. It is enough to take our bearings from Bugarach, a fixed point much as the captain bearing the same name never leaves his vessel, according to Jules Verne. It is near him that we need to concentrate our search for the treasure. In fact, a good seat at the table is inevitably "not too far from the Captain" and "Under the command of Captain Bugarach, there is nothing to fear. A favorable wind is in his cap and he has only to take it off to produce a quartering wind." This wind, Verne tells us, is northeasterly, the direction that leads us to the salt spring. It will then be sufficient to guide us over the "oppositions" of shadow and light, like Eustache Oriental. Monsieur Desirandelle thought that the captain was going to take off his hat, then bend over: as if to make a gnomon!

me, because it is not for drinking!" How do we not think of Sals again? Marcel Lornans goes on to say: "We will find water in other places beside the port, and according to the *Joanne,* there is the Rehhi River that is partially covered by Oudinot Boulevard." It so happens that the Rehhi's apparent source, according to the *Joanne* of 1885, is some three thousand feet from its mouth, in the middle of a narrow gorge whose steep sides consist of recent limestone formations that are rich in fossils. We might think we are precisely near the sources of the Sals in this little gorge made of fossil-rich, limestone cliffs whose stones are identical to those used by Saunière to build his artificial grotto.

We can further note that near the source of the Rehhi River there was a small monument serving as a guard room from which two canals emerged that fed different fountains. Now, beyond the gorge, near the ancient Gabelous guard house, there are two draining galleries and there, just as at Bain de la Reine in Oran, a quake has pulled down the lower levels.

A TREASURE FOR THE TAKING

Now that the sites in this region have been precisely described, we can note that a number of details are also furnished concerning the treasure. It is apparently looking for an owner, and Clovis Dardentor asks: "When the fatal hour sounds, to whom will this vast fortune go? Who will take possession of the houses, the valuables of the former Perpignan cooper, nature having given him neither a direct nor indirect heir, not a single property that has a succession?" Clovis restates this question on several occasions.

Now, this treasure is inexhaustible, and "it is not the fuel that is lacking," shouts Clovis Dardentor, patting his waistcoat pocket, which gives off a metallic sound. All that is required is to look. "An adoptive father, wealthy with two million, resolved to remain a bachelor, is something no one from any latitude of this sublunary world would turn down." Nor anyone in a subterranean world, I might add. This royal gold[51] will permit

---

51. Moktani the guide is "royally" rewarded by Dardentor. Furthermore, we might ask if "the superior oxygen" that fills his chest doesn't give him blue blood.

everyone to make "gilt-edged dreams," and Jules Verne writes at the end, *a propos* of Louis Elissane: "There are proprieties/properties[52] in this marriage and a lot of cash as well." We can also cite the allusions made to the general treasury, the stock exchange, the bank quarter, and so on.

Jules Verne never stops confirming the treasure's royal origin: "It is definitely a superb vocation, this vocation of soldier . . . when one has the taste and since you have the taste . . ." Taconnat goes on: "It's in the blood . . . that we have been given by our elders, the brave merchants of the rue Saint Denis, from whom we have inherited our military instincts."[53] Saint Denis evokes the royal basilica, the necropolis of the French sovereigns. We can wager that the blood he refers to must be royal. Clovis Dardentor, whom Jules Verne describes as "such a high figure," is therefore going to lead us into the country to which the descendents of the Merovingians allegedly retreated.[54] Jean Taconnat says: "At the price of a few hundred francs we have tread on the ground of the other France! Nothing but that fine phrase is worth money, my little Marcel! . . . And then, who knows?" Asked what the words mean, Jean replies, "What they usually mean and nothing more." Couldn't this other France be the Razès?

The first chapter, however, alludes to a "dual heritage." If we hold on to the royal Merovinigan treasure, we must still look for the other source. The "pharamineux"[55] tall tales of Cicerone in Palma concerning the ancient exchange of that city seem to relate to Solomon's Temple and bring to mind the treasure first pillaged in Jerusalem by Titus and then stolen in Rome by the Visigoth Alaric. Because of Palma in Majorca and Perpignan, we can also consider the history of Blanche of France, wife

---

52. [The French word for both of these is *propriétés.* —*Trans.*]

53. Jules Verne is again making a joke, because the principal trade conducted on the rue Saint Denis in Paris is prostitution and the military instinct would provide a strong impetus for the warrior's rest.

54. Those Fainéant [Lazy] or Fénian Kings who we are reminded of by the Fénouan in the book.

55. Evocative of the Merovingian Pharamond. [*Pharamineux* means "tremendous." —*Trans.*]

of the prince of Castille, Fernado de la Cerda. Persecuted after the death of her husband and driven off the throne of Catalonia by Sancho, she found refuge in the Razès. Legend has it that the treasure she gathered to support the cause of her son, Alphonse, remains in the region.

AND IF THE CATHARS . . .

There is yet another possibility, and it is even more extraordinary and fascinating to explain this second source of treasure. In 1243, Occitain fell under the combined assaults of the northern barons and the Church. One of the most beautiful civilizations of all time was well on the way to being destroyed by fire and iron. Many tears have been spilled over genocide and crimes in the world, but this one is far too often over-looked: A people were subjected to all forms of violence, torture, rape, pillaging, and death in the name of the Christ whose doctrine of love was better defended by the Cathar Perfects than by the religious types shouting, "Kill them all! God will recognize his own!" In 1244, Mont-ségur was besieged. This fortress was the last bastion of Catharism. I will not revisit the story in detail here, but with the situation becoming critical during the siege, negotiations were opened, which might seem surprising. The citadel was on the verge of falling, and yet the crusaders granted the defenders the possibility to withdraw with arms, baggage, and honors of war, excepting those Cathars who refused to abjure, and who would be burned. What a show of clemency for the men at arms, for the defenders were even absolved of the murder of inquisitors slain in Avignon. Further, the crusaders even granted leave to remain there fifteen additional days. We might ask why.

But this does not bring an end to the revelations, for negotiations with the defenders of the site, Pierre-Roger de Mirepoix and Ramon de Perelha, were conducted by Ramon d'Aniort, lord of the region of Rennes-le-Château, who held the entire area in his grip. During this fifteen-day delay for negotiations, it is said that the spiritual and mate-rial treasure of the Cathars was spirited away. A fire was lit on the sum-mit of Bidorta to alert Montségur that all had gone well and the precious trove was housed in a safe location. It so happens that the name of the man who lit this signal fire was Escot de Belcaire and he was the envoy of Ramon d'Aniort.

During the Albigensian Crusade, the Aniorts had fought on the side of the Cathars. The four brothers, Géraud, Othon, Bertrand, and Ramon, joined by their two cousins, gave Simon de Montfort's men a very hard time, and they were excommunicated. They had to give up their castles but oddly, their excommunications were rapidly lifted and they were even given back some of their lands. Aniort Castle was scheduled to be razed, but at the last moment, Louis IX mysteriously reversed his decision and sent a message countermanding his previous order. Why? It is a mystery. I should add that Louis IX received Ramon d'Aniort at court with all the deference due a man who should not be taken lightly.

But let's return to Montségur. It may be surprising to see Escot de Belcaire bringing a letter from Ramon d'Aniort to the fortress. Powerful ties connected Ramon to the defenders of the fortress: He had married Marquésia, sister of Pierre-Roger de Mirepoix, and had given his sister Alice's hand to Jordan de Perelha, son of Ramon de Perelha. But this does not explain what kind of pressures Aniort endured to obtain such favorable conditions for the garrison. We might also wonder about the circumstances in 1247 that led Louis IX to compel Pierre de Voisins to surrender part of his property to Ramon d'Aniort. Would Blanche de Castille have negotiated the surrender of Montségur? Could Ramon d'Aniort have obtained such advantages in return for the promise not to use documents proving that the Merovingian line had not been extinguished? If so, then what had appeared incomprehensible would appear perfectly logical. But if Ramon d'Aniort could have played such a role, if he held enough cards in his hand to force the French royal family to negotiate, would the treasure have been safer on his lands or in the zone he supervised?[56]

---

56. As Elie Kercob rightly notes in issue no. 72 of *Cahiers d'Etudes Cathares* [Notebooks of Cathar Studies], the customarily accepted itinerary for removing the treasure is illogical. At the time, the route would have been almost useless for heavily burdened fugitives because of snow. Furthermore, the ending point normally mentioned, Usson, would reveal itself to be a veritable trap.

There was another cause for surprise: In 1283, Philip III (the Bold), accompanied by his son, the future Philip the Fair, made a journey through the Razès. They of course made a stop at the home of Pierre de Voisins,[57] lord of Rennes, who in fact governed almost the whole of this region on behalf of the king of France. The sovereign's travel in this region was no doubt motivated by preparations for the war against the king of Aragon. Philip the Bold would have wanted to secure the neutrality of the local lords, who were vassals of the Aragon king for some of their lands. But Philip the Bold does not seem to have had this as his only purpose and he paid a visit to Ramon d'Aniort. He was warmly welcomed by Ramon, his wife Alix de Blanchefort, and his young brother, Udaut d'Aniort, whom Philip the Fair wished to make his companion in arms but who preferred to become a Templar.

How could the King come to honor these Aniorts, two of whose uncles were Cathars, when even Alix de Blanchefort was the daughter of a heretical faydit lord who had given Simon de Montfort a hard time? It is true that the Aniorts were also relatives of the king, but through marriage and by the interposition of the family of Aragon.[58]

On leaving, Philip the Bold stopped by Pierre de Voisins's for lunch. An agreement must have been concluded and the Voisins were charged with seeing that it was honored, for Pierre III de Voisins, now a widower after the death of his first wife, eventually married Jordane d'Aniort, cousin of Ramon.[59] As a direct lineage, the Voisins family was extinguished at the beginning of the sixteenth century with the last heiress, Francoise, only daughter of Jean II de Voisins. The baroness of Arques and Cousan, she married Jean de Joyeuse in 1518, who thus took possession of the Voisin family lands.

---

57. Philip the Fair was the godfather of the eldest son of Pierre III de Voisins.

58. Philip the Bold was married to Isabelle of Aragon, daughter of James I of Aragon, himself a nephew of Sancia of Aragon and Géraud d'Aniort.

59. I will add that while the Aniorts always protected the Templars on their lands, Jacques de Voisins succeeded in saving some Templars after the arrest ordered by Philip the Fair. Aware of the orders sent to his father, he warned the soldier monks, who made their way to Aragon.

I should also say a word about the Hautpoul family, one of the oldest and most illustrious of the Languedoc. Its founders were known as the kings of the Black Mountains, where they owned the gold mine in Salsignes. The ruins of their first castle, dismantled by Simon de Montfort in 1212, can be seen near the Nore Forest, quite close to a cave where legend has it that a fairy, much like Mary Magdalene or Melusine, spent her time combing her long golden locks. Pierre-Raymond de Hautpoul was at the siege of Antioch at the side of the count of Toulouse when, as if by a miracle, the count discovered the Holy Spear. During the Albigensian crusade, the Hautpouls were also dispossessed of their evocatively named castles located on the banks of the Orbiel: Cabaret (from *capet arietis*, "ram's head"), Quertinheux, Tour Regine, and Fleur Espine. In 1422, Pierre-Raymond d'Hautpoul married Blanche de Marcafava, daughter and heiress of Pierre de Voisins. In 1489, the alliance between the two families was renewed several times. In 1732, François d'Hautpoul wed Marie de Negri d'Ables, who brought as a wedding present the lands of the ancient Aniort family. They had three daughters: Elisabeth, who lived and died a spinster in Rennes; Marie, who married her cousin Hautpoul-Félines; and Gabrielle, who married the Marquis Paul-François Vincent de Fleury. Elisabeth had quarrels with her sisters to whom she refused to communicate the family's papers and titles on the pretext that it was dangerous to consult these documents ceaselessly and that it "would be a good idea to decipher and distinguish what was the family's and what was not." Gabrielle took the Blanchefort title and left to her husband, Paul-François Vincent de Fleury, the responsibility of managing the baths.[60] It was only in 1889 that the Fleury family left Rennes-les-Bains, and shortly afterward Béranger Saunière became in some way the guardian of the premises.

Regarding the Hautpouls, an incident of note occurred in 1870: The notary with whom the family papers had been deposited refused to turn

---

60. The Spanish Archives mention a De Fleury who was a Templar commander at Carcassonne. The De Fleury arms were a field of gold with three roses in gules, placed 2 and 1.

them over to Pierre d'Hautpoul on the pretext that he could not relinquish possession of such important documents without committing a seriously imprudent act.[61]

. . . HAD CONCEALED THE GRAIL ON BUGARACH

With this history in our pocket, let's look at the Grail. In Verne's story, can we see in the Montsalvat of the quest a Mount of the Valley of Salt (*sau-va* in Provençal): the Bugarach? Perhaps we should not be surprised that this peak was given this name only around the time of the fall of Montségur. According to Vladimir Topentcharov,[62] the name Bugarach came from Bulgarians, Bogomils, and *boulgres*—names given to the Cathars.

Perhaps this name was bestowed after the Cathar heritage had been buried beneath the protection of this new Mount Tabor. More significant and perhaps connected, the image of the Grail is depicted in black and white, like the Beaucéant of the Templars [Templar heraldic banner], on the walls of the church in Bézu.[63] Also, it is said that there is a direct link between the Grail Quest and Solomon. In fact, legend says that it is the sword of Solomon that Lancelot sees in the hand emerging from the lake—a fabulous and magical sword that, according to legend, Godefroy de Bouillon possessed. In *Parsifal*, Wolfram von Eschenbach tells us he took the quest of the Grail from a text originally written by the pagan Flegetanis, who was of Solomon's line. There is perhaps no antimony between the Grail and Solomon's treasure, on condition it is not viewed as a "Jewish" hoard, with all due

---

61. Among these documents were supposed to be genealogical papers stamped with Blanche de Castille's seal and proving the existence of the descendants of the Merovingian kings.

62. See Vladimir Topentcharov, *Boulgres et Cathars* (Paris: Seghers, 1971).

63. It is similar to the alternating black and white representation of the Grail that we can see in the sixteenth-century *Book of Hours of Caillaut and Martineau*.

On the toponymic plane, we should also note that the rune used by the Visigoths to designate the chalice, the Grail, replaced an ancient rune meaning "ark," and the rune for "man" was replaced by that of "tomb."

respect to the Israeli agents who are regularly carving furrows in the plateau of Rennes.

In any case, the Cathars always oversaw the region. The last known Perfect, Guilhem Bélibaste, who burned at the stake in 1321, lived in Arques. It was also in Arques where there lived, some years ago, a man named Deodat Roché, who carried the completely inappropriate "title" of pope of the Cathars. This is the area where the doctrine survived longest despite persecution. Jean Duvernoy writes: "In the sixteenth century, it was only in the pastures of Arques, and there only around the shepherd's fires, that the Cathar credo and mythology were still recited, the latter a singular blend of traditions out of the Greek Orient, humble mountain piety, and dreams of revenge. It is these shepherds, alas, to whom we owe the most complete account of Catharism to be preserved."

We might also compare the book closed by the seven seals of the Apocalypse, depicted in the church of Bugarach next to the Grail chalice, to that secret book called the Book of Seals, which was solemnly opened on the Cathar feast day of Bêma. It was certainly Catharism that Colbert found of interest when, while he was hunting for the Rennes-le-Château treasure on behalf of Louis XIV, he gave a trustworthy man the task of going to Carcassonne to copy the inquisition files concerning the Albigensian crusade.

Given all of this, perhaps we should wonder if the Grail was hidden in the Bugarach region. This seems to be what Jules Verne means to say when he makes a mistake about the name of the site Khrafalla, which he calls Kralfalla. It seems this would be a pretext for invoking the Grail. What are in the names Kralalla and Khrafalla? Verne has already substituted *K* and *Kh* for the *g* sound in this book, using this code here; it would give words close to Grail in these two names. Interestingly, he repeats this offense when he writes of Sidi-Kraled instead of Sidi-Khaled and the people of Beni-Amer whom he transforms into Beni-Amor (in other words, the Sons of Love). What better designation could there be for the Cathars, who proclaimed themselves messengers of love and saw Amor as the opposite of Roma?

Figure 1. Harry is invested with powers and is somewhat of a magician. The Underground City

Figure 2. Simon Ford holds one key to the adventure. The Underground City

Figure 3. His name, Jack, brings to mind that of the popinjay. The Underground City

Figure 4. James Starr, next to him a book (no doubt the Gospel of John) on which rests a T-square next to a compass. The Underground City

Figure 5. The circular symbol of the barrel entrance from the engraving on the frontispiece. Clovis Dardentor

Figure 6. The hermitage of St. Anthony in the Galamus Gorge. The Temptation of St. Anthony *painting by David Teniers*

Figure 7. Koubbas—these are the tombs of sacred figures, veritable arks that are reminiscent of the tombs of Arques. Clovis Dardentor

Figure 8. The vignette of the dragon with the crocodile head on the title page of The Castle of the Carpathians.

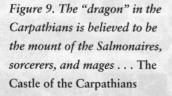

Figure 9. The "dragon" in the Carpathians is believed to be the mount of the Salmonaires, sorcerers, and mages . . . The Castle of the Carpathians

Figure 10. Frik was regarded as a sorcerer, a summoner of fantastic apparitions. The Castle of the Carpathians

Figure 11. The Masonic standard: It is squared, edged with six pales decorated with rains (branches) of periwinkle (Provence), and contains a world (globe) bearing a crescent and the sun, and an antique vase in which a flame is burning. Hypnerotomachia Poliphili *by Francisus Columna*

AMOR VINCIT
OMNIA.

Figure 12. Phileas Fogg: His feet are square, his right hand is placed over his heart, and his left hand is propping up his right. Nearby there is a fabric whose subtle arrangement of folds delineates a scythe. Around the World in Eighty Days

THE GRAIL CUP AND THE SALT OF ETERNAL LIFE

Jules Verne leads us on the trail of the Grail, that cup that was also named in ancient times *coppe, cuve,* and *cave,* as in cavern. In this regard, we cannot help but note the emphasis Verne places on barrels. On numerous occasions he reminds the reader that Clovis Dardentor is a cooper: "It was this cooperage industry, which was so important in the region, to which he devoted the majority of his time and intelligence." The former cooper, accustomed to *cercler*[64] and "rolling," should be the one to lead us to the spring of the circle, beneath the rollers. "In the name of a barrel," as Clovis says, "Captain Bugarach himself is shipping barrels next to the salted foods, a source of considerable exports." All these "warehouses loaded with casks and barrels, these barrels of the Danaids[65] tabled up to the bung," are they to be sought in the silos dear to Father Boudet? After all, wouldn't Formentara, mentioned by Verne, be the "land of wheat?"

The barrel has yet another meaning: In Catalan, the native language of the hero from Perpignan, it is *cuva,* pronounced kou-ba. It so happens we encounter koubbas throughout this journey from Sidi Daoudi to Sis-abd-er-Salam. These are the tombs of sacred figures, veritable arks that are reminiscent of the tomb in Arques. Several of these koubbas are depicted in the book's engravings, and those who are familiar with the Stations of the Cross in the Rennes-le-Château church will recognize this koubba on more than one painting[66] (see figure 7, p. 112c).

Both the sacred tomb and the sacred trove fit perfectly with the dynastic problem posed by the survival of Merovingian heirs, and there is no question that it is necessary to search for the keys near the Sals River. Verne provides repeated clues in this vein, with his growing collection of

---

64. [This refers to "binding with hoops," but in French *cercler* also evokes the word *circle,* which, as we've discovered, is Verne's underlying purpose. —*Trans.*]

65. [*Tonneaux de Danaïdes* is an idiomatic expression for denoting an endless task. —*Trans.*]

66. The round trip lasts forty days, one for each station in the Stations of the Cross.

allusions to salt: Rivesaltes wine (banks of the Sals), Madame Elissane's smelling salts, the salted food shipped by Captain Bugarach, sites such as Aïn Sba (within close proximity to Salt Rock, the salted lakes, the hectares of cotton permeated with salt), and so forth. We should also note, however, the constant appearance of the mines is also associated with water and the idea that rivers reemerge from underground. For example, the Tafna Jules Verne mentions emerges from a grotto but at certain times gushes up in a prairie by means of a spring connected to the grotto by an underground channel. Similarly, he makes several other allusions to subterranean trips beginning at diverted riverbeds.

Jules Verne has left us an important message here, but we should not cease our investigations with *Clovis Dardentor,* for in other works, the author has scattered elements like the pieces of a gigantic puzzle, as if he could not resist the desire to show off his knowledge before devoting an entire book to this enigma. In *The Will of an Eccentric,* there is a cart (Rhedae) hung with red drapery (reign), a tomb appearing like a kind of Solomon's Temple with its "crystal candleholder with seven branches," and an allusion to Constantine and the phrase *"in hoc signo vinces,"*[67] and another to "a new Lazarus burst from the tomb." We can also find Max Real, a royal name; Syracuse; the rich city of salt and its salt marshes; Salt Lake City; Salina; the salt needles; the guides accompanied by black men carrying mine lamps; and the "devil's chair." Too, there is the "incomparable wonders of these caves that have only surrendered a portion of their secrets. Do we have any idea of what they might still be reserving for the world's curiosity, and will we not one day discover an entire new and extraordinary world in the entrails of the world?"

In Search of the Castaways has a salt island; the Salinas; St. Anthony's Cape; the balanced boulders; the landmarks that are no longer in their rightful places; Salinas Lake (dry); Table Mountain; Signals Mountain; the chessboard; the thermal waters; the ferruginous springs; the ox-drawn carts; the Crown Hotel; the gold mines; the wagon fortress;

---

67. ["In this sign you will conquer" refers to Emperor Constantine's vision of the cross that led to his conversion to Christianity. —*Trans.*]

the salt spring; Thabor Island worthy of the shepherds of Arcadia; and Pagnol, who says: "We are passing through, that's all, like the honest man on earth, doing as much good as possible. *Transire benefaciendo,* that's 'our' motto."[68]

I can cite other novels, but none seems to have been devoted exclusively to the Rennes-le-Château affair except *Clovis Dardentor.* Once Jules Verne's knowledge concerning the mystery of the Razès has been exposed, however, two questions remain: How did he know and why did he wish to leave posterity a coded message about it?

68. One of the false tombs of Rennes-les-Bains bears the inscription "He passed through doing good."

6

JULES VERNE AND FATHER BOUDET'S SECRETS

THE ROSE, THE CROSS, AND THE GREAT ARCHITECT OF RENNES-LE-CHÂTEAU

Who could have so thoroughly informed Jules Verne about the affair at Rennes-le-Château? We have studied his ties with Freemasonry—could it have been within the context of this society that Jules Verne was made aware of the secrets of the Razès? It is said that Freemasonry was founded by the Templars who managed to escape Philip the Fair's minions. Evidence seems to indicate that the Order of the Temple knew the secrets of this region, but this origin is undoubtedly more legendary than real.

In any case, there is a strong possibility that Jules Verne obtained this information through the intermediary of the Freemasons, for since 1864 he had been director of Hetzel's *Magasin d'Education et Récréation* [Department of Education and Recreation] at the side of Jean Macé.[1] Speaking of him, Verne wrote to his publisher: "I love him and I owe him more than I do you . . . He is my special director." Nor should

---

1. Jean Macé was a member of the Alsace-Lorraine Lodge in Paris.

it be overlooked that he was a friend of Hignard, with whom he made his first trip to Scotland and who was also a Mason.[2]

In fact, Masonic themes are not excluded from Rennes-le-Château. Not only is there a Masonic tomb in the cemetery in Rennes, but also according to Gérard de Sède, the sculpted monument to the dead in church in Couiza is a precise recapitulation of the table of the Rosicrucian Scottish Knight grade created in 1760. Indeed, we can detect notable similarities.[3] Furthermore, the Stations of the Cross in the church of Mary Magdalene in Rennes-le-Château also seems connected to Scottish Freemasonry. The eighth station shows a woman in widow's veils holding the hand of a child wearing a Scottish tartan. In the ninth station a knight who has no orthodox purpose there evokes the grade of the Charitable Knight of the Holy City [CKHC] of the Scottish Rectified Rite. It should be noted that this grade was founded at the congress that took place in 1778 in Lyon through the impetus of the archaeologist Alexandre Lenoir, who was related to the Hautpoul family (Olivier d'Hautpoul was the son of Angelique Lenoir), and that François d'Hautpoul was later elder of the Carbonari Lodge in Limoux. Under the pseudonym Jean Kotska, the ritual of the CKHC was first published in 1895 by Jules Doinel, conservator of the Archives of Aude and leader of a gnostic sect.

A connection certainly seems to exist between the decoration of the

---

2. In the unpublished version of *A Journal of Travels in England and Scotland,* held by Jean-Jules Verne's heirs, the Masonic temples he saw over the course of his journey were cited in minute detail. According to Serge Hutin, Hignard was the elder of a lodge of which Gérard de Nerval was supposedly a member. It is curious to imagine Nerval employing the language of the birds; adorning himself with jay feathers; and evoking the "queen of the Midi" crowned with stars, one of her feet placed on a bridge, the other supported by a wheel, and one of her hands resting on a high prominence while another peak rises up across the sea on which the name of Meroveus is inscribed.

3. See René LeForestier, *La Franc-Maconnerie Templière et Occultiste* [Occult and Templar Freemasonry] (Paris: La Table d'Emeraude, 1987). The model of this monument to the dead is not unique, however, as Gérard de Sède seems to say. Moreover, he altered the photo in this book.

church and the 18th Grade of the Rose+Cross of Scottish Freemasonry.[4] Roses and crosses, moreover, decorate all stations in the Stations of the Cross. We can also see in the church of Bugarach the lamb of the Holy Zion (Sion) accompanying the Book sealed by seven seals, symbol of the Scottish Master of St. Andrew. In addition, the angels on the font in the church in Rennes-le-Château seem to be prompting us to follow the progress of the journeyman. There are also the two tombs for Marquis de Fleury in the cemetery of Rennes-les-Bains on one of which we can read "He passed through doing good." This phrase has connections with Rosicrucian symbolism.

We may also wonder if much of this information was given to Verne by Hetzel, who was a curious fellow. He was a minister under Cavaignac and was banished in 1851. He was responsible for preparing the clandestine edition of Victor Hugo's *Châtiments* [Punishments]. Hetzel was a friend of Lamartine and was his confidant during the heated days of 1848,[5] he was a secret agent in Germany, and he introduced Jules Verne to George Sand.

GEORGE SAND AND THE MERRY LABORER

George Sand's work is rarely granted the attention it deserves not only literarily, but also with respect to secret societies. It was she who wrote: "I truly believe there is a great work to be done on the occult history of humanity." In a certain fashion it can be said that *Consuelo* partially responds to that intention.[6] In *Histoire de ma vie* [Story of My Life], George Sand describes her detachment from the church and her attraction to nature and its paganism and adds: "I have devoted myself to the occult sciences." Smitten with idealism, Sand considered that religions most often served as limits on the spiritual. She was won over by the philosophical ideas of Pierre Leroux, whom she defended in her

---

4. This grade was introduced by Charles Edward Stuart, but, according to legend, it was created by Godefroy de Bouillon.
5. [This was a time of revolt in Europe. —*Trans.*]
6. Readers of *Consuelo* will learn a great deal about the *consolamentum* of the Cathars.

works from 1837 on. Leroux was in search of a new religion that could supplant Christianity, and he taught the reincarnation of souls. George Sand synthesized his beliefs: "I believe in eternal life; I believe in eternal humanity and in eternal progress, and as I've embraced in this regard the beliefs of Monsieur Pierre Leroux, I refer you to his philosophical demonstrations." Under the influence of these ideas, George Sand wrote *Spiridion* (which Jules Verne alludes to in *Clovis Dardentor*), *Les Sept cordes de la Lyre* [The Seven Strings of the Lyre], *Le Compagnon du Tour de France* [The Journeyman of the Tour de France], *Horace, Consuelo, La Comtesse de Rudolstad,* and more.

Just like Hetzel, George Sand was closely involved with the events of the Revolution of 1848. In her work we can find defenses of the Revolution's ideals, but we can also note some very distinctive hidden messages. For example, knowing the secret meaning (connected to the Cathar church) of the song of the herdsman in the land of Oc, we can wonder when George Sand writes: "One cannot be a perfect laborer unless one sings to the oxen, and this is a separate science that requires a particular taste and method."

Those who are fond of surprises and who have a talent for reading between the lines and finding the hidden meanings of words can read *Jeanne* and stroll with its characters toward the rock of Ep-Nell (headless), near those piebald stones that move. They can visit the cave and sit down on the bench worked into the rock. They can search for the treasure beneath the druidic stones; search for the gold and silver chariots of the Gallic chieftains; weep with the Madeleine of Canova, contemplating the cross she has manufactured from two reeds; and dream on the banks of the hot water springs and the ponds that hold mineral springs: "You are looking for treasure beneath the stones? It is in the water you must search. This is where the true treasure lies." There, it is said, lies a treasure so vast that no one will ever see the end of it.

Just what secret was kept by George Sand, descendant of Aurore de Koenigsmark and whom Victor Hugo called "the greatest of her time and perhaps of all time"? We can see why George Sand, who was thoroughly aware of everything concerning Freemasonry and traditional teachings, would have had such influence on Jules Verne.[7] Not surprisingly, in *Spiridion* we find her defending Johannine and gnostic ideas such as those of Joachim de Flores. It should be noted in passing that Spiridion was the name of a fourth-century Greek bishop who continued his vocation as a shepherd even after his ascension to this position. He prayed to his dead daughter Irene to tell him where she had hidden a certain trove, and his prayers were apparently answered. Numerous Venitian images depict him as a Greek monk standing on either a shrine or a tomb.

ALEXIS AND AXEL

We know that Sand liked the works of Jules Verne and recognized him as "an admirable talent with the heart necessary to enhance it." She encouraged the writer to continue down his path, and for his part, Jules Verne deferred to her as to a teacher, writing to her: "Madame, your letter fills with joy a newcomer to this literary world that you illuminate and warm with every word that emerges from your pen. . . . Do me the honor, Madame, of believing in the profound devotion of your respectful admirer."

But Sand's influence extends farther. If we compare *Journey to the Center of the Earth* by Jules Verne to *Laura or the Journey in the Crystal* by George Sand, we can note truly striking resemblances. The drunkenness of the hero Alexis (in *Laura*), provoked by amorous musings, alcohol, and fever, cannot help but recall the lessons Axel learned in the abyss in Verne's novel. Like George Sand, Verne used the device of the found manuscript. As for the scholar Liddenbrock, like Herr Hartz in *Laura*, he is a foreign (German) scientist devoting himself to an open science of metaphysics and dreams. George Sand describes stones, plants, and animals with the help of scientific terms intended to increase the reader's

---

7. She influenced several others, as well. Those who are curious should read the strange sonnet dedicated to George Sand by Gérard de Nerval and analyzed by Jean Richier in *Nerval: Expérience et Création* [Nerval: Experience and Creation] (Paris: Hachette, 1970).

knowledge, much like Verne includes interminable lists of crustaceans and fish. Alexis becomes a mineral merchant, similar to Axel's uncle, who is a mineralogist. Alexis witnesses the unfolding of her adventure between two uncles and a female cousin, while Axel's uncle, a cousin, and a guide intervene in his. Alexis's uncle metamorphoses into a kind of god of the volcanoes, and Axel and his uncle gain entry into the earth through a volcano's orifice. Both stories end with the marriage of the heroes to their cousins.

There are other similarities: The scholar Tungténis, just like Liddenbrock, admires the ugliness of antedeluvian animals. The Paradise discovered by Nasias and Alexis consists of a volcano, "a black needle in a gold ring" (a kind of gnomon), and the entrance to the earth is found thanks to the shadow of a volcano in *Journey to the Center of the Earth*. (Additionally, this passage brings to mind the Grail: "It was an island . . . hollowed into a cup . . . in the middle of a volcano of prodigious height.") Like Axel, Alexis is initially put off by science; he has no desire to become a scientist, distrusting the ungrammatical names it assigns things. Like Axel, Alexis feels the fascination of vertigo.

Interestingly, the similarities between Sand's novel and Verne's did not seem to have charmed George Sand, who notes in her diary: "I am now reading *Journey to the Center of the Earth* by Verne. Up to this point, it resembles my *Journey in the Crystal* a little too closely." Nonetheless, it seems the idea for *Twenty Thousand Leagues under the Sea* was given to Verne by George Sand, who wrote him: "I hope you will soon lead us into the depths of the ocean and have your characters travel in those diving machines that your science and your imagination make it possible to perfect." Regarding Sand's influence, Verne told Hetzel that he needed the eloquence of George Sand for this work, and he placed her novels on the shelves of Captain Nemo's library. In addition, several characters in his books bear the name Sand, with some (such as Mathias Sandorf) having it as part of their surname. There can be no doubt that the famous novelist exerted both literary and occult influence over Jules Verne.

UNDER THE SIGN OF DELACROIX, OR THE SECRET OF THE ANGELS

George Sand was a close friend of the painter Eugene Delacroix, who painted a number of portraits of her starting in 1834. He made several visits to George Sand's house in Nohant in 1842, 1843, and 1846, and Maurice Sand, the writer's son, worked for a time in the master's studio. Sand also dedicated a humorous piece to Eugene Delacroix, the well-known house painter in Paris—a farcical text entitled "Lament on the Death of François Luneau"—and Delacroix's painting *L'Amende Honorable* [Making Amends] was influenced by her book *Spiridion*.

This painter who admired Nicholas Poussin, to whom he attributed the merit of an art "professing mute things," was an unusual fellow, in his own right [8] and was an odd painter of odd paintings, proof of which can be found by visiting the Chapel of the Holy Angels in Saint Sulpice in Paris. Interesting for our purposes, the paintings in this chapel have a direct connection to the affair of Rennes-le-Château. It was to Saint Sulpice that Saunière went to request information after he found the parchments at the foot of the altar of his church. Delacroix decorated the Chapel of the Angels with three paintings. One of them depicts St. Michael felling a dragon. In it the saint is depicted as victorious over this demon guardian of the threshold who curiously looks like Poseidon, god of the sea and earthquakes.

Another painting depicts Helidorus driven from the Temple. Helidorus was the prime minister of the Syrian king Seleucos of the second century BCE. Seleucos gave Helidorus the task of pillaging Solomon's Temple. What a coincidence! The story goes that while Heliodorus was sacking the premises; there appeared a knight covered in gold and riding a white horse. The animal knocked over Helidorus and trampled him while angels whipped him. [9] This is the scene depicted by Delacroix.

Delacroix shows us the two columns of the Temple, Jakin and Boaz,

---

8. It has been often repeated that he was the bastard son of Talleyrand, who was, among other things, grand master of the Grand Orient of France.
9. See the Book of the Maccabees.

and the high priest Onias. Two wingless angels float in space on either side of the horse. One detail particularly draws attention: Scattered down the steps of a staircase is part of the Temple's treasure. Chests, jewels, and sacred vases all seem to flow down the stairs. A soldier can be seen fleeing with a gold vase on his shoulder. In another important detail, another soldier wears a starry Phrygian bonnet, like a shepherd of Arcadia. This bonnet reminds us that the legends of Pelops and Midas took place in Phrygia. Pelops, son of Tantalus, conquered Arcadia with the help of a winged horse. Midas ruled the Pactole, the river that transformed everything into gold. In one more detail in the painting, we see that the veil is being lifted by the wind. Will this wind disclose the mysteries of the Holy of Holies?

If we can believe Henri de Lens, this painting by Delacroix was composed based on representations of the heavenly planisphere.[10] If this is so, one of the angels can be linked to the constellation of Andromeda; the bearer of the vase is Aquarius, the Water Bearer; and the second angel is Antinoïs. The man wearing the Phrygian bonnet becomes Cepheus of the starry bonnet. We also cannot help but compare the horse to Pegasus, the illustrious winged horse, the "horse of God."[11] In addition, we can find similarities between the gold "abacus" on top of which a gold ball is sitting and the iconography in the churches of the Razès.

JACOB AND THE GUARDIAN ANGEL
OF THE FORD

Facing the painting of Heliodorus is another painting by Delacroix: *Jacob Wrestling with the Angel.* On a night when Jacob had traveled near a ford, an angel sent by God wrestled with him. The fight lasted throughout the night; only at dawn was Jacob beaten, wounded, and

---

10. See Henri de Lens's enthralling book, *Cent Trésors, une énigme* [One Hundred Treasures, One Mystery] (Paris: Ed. Albatros, 1976).

11. On the slopes of the Cardou near Rennes-les-Bains there is a boulder called *lampos,* which at certain times of the day looks like a horse. There is a similar rock near Les Salines.

with his left thigh paralyzed. We will skip over the symbolic value of this strange story, but at dawn the angel left after changing Jacob's name to Israel.[12] Jacob then named the site of the combat Pniel, meaning "face of God." The scene in the painting takes place at the foot of an imposing tree. On the right side a caravan passes. Jacob's hat and a spear are lying on the ground. Behind him stands a black rock and a white rock and a single row of three oaks.

Robert Graves[13] finds Jacob a kind of sacred king who has usurped the succession. But Jacob also brings to mind his dream of the ladder on which angels climb and descend. When he awoke from this dream he said: "The Eternal One is certainly in this place and I knew it not! And fear took him and he said, 'This place is terrible. Here is the house of God and the gate of heaven!'" With this, Jacob arose, took the stone that he had used as a pillow, set it upright, and poured oil on its top. To this place that had borne the name of Luz he gave the new name Bethel (House of God). Interestingly, over the porch of the church of Mary Magdalene in Rennes-le-Château is the phrase *Terribilis est locus iste* (this place is terrible).

If we look closely at Delacroix's painting, we can see a small thread of flowing water.[14] As for other symbolism, we can look at the inscription of the seventh station in the Stations of the Cross in Saint Sulpice (which is quite near the painting) and read: *Retire-moi de la bove que je n'y reste pas enfonce. P.S. LXVIII.*[15] The play on the identical representation of the V and the U permits the word *boue*[16] to be written as *bove,* referring to a grotto or cavern. If we refer to the numbers in the inscription to find the corresponding Psalm (68 in the Hebrew Bible and 69 in the Latin Bible), we can see that it is a "Lamentation of the Master Chanter on the Air: Of the Lilies . . . of David."

---

12. In Hebrew Jacob means "measure of time."

13. Robert Graves, *The White Goddess* (New York: Farrar, Strauss, Giroux, 1966).

14. We can compare this to the "Baptism of Jesus" in the church of Mary Magdalene Church.

15. [Pull me from the mud/cave so that I do not remain buried there. P.S. LXVII. — *Trans.*]

16. [*Boue* = "mud." —*Trans.*]

THE GNOMON AND THE SYMBOL
OF THE HOLE

There are quite a few other unique features in Saint Sulpice beyond Delecroix's paintings. The gnomon, for example, with the copper line that traverses the church, marks a meridian. There is also a statue of St. Peter seated on a throne stamped with the Seal of Solomon. In addition, there are the letters P and S looming above the north and south portals, the cross of St. Anthony, and a thousand other details.

Included among these are the fonts and the St. Martin Chapel, with its painting that depicts a small bridge and a white-water river near a wheel or circle. In the sacristy there is another painting of St. Michael felling a dragon and a scene taken from the Book of Tobias. In the St. Vincent Chapel there is Anne of Austria watching over the future Louis XIV and another infant. Who is this second child? It might bring to mind a possible connection to the mystery of the man in the iron mask. Another surprise awaits in the St. John the Baptist Chapel: the mausoleum of the abbot Languet de Gergy. According to the inscription on this odd monument, the abbot "procured for the poor the treasures of the rich and for the rich the prayers of the poor." We could just as easily say that he, too, "passed through doing good." But perhaps the most interesting detail is the group of four canvases by Signol.[17]

Let's first look at *The Crucifixion:* The crucified one is depicted on Golgotha (place of the skull), with the two thieves in fairly distinctive positions. At their feet are the Virgin, St. John, Joseph of Arimathea, Nicodemus, and, most important, Mary Magdalene. In the foreground soldiers are gambling with dice for Christ's robe, and at the very bottom, some odd pebbles can be seen. What do they represent? He who looks will find. The text placed above the head of Christ on the cross is depicted in its entirety, which is fairly rare. But if we take a closer look, we can see that it is reversed. It would require a mirror to read it

---

17. Two of these paintings allow the discovery of the key "Mortépée," which applies to the decoding of the text of the tomb of Marquise de Blanchefort.

normally. Here we are in the middle of a topsy-turvy world where every-thing is reversed.

The second painting is *The Resurrection of Jesus.* In it Christ emerges from the tomb, pointing at the immense tombstone and holding a cross. In the third painting, *The Ascension of Jesus Christ,* Christ rises toward heaven, leaving the chalice and the Eucharist in our world. Finally, there is the fourth painting, *The Betrayal of Judas,* in which St. Peter is shown drawing a sword and St. John is on his knees begging. In the distance we can see rocks, olive trees, and a cave.

There is a peculiarity to be found in these last two canvases: the artist's signature includes an anomaly. EM SIGNOL becomes in one EM SIИ OL and for the other EM GIGИ OL. It should be noted that on the one hand, we are again dealing with a reversal, and on the other hand, Signol is the symbol of the hole (ole) and the reverse of Longis.[18]

Finally, when leaving Saint Sulpice, we can see the fountain in the square that is named the Fountain of the Four Cardinal Points because the statues are those of Bossuet, Fénelon, Massillon, and Fléchier. Its counterpart might be the Fountain of the Four Ritous (the four parish priests) near Rennes-le-Château.

THE SOPRANO AND THE HAPSBURGS

We have seen that through Hetzel, Jules Verne was influenced by George Sand, whose friend Delacroix painted works in the Chapel of the Holy Angels in the odd Saint Sulpice. Regarding these details, the seeker should always keep one principle foremost in mind: It is necessary to close the circle. Until the serpent bites his tail, nothing is proved. We therefore need to establish connections that lead us from Béranger Saunière and Rennes-le-Château to Jules Verne and George Sand.

One connection is provided by the soprano Emma Calvé. Fascinated with occultism, she diligently followed the conferences of Papus, was

---

18. Longis-Longinius is the Roman soldier who stabbed Christ's side with his spear. The Grail cup traditionally accompanies this spear and it is said to have been part of the Hapsburg dynasty treasure.

a member of the Theosophical Society, and followed the teachings of Ramakrishna's disciple Swami Vivekananda. There is a photo of her decorated with a symbolic motif and dedicated thus: "To monsieur the Count de Saint Germain, the great chiromancer who has told me such truths. Emma Calvé, 1897." This beautiful opera singer was an odd character, a celebrated diva in her time who seems to have spent a great deal of time in the occult milieu of Saint Sulpice. It was through these means that she met Béranger Saunière. Formerly the mistress of Jules Bois,[19] she became the mistress of the parish priest of Rennes-le-Château. What was the origin of this love affair? Had the diva been cast into Saunière's arms as a means of keeping a hold over him? Whatever the truth may be, the fact remains that the soprano, who had been swimming in debt, rapidly found herself out of her difficulties once attached to Saunière. She wrote in her journal at the end of 1893: "Still 100,000 francs of debt. Why so much weariness? What is the use of working so hard?" and she noted a year later: "I've settled everything, thank God. I am buying Cabrières."[20] Perhaps this money came from Béranger Saunière or even from those who ordered Calvé to seduce the priest. It is almost certain that Emma Calvé bore a child of Saunière's, a little girl who was born in Rodez and who died at the age of fourteen. She was raised in a family with a passion for the occult.

Shortly before her death and once again in debt, Emma Calvé sold her château in Cabrières to her friend, Madame Hurbin, chatelaine of Creissels, who for more than ten years was tutor to the Hapsburg children. As we have learned, a Hapsburg archduke, known as the "foreigner," paid several visits to Béranger Saunière in Rennes-le-Château. These visits eventually lead to the accusation that Saunière gave intelligence to the enemy during World War I. Interrogated by the counterespionage service after the war, Archduke John of Hapsburg declared that, no longer believing his family was safe, he had come to Rennes

19. Bois was famous for his duel with Stanislas de Guaïta.

20. Cabrières is near Aguessac, in the Aveyron region. It seems that the *Book of Abraham* mentioned by Nicholas Flamel was stored at the Château de Cabrières during the seventeenth century.

in search of a refuge and to prepare for his family's arrival there. Since that time, it seems that Archduke Rudolph of Hapsburg, sixth child of the last emperor of Austria-Hungry, visited Rennes-le-Château in 1976. It also seems that John of Hapsburg met Father Boudet in Axat several times. He presented himself under the pseudonym Monsieur Guillaume and found lodging with the priest's sister-in-law.[21]

Father Saunière moved in interesting company indeed! It is true that he also welcomed into his home the Lazarist Ferrafiat; the state secretary of the fine arts Dujardin-Baumetz; the woman of letters Andrée Borguière, who had no fear of calling herself the viscountess of Artois; Marquise de Bourg de Bozas; and the countess of Chambord, the wife of the last representative of the elder branch of the Bourbons, who had a claim to the crown of France. It is also true that he owned several bank accounts in Perpignan, Toulouse, and Paris, as well as an account with the Fritz Dörge Bank on Lajos Kossuth Street in Budapest.

We should not overlook that the Hapsburgs had a long-standing claim to legitimate rule over the whole of Europe, contesting the claims of the dukes of Lorraine.[22] Their motto was quite explicit: A.E.I.O.U. *(Austria Est Imperare Orbi Universi).* Was Béranger Saunière a supporter of the Hapsburg dream of ruling the Continent? It is true that their treasure included the famous "spear of destiny,"[23] companion to the Grail and supposedly brought back from the East by Raymond de Saint Gilles? In his fascinating book *The Spear of Destiny*[24] Trevor Ravenscroft writes: "The symbol of the Merovingians was the ancient Tribal Spear, which denoted spiritual leadership under the Tribal God and the terrestrial power of life and death over all Frankish kinfolk."

Added to this mix is a curious drawing by the initiate Albrecht Dürer representing the crown of the Holy Empire with the inscription *Rex*

---

21. This information was provided to Gérard de Sède by the Benedictine Dom Louis Gaillard, a professor at the Catholic school of Lille (in a letter dated March 18, 1968).
22. According to the history of St. Sigisbert by Reverend Father Vincent (1702), the Hapsburgs could rightfully claim the heritage of the Merovingians.
23. This spear was of particular interest to Adolph Hitler.
24. *The Spear of Destiny* (York, Maine: Weiser Books, 1982).

Salomon—per te reges regnans.[25] In order to attain this universal sovereignty, the Hapsburgs sometimes made use of secret societies.[26] But what connection was there between the Hapsburgs and Jules Verne? Quite simply, it was ties of friendship. During his travels in Algeria and Italy in 1884, Jules Verne stayed in Venice at the Oriental Hotel. There he received a visit and books on the Balearics from Louis Salvator of Tuscany, archduke of Austria and nephew of Emperor Francis Joseph. Jules Verne even wrote on this subject in *Clovis Dardentor*: "All he needed was to shut himself up in a library, on the condition that library owned the work of His Highness the Archduke Louis Salvator of Austria." He provided more detail in footnotes: "Louis Salvator of Austria, nephew of the emperor, last brother of Ferdinand IV, grand duke of Tuscany, and whose brother, while sailing under the name of Orth, never returned from a voyage in the seas of South America."[27] Further on, he specified: "To read a text on the Balearics that is so complete and precise, to look at its color plates, the views, the drawings, the sketches, the diagrams, the maps that make this work without peer—it is in fact an incomparable work for the beauty of its execution and its geographical, ethnic, statistical, and artistic value . . . Unfortunately, this bookseller's masterpiece is not available for sale in the trade." We can also note that the Hapsburgs supported the undertaking of the Baillard Brothers in Sion Vaudémont, told by Maurice Barrès in *La Colline Inspirée* [The Mystic Hill].

It is the story of the life of Jean Orth, the prince who abdicated his birthright to live a fraternal existence in the service of an anarchist ideal, that Jules Verne describes in his novel *The Survivors of the Jonathan*. The Kaw Djer is none other than Jean Orth, who left the Austrian Court after the tragedy of Mayerling. Jules Verne maintained a regular written correspondence with the archduke of Austria and by this means seems

---

25 [King Solomon, it is through you that kings reign.]

26. For example, François III of Lorraine, who achieved the crown of the Holy Empire by marrying Marie-Teresa of Hapsburg, was a Freemason and an alchemist and was affiliated with the Gold Rosicrucians. On his tomb an angel is depicted holding the crown out to him.

27. Louis Salvator's vessel, the *Nixe*, was shipwrecked off Cape Matifou, Algeria.

to have been kept informed of Jean Orth's life, about which the Austrian court officially maintained complete silence. Before 1905, then, he was abreast of events that were otherwise known only after 1907. Béranger Saunière and Jules Verne thus seem to have had similar relationships, but that of Verne predates that of Saunière.[28]

The Hapsburgs, then, would have been very well placed at the keystone of the arch of this affair, for they spent time with Emma Calvé, Béranger Saunière, Jules Vernes, and Father Boudet, that strange priest who "taught" Saunière and who applied to his work on Rennes-les-Bains the same rules used by Jules Verne throughout his writing: the methods of the Ars Punica, or Punic language, that Boudet discusses in *The True Celtic Language and the Cromlech of Rennes-les-Bains.*

28. Jules Verne had other noble friends: the count of Paris, the counts of Montmorency and Eu. In fact, he wrote his family: "These Orleans are fine folk with open minds. They do me the honor of liking my books as well as myself a little."

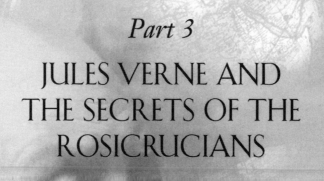

Part 3

JULES VERNE AND THE SECRETS OF THE ROSICRUCIANS

JULES VERNE AND THE ROSICRUCIAN ORDER

ANATOLE FRANCE AND THE ANGELS OF SAINT SULPICE

As we have just seen, Jules Verne was extensively informed about the mysteries of Freemasonry and knew everything concerning the enigma of Rennes-le-Château, but he was not alone in this knowledge. While all details of this knowledge cannot be revealed in this one book, I must furnish a few additional trails to follow, for well-known authors who were abreast of this affair number well over a dozen. Those whose curiosity has been piqued can read *La Révolte des Anges* [The Revolt of the Angels] by Anatole France. In this novel, angels who have fallen from heaven take on the appearance of human beings and make plans to win back their power and topple God in order to put their leader, Lucifer, on the throne of the universe. In this process, Lucifer brings the light of liberating knowledge to humanity. It goes without saying that critics of France's writing have regarded this novel simply as an attack on religion and a satire on society of the era in which it was written. The more perspicacious have taken note of an anarchistic tone in this book. Who, however, has perceived the real message this novel contains?

In the book much of the action takes place in the shadow of Saint

Sulpice, specifically in the Chapel of the Holy Angels in which we see Father Guinardon, "sturdy as an oak," restoring the paintings by Delacroix. The story unfolds between the teashop of the Four Bishops[1] and the Esparvieu Library, whose librarian one day discovers "the most precious relics of Israel all lying in a disordered heap, gaping and crumpled." The reader must pay the closest attention to the most minor details in the book: Zéphyrine, a painter's favorite model who had lent her golden hair and polished shoulders to so many Magdalenes, Marguerites, sylphs, and mermaids; the way in which Guinardon restores the paintings, filling up the cracks that have emerged due to the sinking of the walls or, more likely, to a seismic disturbance; the two hundred thirty-eight letters that have disappeared in the adventure and which form part of Gassendi's correspondence with Gabriel Naudé.[2]

In the book we can note allusions to Freemasons, the scepter of St. Louis, the six hundred pearls of Queen Marie Antoinette's necklace, the imperial mantle of Charles V, the tiara wrought by Ghiberti for Pope Martin V, the Colonna, Bonaparte's sword, and the ring Charlemagne supposedly placed on a fairy's finger. While following the pilgrimages of the fallen angel, Arcade, we might ask why the Everdingen Bank and its branches are marked by red crosses.

Of course, there are people who see mystery everywhere and seek to move from comparisons to conclusions where only coincidences exist. In addition, Anatole France had a reputation for being a skeptic and a rationalist, but this did not prevent him from having a pronounced taste for esoterism. Furthermore, he handled the language of enigmas quite skillfully, as we can see in *L'étui de nacre* [The Mother-of-Pearl Case], and he did not scorn using the language of the birds. He also attended séances and was something of a treasure hunter, which led him to excavate tumuli in Brittany. What is the proof of his taste for the occult? His

---

1. See the Fontaine des Quatre Ritous (the four parish priests) in Rennes-le-Château.
2. One of the very first to take an interest in the Rosicrucians.

armchair,[3] recently displayed by Parisian antique dealers, stands surety for it. Moreover, he wrote in the February 15, 1890 issue of the *Revue Illustrée:* "A certain knowledge of the occult sciences has become necessary to grasp a large number of the literary works of this time." As a friend of Maurice Barrès and Victor-Emile Michelet, it was through Michelet that he knew Papus. In the June 1, 1890 issue of *Le Temps* he wrote: "This ancient house[4] is amiable for the fact that is it open to all novelties. Everything is taught there. I would wish only that the rest be taught there as well. I would like a chair of magic to be created there for Monsieur Papus."

In his other books such as *L'anneau d'améthyste* [The Amethyst Ring] are mentioned the capture of Jerusalem by Titus; Clotaire II; the Grail; a gold ciborium; a Eucharist chalice that holds a ball and a die; and the priest Guitrel, who has more than one thing in common with Father Saunière.

ANATOLE FRANCE AND COUNT DE GABALIS

Anatole France's novel *La Rôtisserie de la Reine Pédauque*[5] is largely inspired by a book by Montfaucon de Villiars: *Le Comte de Gabali*[6] [The Count of Gabalis]. The author even winks at the reader to emphasize this borrowing when Monsieur d'Astarac says: "Know well, my son, Salamanders are not to be betrayed without punishment awaiting you. Their vengeance on the perjurer is of the cruelest," a phrase that brings to mind the mysterious circumstances surrounding the death of

---

3. [One of these séances, which took place on the rue de Trévise, was described by Frédéric Boutet in *Les Aventuriers du mystère*. [The Adventurers of the Mystery]. This is a large armchair whose feet and armrests terminated in cloven hooves. In addition, the back of this chair is topped by a goat's head with a magnificent pair of horns—the goat being a well-known symbol for Satan. —*Trans.*]

4. [This refers to the College of France. —*Trans.*]

5. [Published in English under the titles *The Queen Pedauque*, *The Romance of Queen Pedauque*, and *At the Sign of the Queen Pedauque*. —*Trans.*]

6. It first appeared in Paris on November 21, 1670, and was published by Claude Barbin. Its subtitle is "Conversation on the Secret Sciences."

Montfaucon de Villars.[7] In any event, whole pages in France's novel have been taken from *Le Comte de Gabalis*. Why? The answer does not seem very hard to find.

Nicolas-Pierre-Henri de Montfaucon de Villars was born in the Aude, in the Alet diocese quite close to Rennes-le-Château.[8] Following a brilliant career as a theology student in Toulouse, he was ordained, then made his way to Paris where he frequented libertine haunts and took part in the Fronde.[9] He was eventually imprisoned on the orders of Mazarin and was freed only after Mazarin died in 1661. Although he had murdered his uncle, this caused him no real unease, for he no doubt had the benefit of powerful protectors. In March 1675, however, Abbot Montfaucon de Villars was assassinated while traveling on the road from Mâcon to Lyon.

Was this murder an act of vengeance on the part of his cousins or the Rosicrucians, as some claim? Had he even been initiated into the order, as Gerard de Nerval believed? Had he betrayed certain secrets, although in veiled form, in *Le Comte de Gabalis?* Voltaire wrote, half seriously and half ironically, as was his habit: "Villars, famous for his *Comte de Gabalis,* was slain by a pistol bullet. It was said he had been murdered by the sylphs for having revealed their mysteries." Cruel irony. Villars himself wrote: "Ever since the blessed Raymond Lulle pronounced the decree in his testament, an executioner angel has never failed promptly to twist the neck of all those who have discreetly revealed the philosophical mysteries." It is certain that the theories contained in a joking form in *Le Comte de Gabalis* correspond clearly to the Rosicrucian theory of

---

7. [The priest Montfaucon de Villars was killed in 1673 on his way to Lyons. Some maintain that he was murdered because his books revealed too much. Lamy discusses the death here and postulates it's possible causes. —*Ed.*]

8. He was descended from Arnaud de Baccallaria, lord of Villars, the architect of the fortress of Montségur.

9. See *La race fabuleuse* by Gérard de Sède concerning the connections between the Rennes mystery and the Fronde. [The Fronde refers to the civil war that took place in France during the mid-seventeenth century. It takes its name from the French word for "sling" and refers to the rioters in Paris pelting stones at the windows of Cardinal Mazarin and his supporters. —*Trans.*]

the three worlds and the elemental spirits. The very name of the count, Gabalis, is the word Paracelsus (claimed by the Rosicrucians as one of theirs) gives to the vital energy that propels the world.

I believe that the Rosicrucian aspect of *Le Comte de Gabalis* counted for a great deal in Anatole France's decision to use it to write *The Queen Pedauque*. As we will see, there are very strong connections among the Rosicrucian order, the affair of Rennes-le-Château, and authors such as Jules Verne who have left us encrypted novels on this subject.

THE ROSICRUCIAN ORDER IN THE NINETEENTH CENTURY

The existence of the Rosicrucian Order was first noted in 1632 when posters were put on the walls of Paris by the Brothers of the Rose+Cross. Then, in 1710, Sincerus Renatus published in Breslau *The True and Perfect Preparation of the Philospher's Stone by the Fraternity of the Rosy and Golden Cross*. These fraternity members met in local groups called *circles*.[10] These groups grew fairly large in southern Germany, and starting in 1755, they spread into the rest of Germany, Poland, Bohemia, Hungary, and Russia. Among their famous adepts was François de Lorraine, who held the grade of Rex Solomon, a strange figure we discussed earlier who was initiated into Scottish Freemasonry and who gained the crown of Austria by marrying Maria-Theresa of Hapsburg in 1736.

In 1745, Martinez de Pasqually, another mysterious figure, founded the chapter of the Scottish Judges (within the framework of Freemasonry) in Montpellier. For fifteen years he traveled throughout the Midi region of France. In 1760, in Toulouse, then Foix, he founded a secret society called The True Mason Knights Elect Cohen of the Universe, whose high grade carried the title of Réau-Croix. The doctrine he offered in his treatise on the reintegration of souls was fairly close to the one espoused by the Cathars. It was under his influence that Jean-Baptiste Willermoz introduced into Scottish Freemasonry the grade of

---

10. A term that should alert the attentive readers of Jules Verne.

the Benevolent Knight of the Holy City. The expansion of these doctrines was assured by Louis-Claude de Saint-Martin (1743–1803), also known as the Unknown Philosopher. In 1787, while traveling to London, Louis-Claude de Saint-Martin was made a member of the Order of the Unknown Philosophers, founded in 1643, and was made a child of the Brothers of the Orient (Rosicrucian Order).[11]

The eighteenth century, the era of illuminism, was also that of the famed Count de Saint-Germain, who some said was immortal. This one-of-a-kind individual, who was referred to by various names[12] (Marquis of Montferrat, Count of Surmont, Count Weldone, Count de Bellemare, Count Tzarogy, Count Solitkoff) in accordance with a procedure dear to the Rosicrucians, arrived in France in 1758 with the Marechal de Belle Isle, count of Gisors, knight of the golden Fleece, and grandson of the lord high treasurer Fouquet. What a coincidence! He was very likely the eldest son of François II Rackoczi, descendent of the sovereigns of Transylvania.[13] Because Marechal de Belle Isle was also a "lost king," what he told Madame de Genlis is interesting to compare to the history of the alleged descendants of the Merovingians: "All I can tell you about my birth is that at the age of seven, I wandered the depths of the forests with my governor . . . and that my head was the opening bid." This theme also exists in the history of the mythical founder of the Rosicrucian Order, Christian Rosenkreutz. George Sand introduces Count de Saint-Germain into her two most beautiful novels: *Consuelo* and *La Comtesse de Rudolstadt* [The Countess of Rudolstadt].

In the nineteenth century, Stanislas de Guaïta founded the Kabbalistic Order of the Rose+Cross. He was a close friend of Maurice Barrès, whose

---

11. See Jean-Michel Angebert, *Le livre de la Tradition* [The Book of the Tradition] (Paris: Robert Laffont, 1992).

12. The very name Saint-Germain comes from Sanctus Germanus, the "holy brother," as well as the "good cousin."

13. Transylvania plays an important role in the history of the Rosicrucian Order. Comnius, said to have been the spiritual father of the Freemasons and a friend of J. V. Andreaus, made many visits there. George Sand and Jules Verne clearly knew the importance to be attributed to Transylvania as well as the importance of its name, which is quite rich symbolically and evocative of the journey through the wilderness.

novel *La Colline Inspirée* is also worth reading from the perspective we are examining in this book. Barrès[14] wrote that Verne was "this master who wishes nothing more than to be an elder brother for us." Can we interpret this to mean an elder brother of the Rosicrucian Order?[15]

We should also look to Josephin Péladan, founder in 1891 of the Rosicrucian Order of the Temple and the Grail. He was a descendant of a Cathar family and perhaps held teachings learned first-hand.[16] From March 28 to April 30, 1893, he organized at the Palais du Champ du Mars an open Rosicrucian Salon under "the tau, the Greek cross, the Latin cross, the Grail, the Beaucéant, and the Cruciferous cross is in Roman Catholic communion with Joseph of Arimathea, Hughes de Payens, and Dante." There should be no surpise in finding Eugene Delacroix among the exhibitors at this salon.

This is not the only connection that existed at this time between the Rosicrucians and the affair in Rennes. Jules Bois, long acknowledged lover of Emma Calvé, was involved in the "war of the two roses" that pitted two Rosicrucian societies against each other. After issuing numerous attacks in the press against Stanislas de Guaïta, Jules Bois was one day greeted by the appearance of two witnesses sent by his rival: Victor-Emile Michelet and Maurice Barrès. Another duel pitted him against Papus. Emma Calvé, who, as we've learned, was also the mistress of Béranger Saunière, maintained close relations with Joséphin Péladan.[17]

There are numerous roses and crosses serving as decoration in the

---

14. Maurice Barrès was a guest at Jules Verne's home in Amiens.

15. A cenacle of the Elder Brothers of the Rosicrucian Order still exists today. Their studies seem mainly focused on alchemy.

16. The theory of a Cathar-Rosicrucian line of descent has been suggested many times, seemingly rightfully so (see Jean-Michel Angebert, *Hitler et la tradition cathare* [Hitler and the Tradition of the Cathars] (Paris: Robert Laffont, 1971). For his part, Maurice Magre sees Christian Rosenkreutz as a Cathar initiate who received instruction from Albigensians who found a haven in Germany. F. Wittemans *(Histoire des Rose+Croix)* also maintains this theory of a Cathar line of descent, but adds to it the Templars and Hussites.

17. Péladan's society included among its members Count de la Rochefoucauld, whose family, according to Gérard de Sède, owned vast forests in the Aude and had brought the Stublein family down from Alsace to oversee them. It was Eugéne Stublein who made a copy of the inscriptions on the tomb of Marquise de Blanchefort before Saunière removed them.

churches in the Razès. In Rennes-le-Château there are roses depicted on certain tombs, including the double sepulchre of Paul-Urbain de Fleury, with its inscription "He passed through while doing good." In Rennes-les-Bains there is a cross decorated with roses and bearing the inscription *In Hoc Signo Vinces, Domino Vie Rectore, Petrus Delmas Fecit,* 1856.[18]

Of note in the history of the Rosicrucians and their connection to Rennes-le-Château is that Father Gaultier, a seventeenth-century Jesuit, attacked the Rosicrucian Order, accusing it of being an offshoot of Lutherism. He wrote: "It is not of no account that the general Sabbath spoken of in the dreadful pacts made between the devil and the so-called Invisibles in 1623 is held in the neighborhood of the labyrinth that lies in the Pyrenees." What could he have meant by this? To what place was he referring?

THE WORLD TOUR OF A ROSICRUCIAN

Now we return to Jules Verne, in whose work there are numerous allusions to the Rosicrucians—from the grade of the Réau-Croix mentioned in veiled fashion in *From the Earth to the Moon* to the name of the realm in *Bourses de Voyage* that openly bears the name of "Rose+Cross." The device that figures on the tomb of the Marquis de Fleury in Rennes-les-Bains figures, in its Latin form *(Tranisire Benefaciendo)* in his novel *In Search of the Castaways,* and the character Paganal even declares: "That's our motto."

Amidst all this symbolism, Philip Jose Farmer invites us to read *Around the World in Eighty Days* again, with a perspective of Phileas Fogg as an earthling who has been raised by extraterrestrials and who

---

18. The winged messenger inviting Christian Rosenkreutz to the royal wedding bore a letter with a seal bearing a cross and the inscription "Under this sign you will triumph." The text of the letter itself reads: "This day, this day, this day, is that of the royal wedding. If your birth has merited it for you, if God has predestined you this joy, then make your way to the summit crowned by three temples, and you will witness the story personally." Incidentally, this quest could be achieved only by those carrying water, salt, and bread.

owns an elixir of long life.[19] All the characteristics of a Rosicrucian appear in what Marie-Hélène Huet writes concerning Fogg:[20]

> He transcends time, a Byron who has lived a thousand years without aging. . . . The character is not merely mysterious or impenetrable, he is quasi- omniscient. Had he traveled? Most likely, as no one had a better map of the world than he. There was no spot so remote that he does not appear to have some special knowledge of it . . . His words were often regarded as being inspired by second sight, as so many events would always eventually justify them.

After referring to these passages, Marie-Hélène Huet goes further, asking: "Is it an exaggeration to write that Phileas Fogg appears clad in all the divine attributes, such as science, majesty, and authority over all the elements?" And with respect to the Reform Club, the "circle" of which Phileas Fogg is a member, couldn't its initials—R.C.—be based on Rose+Cross?

We can also take note of the Rosicrucian elements in *Mathias Sandorf*. From the beginning, Jules Verne alerts us by talking about florins and kreutzers,[21] two coins evoking the flower exemplified by the rose and the cross. Mathias Sandorf himself (who in the book's engravings resembles Hetzel) possesses Rosicrucian characteristics: "He regarded her with an irresistible fixity, as if he was emitting a magnetic power from his eyes. He seemed to be gaining entry into her brain, where thought was going dark, with his own life and will." Another passage tells the same: "He could be heard murmuring this sentence borrowed from Indian legends: Death does not destroy; it only confers invisibility." In addition, Sandorf changes his name and belongs to a political secret society; he "resuscitates" the dead, or at least knows how to put people into a catatonic stupor and then revive them; and he heals for free.

---

19. Philip Jose Farmer, *The Other Log of Phileas Fogg* (New York: DAW Books, 1973).
20. Marie-Hélène Huet, "Exploration du jeu," in "Jules Verne, le Tour du Monde *Revue des Lettres Modernes* (Review of Modern Letters).
21. This method was also employed by Gerard de Nerval in *Angelique*.

This cannot help but bring to mind the laws a Rosicrucian must observe:

- The prohibition of exercising any profession except that of healing the sick at no charge
- Prohibition on the compulsory wearing of special dress reserved for the brotherhood, with dress instead being adapted to local custom
- The obligation for each brother to present himself on the appointed day at the dwelling of the Holy Spirit (refer to *Around the World in Eighty Days*)
- The obligation for each brother to ask a worthy person to succeed him if necessary (*Mathias Sandorf* finds this person in Bathory)
- The letters R.C. should serve as seal, ensign, and sigil[22]

The themes contained in the Fama Fraternatis (Laws of the Brotherhood) of the Rosicrucian Order can also be found in the work of Jules Verne. In fact, as shown in Verne's words, the Rosicrucians believed that humanity recorded a constant progress marked by the exploration of unknown regions, scientific discoveries, and the increase in the number of scientists, but that danger came from fanaticism, the abuse of respect for authority, the lack of understanding among scientists, and their refusal to communicate their discoveries. The primordial Rosicrucian books include the M Book[23] and Proteus.[24]

Jules Verne's encoding of his work was perhaps a reference to the warning that appears at the beginning of *The Chemical Wedding of Christian Rosenkreutz:* "Mysteries made public become cheap and

---

22. This is why René Descartes, after displaying an interest in the Rosicrucans and after he was no doubt initiated into the order thanks to the mathematician Faulhaber, signed his works R.C. It should be added that, as prescribed by the rule, he practiced medicine for free. His principle stating that nature abhors a vacuum is a Rosicrucian law.
23. Could this be the *Liber Mundi, Liber Mirabilis,* or *Mutus Liber,* or some other book?
24. An allusion to this mythical figure appears in *Mathias Sandorf.*

things profaned lose their grace. Therefore, cast not pearls before swine nor make a bed of roses for an ass." It seems Verne has respected this warning to the letter, but this should not prevent us from further analyzing his work. To do this we should now turn to two of the oddest novels he wrote: *Robur the Conqueror* and *Maître du Monde* [Master of the World].

ROBUR, THE ROSICRUCIAN MASTER

The storyline of *Robur the Conqueror* is quite simple. It begins when, throughout the world, strange lights and noises occur in the sky and observers cannot define them. (Today we would call these unidentified flying objects, or UFOs). Robur, a brilliant scientist, has created a heavier-than-air machine capable of flight and he has named it the *Albatross*. Other scientists are averse to the notion that objects that are heavier than air can fly. For a while they simply grimace at Robur, which allows them to avoid asking questions, but they eventually reject him and call him a lunatic. As a result, Robur shuts himself up in his solitude and his pride. Soon, to show that he is right, he has two scientists kidnapped and takes them on a trip around the world in the *Albatross*.

As the story progresses, Robur's meglomania grows until, in the companion novel, *Master of the World*, it gains the upper hand over his scientific genius. This presents for Verne the means for him to lose what cannot be salvaged in order to preserve the rest. On the one side, we have scientists who refuse to believe the evidence of their own senses; on the other, we have a brilliant individual. It is not hard to see where the author's favor lies. It is not difficult to see that he prefers the misunderstood genius to those whose self-importance is larded with diplomas. He must handle everything with kid gloves, however, and try to please everyone, so Verne changes his hero's character a bit. The reader can make of it what he will: Those who are not worthy will regard the petty types represented by Uncle Prudent as the heroes of the story; the rest will recognize the genius of Robur. At least, this is what Verne seems to be telling us.

The most important aspect of the matter, however, is the fact that Robur possesses the characteristics of the Rosicrucians.[25] He appears much younger than his age, as if he owns the miraculous elixir of life. He introduces himself by saying: "A citizen of the United States, my name is Robur. I am worthy of this name. I am forty years old, although I look only thirty. I have an iron constitution, rigorous health, remarkable muscular strength, and a stomach that even the world of ostriches would regard as excellent. That sums up my physical description."

In this novel, where he speaks a certain jargon for the outside, as Father Boudet would say, Jules Verne stresses the name Robur. His character even says, "My name is Robur. I am worthy of this name." The connection is further underscored in the book's title: *Robur the Conqueror*— that is, R.C., the signature of the Rosicrucians.[26] It is no surprise, then, that this book, too, makes some allusions to Rennes-le-Château. Some of the details Verne highlights are the Paris Meridian[27] and the origins of the Franks. In addition, a number of observations made from the sky at specfic hours can be reconciled only if we shift them by an entire hour (with respect to the sun's position) and place them in the Rennes-le-Château region. Perhaps this is the "unique focal point" Jules Verne invites us to explore. Here we find the Mount Royal mentioned in the book. Anyone familiar with this corner of the Razès region would lose all doubt upon reading this passage from Robur, who is supposedly flying over the United States:

> Toward five o'clock, after crossing the Black Mountains covered by pines and cedars, the *Albatross* flew over the territory that

---

25. Verne emphasizes this aspect when he says that the most beautiful Masonic Lodge can be seen in Philadelphia. It is an allusion to the Rosicrucian Freemason relation and the meaning of Philadelphia being synonymous with the Rosicrucian's highest purpose— brotherly love.

26. Another key to the book resides in the name of one of the other characters: Uncle Prudent, the word *prudent* being a key.

27. For a time the *Albatross* follows the Paris Meridian and nothing can force it to deviate from this straight course. Following it so strictly would inevitably lead to flying over the region of Rennes-le-Château.

has rightfully been called the badlands of Nebraska—a chaos of ochre-colored hills, pieces of mountain allowed to tumble to the ground that broke during their fall. From a distance, these blocks took on the most fantastic shapes. Here and there in the middle of this enormous game of knucklebones, one could spy the ruins of medieval cities with forts, keeps, crenelated castles with round towers.

How many medieval fortresses exist in the United States? Here, it seems, the landscape is actually sited in the Razès, not far from the Black Mountain in the Corbières Range with its ochre hills. The allusion to fossilized human remains that follows this passage could only delight the current owner of the castle of Rennes-le-Château, who has long maintained that the fossils of giant men can be found in this region.

We won't look closely at the various references to auriferous zones, a silver river, Salt Lake City (the Mormon capital on the banks of the Great Salt Lake), Oran, the dotted lines on maps that are reminiscent of Father Boudet's triangulations connected to a needle. We can end our consideration of *Robur the Conqueror* with this important passage from the book: "No, never has a black man since Toussaint Louverture, Soulouque, and Dessaline, excited so much mention." What is the reason for this allusion to two emperors and a Haitian general? Quite simply their names permit Jules Verne to tell us the gold of Roco Negro[28] can now be found by looking: Louverture, Soulouque, Dessaline, or, if you would rather: the opening beneath the oak of Salines. C.Q.F.D. Ce Qu'il Fallait Démontrer (something that requires demonstration). [The three names together mean the opening beneath the oak of Salines.] It so happens that the oak figures prominently in the Delacroix painting of Jacob wrestling with the angel and also appears in one of Signol's paintings. It is also connected to the very name of Robur: This well-deserved name

---

28. In *Master of the World,* Jules Verne tells us in his way that the gold is no longer at Roco Negro, but that the local clues leading to this spot are valid. The treasure has simply been moved. I will leave it to the perspicacious reader to find the relevant passage.

comes from the Latin and serves as the root of one of the French words for oak: *rouvre*.[29] We will see that this name also refers to one of the branches of the Rosicrucian Order.

Master of the World (what a title!) is the sequel to *Robur the Conqueror*. Having lost his first machine, Robur has constructed a new one that, in addition to flying, has the distinction of being able to go beneath the water, over the water, and on the ground. Robur seeks to be master of the air much like Captain Nemo wishes to be master of the oceans. It is clearly a Promethean ambition that causes him to say: "I am the master of this seventh part of the world that is larger than Australia, Oceania, Asia, the Americas, and Europe, this aerial Icaria that millions of Icaruses will one day inhabit." Robur displays pride in this black pavilion sowed with stars and with a gold sun at its heart. He is a little like Lucifer, the rebellious light bearer. Robur issues a kind of challenge to God, which is why he eventually will be toppled from his place, but he also brings teaching, and part of his discourse can be interpreted as "There are secrets that are not right for all men to know, especially if they are not prepared, and it is important not to reveal all to the profane if they have never received initiation."

A portion of *Master of the World* takes place on a mountain (or at its foot): the Great Aerie, where the heroes go in search of Robur. Interestingly, in the region of Rennes-le-Château there is an Eagle Peak right next to Les Salines, and the mountain figuring in Jules Verne's novel bears a strange resemblance to Bugarach. Furthermore, it seems that the road to it in the novel is based on the one that leads to Les Salines.

For a time, the main problem to be resolved in the novel is how to enter the Great Aerie. Strange phenomena—lights and smoke—occur there and people wonder, "Just what is going on in the belly of the Great Aerie?"[30] If we were to seek information at the site in the Rennes region, we would be told that strange UFO-like lights are sometimes

---

29. Robur, a palindrome, indicates the colors red and royal purple.
30. Jules Verne also alludes to underground canals and a cavern, a lake that empties and refills, Lake Saint Clair, and so forth.

seen emerging from Bugarach, as if from inside the mountain. It is no surprise, then, that Jules Verne's Great Aerie is described as a "region inhabited by monsters of the air."

Once again, the story begins to revolve around a treasure hunt.[31] In fact, the guides who mount the expedition to the Great Aerie and indicate the route to follow are named Harry Horn and James Bruck: The way to pillage (Harry) is to follow the "detour of the river" (horn). Finding the treasure will permit you to press (jam) the jewels against yourself—to wear them as you would wear a brooch (Bruck).

Further, the phrase "my leader had charged me with wresting the secrets from this devil of the Great Aerie" can only remind us of the poem by Labourrise-Rochefort that states the treasure of Rennes is guarded by a demon. Jules Verne builds on this when one of his characters asks: "When should we go hunt for them in the entrails of the mountain?" What do the heroes do? They enter a gorge that is not very steep and follow the riverbed. They advance with the agility of an "isard" (an animal typical of the Pyrenees),[32] and they end up at a stone whose strange silhouette depicts an enormous eagle. In fact, this eagle can be seen sculpted into an enormous rock on the side of Bugarach. Are we to conclude, then, that Bugarach, like the Great Aerie, is a haven for the devil?

The Rosicrucian aspect of the *Master of the World* is perceptible in certain details, from the R.C. of Robur the Conqueror to his physical youth, and from his powers that are depicted as both semi-divine and semi-diabolical to the allusion to Proteus. In the novel, the quest of those in search of the *Dreadful*, Robur's aerial vessel, is copied exactly from a Rosicrucian text:

---

31. It should be noted that the Great Aerie includes a spot named Black Dome, bringing to mind Roco Negro, and that an allusion is made to the exploitation of mines and mineral waters. Another allusion is made to Black Rock and White Mansion, which could just as easily be referred to as Roco Negro and Blanchefort.

32. [This is a species of mountain goat quite similar to the chamois of the Alps. —*Trans.*]

In the middle of the world rises a mountain, both near and faraway; there one finds the greatest treasure and the malice of the demon. The way that leads there can be found only by one's own efforts. Pray and ask the way, follow the guide who is no earthly being and is found inside you, although you know him not. He will lead you to your purpose at midnight. You will need a hero's courage. . . . At the moment you have sight of the castle, the wind will cause the rocks to tremble. Tigers and dragons will attack you. An earth-quake will topple everything the wind left standing, and a violent fire will consume all earthly matter. At dawn, calm will return and you will find the treasure.

GASTON LEROUX AND THE MYSTERIOUS KING

While Jules Verne wrote *Robur the Conqueror,* Gaston Leroux gave us *The Mysterious King.* The connections between the two are the same inspiration, the same Rosicrucian Order, and, if I dare say so, the same Robur. Gaston Leroux is, as most know, the author of numerous detective novels, among them *The Phantom of the Opera, The Perfume of the Lady in Black,* and *The Mystery of the Yellow Room.* One phrase from his work has become embedded in my memory and often springs to mind: "The presbytery has lost none of its charm, nor the garden its dazzle." It is an anodyne phrase—and yet underlying it is the presence of a mystery. What kind of souvenirs would this presbytery evoke?[33]

Of Norman origin, Gaston Leroux first wished to be a sailor, dreaming of foreign shores and unknown worlds on the other side of the sea. Then he wished to be an orator, a man of language. Finally, at the age of twenty, he awoke to the charms of art and resolved to watch

---

33. In fact, this phrase is one Gaston Leroux borrowed from George Sand. It comes from one of her least known works, *Mélanges* [Blends], with a slight difference that makes it less beautiful, I think: In the original, the word *neatness* is used instead of the word *charm.*

the movement of humanity. As Daniel Compère points out,[34] this could describe the very youth of Jules Verne.

Leroux, this enlightened fan of the quest for treasure,[35] gave us his own Robur in *The Mysterious King*. It is a strange story about a leader of robbers with a big heart and an innate sense of justice, who combines the aspect of a naïf with that of an invincible being. This righter of wrongs by theft—half Count of Monte Cristo, half Robin Hood, both Cartouche and Mandrin—rules like a veritable king in the shadows, but does so while retaining an anarchistic spirit.[36] He leads an underground world, a sort of Aggartha in Paris. As the king of the catacombs, he, too, is a kind of lost king.

In the novel, the two letters—R.C.—that appear in the morning painted in red on the doors to the prison of La Roquette, just as the posters of the Rosicrucians appeared on the walls of Paris in the seventeenth century, are also the signture initials of of the king of the catacombs.[37] But why does the protagonist sign things R.C. when Gaston Leroux entitled his novel *The Mysterious King* (which would be R.M.)[38] and the actual name of this character is Robert Pascal (R.P.)?[39] How, though, could the author have done otherwise, for like Verne, Gaston Leroux

---

34. Daniel Compère, "Gaston Leroux et Jules Verne" [Gaston Leroux and Jules Verne], in *Visions Nouvelles sur Jules Verne* [New Views on Jules Verne] (Centre de Documentation Jules Verne. Amiens: 1978).

35. Leroux personally organized a Hunt for the Treasures of Cartouche in the newspaper *Le Matin*. Colleagues of the newspaper had placed sums of money in seven spots in Paris and in the provinces, and Leroux's serial published by *Le Matin* held clues that could put the reader on the scent. This serial later appeared in the form of a novel under the title *La double vie de Théophraste Longuet* [The Double Life of Theophrastus Longuet]. This is a story that deserves to be read for more than one reason.

36. He draws up a contract in the name of the Association Against Society (A.C.S.) Company. [Cartouche is the highwayman Louis Dominique Bourguignon (1693–1721) whose exploits became legendary and earned him a reputation similar to that of Robin Hood. —*Trans.*]

37. ["King" is *roi* in French. —*Trans.*]

38. [R.M. = *roi mysterieuse*. —*Trans.*]

39. Gaston Lerox pirouettes around the question when he explains that the protagonist's father was named Robert Carel.

wished to write a text inspired by Rosicrucianism. As we saw earlier, R.C. is the Rosicrucian signature.

The connection with *Robur the Conqueror* does not stop there, however, for on the doors is also the phrase "*ROBUR mortis viri saluss et sublimitus, profundis, longitudo, latitudo.*" If there are still any doubts, then reading the book will show that Leroux describes his hero as a master of good and evil, and the mysterious king does not hesitate to say, "I am stronger than death! I am life!" Indeed, he is one of the Masters of the World who also appears in the guise of the mysterious Count de Teramo-Girgenti, who, like Saint-Germain and Cagliostro, was supposedly alive during the time of Henri IV and had found the secret of resurrection (a secret that partially consists of going to take the waters every summer). "I do not ressucitate myself. I am resuscitated. All that is required for me to come back to life is that under certain given conditions, certain words are spoken in the presence of my corpse." In addition, the title of one of the chapters of the novel is: "You Will Awaken Among the Dead."

Once again, we should not be surprised to find allusions to Rennes-le-Château in Leroux's work. For example there are references to the "so-called Dagobert chairs with the feet and armrests forming an X over which tapestries of incalculable value had been draped." Other keys are the allusions to the Observatory Quarter of Paris, Saint Sulpice, Saint Vincent de Paul, Freemasonry, a cemetery whose vaults do not remain sealed, the yellowtail coris, Scotland, quill and ink, Benvenuto Cellini and Marguerite de Valois, and to a head in Ingre's *Apotheosis of Homer* which is undoubtedly that of Nicholas Poussin.

Two other significant details in the novel are the name of Mademoiselle Derennes (of Rennes) and the parrot that holds the key to part of the story and bears the evocative name of Solomon.[40] It is he who gives *the key* to the boarders because he lives in the *lodge* (Masonic lodge) of a concierge between Notre Dame de Lorette, the Virgin, St. Joseph, the

---

40. Its real name is Jacquot, an incontestable allusion to the "Children of Master Jacques" and the Sons of Solomon of Companionnage. These are different secret societies.

infant Jesus, the Stations of the Cross, and rosaries. Further, this parrot says: "You are the Marguerite of Marguerites! You are the pearl of the Valois," which is a phrase that must be put into context with the origins of the mysterious Angelic Society[41] to which Gérard de Nerval, among others, belonged[42]—a subject we will revisit.

In truth, this king of the catacombs is quite mysterious. He enters his kingdom through a well that appears "beneath the moonlight like an ordinary well: an iron hoop from which hangs a pulley, through which runs a chain at the end of which is a bucket." According to one of the characters, though, it seems that a person can go "to the center of the earth" through this well, and it seems a fabulous treasure is hidden there. Who would have doubted it? To continue the connection of the R.C. to the Rosicrucian Order, chapter 9 of the novel alludes to the grade of Reau-Cross of the Elect Cohens, and the king of the catacombs rules over "one of the most formidable occult powers like none that has been assembled on the margins of society for a long time," as we are told by Gaston Leroux.

The comparisons that exist between Robur and the Mysterious King are too large to be the work of chance. We might ask if Gaston Leroux and Jules Verne may have belonged to the same secret society or if Leroux may not have received his information from Verne, for, as Daniel Compère tells us:[43]

> It is not impossible that Gaston Leroux and Jules Verne met. It is a simple hypothesis I am venturing, but here are the elements that support it. Gaston Leroux was born in Paris in 1868, but his parents moved to Tréport around 1879. The young boy therefore attended

---

41. See also the Street of the Mists.

42. The entrance to the underground realm of the mysterious king is located precisely at the spot where Gérard de Nerval's body was found. (It has never been certain if he hung himself or was murdered).

43. Daniel Compère, "Gaston Leroux et Jules Verne" [Gaston Leroux and Jules Verne], in *Visions Nouvelles sur Jules Verne* [New Views on Jules Verne] (Centre de Documentation Jules Verne. Amiens: 1978).

the Eu secondary school from sixth grade to the final grade. The school director designated Leroux to be the play companion of Philippe, son of the count of Paris who lived in the Château of Eu. (As a digression, the restoration work on this château was carried out by Gaston Leroux's father, the director of a public works company, who used Viollet-le-Duc's blueprints.)[44]

It so happened that during this time, Jules Verne spent many weeks in Tréport, where his *Saint Michel III* was anchored. He made the acquaintance of the count of Paris to whom he offered the manuscript of *Twenty Thousand Leagues under the Sea*. Daniel Compère believes that it would be very surprising given their close proximity if the young Gaston Leroux, already drawn to literature (he wrote novellas at the boarding school he attended), and Jules Verne did not meet. Could Gaston Leroux have been initiated by Verne? We of course cannot state this as fact, but what is certain is that Jules Verne exercised great influence over Gaston Leroux. There is a certain wink of complicity in the title given a chapter from *The Perfume of the Lady in Black:* "La presqu'ile mystcricuse."[45] Gaston Leroux's novel *Baloo* deals with the same subject as Jules Verne's *Le village aérien* [The Aerial Village]: the link that connects man and ape. Similarly, Daniel Compère feels that *Rouletabille chez Krupp* [Rouletabille at the Krupp's] (Rouletabille is Leroux's detective hero in a series of novels) is almost an homage to Jules Verne. The following passage is from the beginning of the book: "But that's a Jules Verne story you're telling us, my dear scholar . . . I read it when I was a schoolboy. It's called *Les Cinq cents millions de la Begum.*" [Begum's Millions]

While Leroux's novel is more like a torpedo than the cannonball used by Jules Verne, it closely follows the outline of the novel by Verne, who was inspired by the Krupp's factories to create the Stahlstadt in his story. Leroux also has a "submarine" work, entitled *Le Capitaine Hyx*

---

44. [Viollet-le-Duc was a nineteenth-century architect who restored many French monuments, including Notre Dame and the Hotel de Ville in Paris. —*Trans.*]

45. ["The Mysterious Peninsula," a nod to Jules Verne's *Mysterious Island.* —*Trans.*]

[Captain Hyx]. It seems that naming someone Hyx (X) or Nemo (No One) amount to the same thing. This novel has obviously been inspired by *Twenty Thousand Leagues under the Sea.*

I recommend that anyone with an interest in Rennes-le-Château read all Leroux's novels. We unfortunately do not have the space to examine all of his work in detail here, but there is one more work worth noting: *La Reine du Sabbat* [Queen of the Sabbath], whose protagonists are Reginald, Regina, and Reynaldo. The story, whose plot unfolds partially in the Carmargue region of southern France and partially in Bohemia, is a romanticized and somewhat biased tale of the archduke of Hapsburg portrayed by Jules Verne in *The Survivors of the Jonathan:* Jean Orth, barely disguised under the name of Jacques Ork.[46] In this novel, just as in *A Man in the Night* or *Rouletabille chez les Bohémiens* [Rouletabille and the Gypsies], the plot revolves around a dynastic difficulty, the quest for a "chosen one of the race," a descendent of royal origin, a promise of happiness for the people's future. "Won't the blood that has been spilled prepare a marvelous and triumphal dawn for his race?" In *Rouletabille and the Gypsies,* the prince born of an extremely ancient race *(A Man in the Night)* is replaced by a queen foretold by an ancient prophecy: "In this time, a queen will be born to the race, having the symbol of the crown on her shoulder." This was the same way that Merovingian kings could be recognized: through a distinctive sign on the skin. This is the well-known secret of *Le Pieuvre.*[47] Some odd gypsies portrayed by Leroux, who name Odette their "little Queen," invite us to posit an equation.[48] These are odd gypsies who deliver the secrets of Jules Verne to us.

---

46. It is curious to note that *Un homme dans la nuit* [A Man in the Night] exactly describes the conflagration of the Bazar de la Charité in which Archduchess Sophia of the Hapsburgs died.

47. [The Octopus; also slang for "leech." —*Trans.*]

48. Little Queen, or *petite Reine,* is the nickname for Odette. Given that *-ette* is a diminutive ending meaning small, by algebraically simplifying this equation, we get Queen = Od, or Rennes-Aude. It is noteworthy that the hero of *Les Mohicans de Babel* [The Mohicans of Babel] is named Claude Corbières; and that it includes a Count Godefroid de Martin l'Aiguille [*Aiguille* means "needle" in French. —*Trans.*] and a certain Vorski, who claims descent from the kings of Bohemia.

Gaston Leroux fully admitted the influence Jules Verne had upon him. In *A Man in the Night,* he used for inspiration an episode from *Around the World in Eighty Days* and does not seek to conceal this fact. In *Queen of the Sabbath* he again borrows from his mentor, mainly by citing the torment suffered by Michel Strogoff and by entitling one chapter "Mister No Name" (or, in other words, Nemo). He also found inspiration for certain passages in *Castle in the Carpathians* and *Master Zacharius.*

Let's end this section with a phrase from *Rouletabille and the Gypsies:* "Legend recounts how Gypsy tombs were never to be found because they would divert streams from their beds in order to bury the bodies they wished to save from profanation by the *gaje.*" In this regard I can only recommend reading the article by E. Blanc-Lafangere entitled "Lourmarin, Cursed Castle of the Gypsies" (which appeared in the magazine *L'Ere d'Aquarius,* no. 4), which is highly instructive concerning a dwelling once belonging to the Créqui-Lesdiguière.

DOROTHY THE TIGHTROPE WALKER

Next, we'll investigate a book by Maurice Leblanc, father of Arsène Lupin.[49] *Dorothy the Tightrope Walker* starts off in the castle of Roborrey (Robor-Rey, which could mean either "royal oak" or King Robur) near a river whose bed is covered with white pebbles, an ancient fountain with dolphins and sirens, and a sundial erected in a rock garden. A strongbox is stolen from this location. It can be opened only using the key R.O.B. Dorothy, the heroine of the novel, sets off to follow the trail of a fabulous treasure coveted by the abominable d'Estreicher.[50] The key to finding this treasure is provided by the phrase *In Robore Fortuna.* Dorothy says of it: "Four people are joined by a common secret.

---

49. [He is a popular French fictional character who was a brilliant and elegant thief, similar to the English Raffles. —*Trans.*]
50. Is this a clue that we should view him as an Austrian? [Readers will remember Saunière's mysterious "Austrian" connection. —*Trans.*]

Now, the word Roborey uttered by my father on his deathbed gives me the right to find out whether he himself may not have been part of this group, and whether, consequently, his daughter is qualified to take his place." Dorothy's father's name was Jean d'Argonne[51] and her mother's name is Jesse Varenne.[52]

The courageous and pure-hearted Dorothy is accompanied by her adopted children, to whom she does not fail to give a history lesson on . . . the Merovingian kings! The peculiar treasure they are hunting is in fact an inheritance. One day, in 1721, a certain Jean-Pierre de la Roche, the marquis de Beaugreval, made his will and entrusted it to a lawyer with the stipulation that it was not to be read for exactly two hundred years—July 12, 1921. It seems this odd bird who was something of an alchemist had determined he would die on July 12, 1721, and was convinced he would resurrect on that same day in 1921. On that day, the heirs to those who had been entrusted with various medallions were to arrive at the resting site of his mortal remains, follow the instructions to find an elixir, and see that the marquis ingested it. He would then come back to life.[53]

How could this not be another reminder of Count de Saint-Germain and the Rosicrucian Order, one so similar to the details concerning Count de Teramo-Girgenti in The Mysterious King? How could this not bring to mind those iron-bound crypts, especially when we learn that the rendezvous proposed by Marquis de Beaugreval is to take place beneath an elm?[54]

In truth, Dorothy herself possesses these strange "resuscitative" powers and uses them when "she dispels the shadows and decodes the

---

51. The name of a township located near Stenay in the Ardennes.

52. This cannot help but bring to mind the flight of Louis XVI in the direction of Stenay and the Orval Abbey and his arrest in Varennes [by the government of the Convention. —*Trans.*].

53. Maurice Leblanc had no hesitation about comparing this resurrection to that of Lazarus.

54. [This is actually a reference to the famous iron-bound elm that once stood at Gisors, with all its Templar and treasure legends. —*Trans.*]

enigmas. With her magic wand she causes invisible springs to gush forth, and most particularly, she discovers in the most unfathomable places, such as beneath the stones of the old castle and at the bottom of forgotten oubliettes, fantastic treasures whose existence was never suspected." It is not surprising that the letter sent by her father, Jean d'Argonne, would be "stamped with the symbol of the Red Cross."

By using the red line drawn on the map as their guide, the heroes eventually reach the treasure, the object of their quest, at La Roche-Périac. Here, they find themselves near an old clock with two large hands colored with rust. The key to the treasure is a magnificent oak, a *chêne-roi,*[55] which is reminiscent of both Robur the Conqueror and the king of the catacombs. (C.R. is quite close to the signature R.C.) There, near two granite column-like needles that give the appearance of an open door through which the blue sheet of the ocean can be seen, the fortune of the marquis is found in the heart of the robur oak. Maurice Leblanc makes sure to point out that the word *robore* is the ablative of the Latin word *robur,* meaning "strength," "steadfastness," and "energy," and calling to mind the variety of oak known as the *rouvre. In Robore Fortuna:* In the oak, the fortune. This is just another way of saying Louverture, Souslouque, Dessaline.[56] Yet the wise and pure Dorothy renounces her claims to this treasure, thus embodying the other meaning of *In Robore Fortuna:* Fortune lies in the steadfastness of the soul.

While Arsène Lupin does not make an appearance in this novel, he nonetheless inspires it. The mystery Dorothy solves is one Lupin proposed solving in his youth when the countess of Cagliostro acquainted him with it. One of the episodes in *Dorothy the Tightrope Walker* is also directly inspired by another novel by Maurice Leblanc in which Arsène Lupin does not appear but in which some loot has been stashed in an oak. This novel, *La vie extravagante de Balthazar* [The Extravagant Life

---

55. [*Chêne-roi* means "king oak." —*Trans.*]
56. [They phonetically sound out the phrase (in French and English), "the opening beneath the oak of salines."—*Trans.*]

of Balthazar] relates the tale of an inheritance linked to an identifying mark on the skin. Certain clues in this story strongly recall Godefroy de Bouillon, which connects us again to the Merovingian legacy, since Godefroy claimed Merovingian ancestry. In fact, the character of Balthazar was born in Val-Rouge.[57]

We might regard this as another link between Jules Verne and Maurice Leblanc, via the Rosicrucian Order and the affair of Rennes. It is a fact that Maurice Leblanc was greatly influenced by Jules Verne. Arsène Lupin displays a characteristic that is common to a number of Verne's characters, as well as to some in Gaston Leroux's and Anatole France's work: aristocratic anarchism, a synthesis that is more than paradoxical. It was Yves Olivier-Martin who, in the August-September issue of the *Europe Revue* devoted to Arsène Lupin, compared the worldly anarchic aspect of Lupin to a characteristic depicted in Anatole France's *The Revolt of the Angels*. Olivier-Martin described him as "a blend of Des Esseintes[58] and a carbonaro-rentier."[59]

There are other disturbing resemblances between the work of Jules Verne and that of Maurice Leblanc. Jean-Paul Faivre[60] believes that Leblanc was so inspired by Verne that the cryptogram of the Hollow Needle delighted Verne as if it were his own. According to Faivre:

The Hollow Needle, with all the modifications one might wish, is Back-Cup, the lair of that other adventurer, Count d'Artigas, alias Ker Karraje.[61] Back-Cup is an islet that looks exactly like an overturned

---

57. [Red Valley. —*Trans.*]

58. [The jaded aristocratic hero of Joris-Karl Huysmans's highly influential novel *A Rebours*, whom Oscar Wilde recalled in his novel *The Picture of Dorian Grey*. —*Trans.*]

59. [*Carbonaro* (plural *carbinari*) is Italian for coal burner and refers to the revolutionary Carbonari, who fought for the unification of Italy. *Rentier* is a French word for an individual who lives off lands or investments. —*Trans.*]

60. Jean-Paul Faivre, "De Jules Verne en Arsène Lupin, ou le mystère de l'Aiguille Creuse" [Jules Verne in Arsène Lupin, or the Mystery of the Hollow Needle] (Cahiers d'Herne: Jules Verne) [Studies of Herne: Jules Verne].

61. From *Face au Drapeau* [Facing the Flag] by Jules Verne.

cup, and from the bottom of it escapes a fuliginous vapor. Its summit rises some 330 feet above sea level and its flanks, whose slopes are steep and regular, become at its base naked rocks incessantly battered by the surf. A natural arch, another Aval Gate,[62] forms the handle of the cup: it too is hollow, an enormous cavern hollowed into the rock. A false volcano whose eruptions are due to the fires, like those in *Master of the World,* are lit to keep away the harmless fishermen and those who are indiscreet." This place also recalls Captain Nemo's last port of call: the small grotto that was enlarged almost to the size of an underground town, topped by a conical hill that stood alone, unconnected to any of the surrounding hills. Ker Karraje's booty is in Back-Cup just as Arsène Lupin's is stashed in the Hollow Needle. The half-underground half-underwater exit of the Hollow Needle bears a strong resemblance to the entrance into Back-Cup.

This resemblance is most likely no coincidence, especially given that Maurice Leblanc employed the same Rousellian processes and cryptographic techniques as Jules Verne. One of these compels the hero of *813* to make exactly the same kind of error made by Pagnol in *In Search of the Castaways:* He translates A PO ON as Apollo instead of Napoleon. In *Un monde connu et inconnu: Jules Verne* [A World Known and Unknown: Jules Verne], Christian Robin makes the additional and very astute observation that in *Le Bouchon de Crystal* [The Stopper], Maurice Leblanc gives indirect homage to Jules Verne by masking his hero under the name of Doctor Vernes, who owns an automobile that is quite comparable to the comfortable Verne machines. And François Raymond speaks of Arsène Lupin as "this modern Proteus" and writes: "This dual presence, not only of the chronology in the cryptogram, but of Chronos himself, as guardian of the treasure, is borrowed by Lupin not from *The Gold Beetle* or even from Sherlock Holmes. It is taken from Jules Verne, the grand master of these kinds of games."

---

62. [A fourteenth-century fortified gate in the southern French town of Mirepoix. —*Trans.*]

Before "The Sign of the Shadow," a novella starring Arsène Lupin, the Scartaris designated in Saknussem's cryptogram was already the stylus of an immense sundial whose shadow on a given day marked the center of the world. The ebb and flow of the tides by turns open and close the second hole of the Needle, thus isolating and uncovering the treasure island of Périac (Dorothy), just as they close off or give access to Nemo's crypts, and Ker Karraje's lair. These are "the great equinoctal tides" that permit only those at the "helm" to attain the "riches of the proconsul," like "the providential tidal bores" of Jules Verne—to allow access to an island or form a blockade around it. A place of salvation, marvels, or treasures, the island is a circle in the center of which time usually threads itself. The land at the pole and the island of the volcano are transpierced by the eternal return.

THE ORDER OF WOOD SPLITTERS
AND COAL BURNERS

We have seen what kind of relationship exists between *Dorothy the Tight-rope Walker, The Mysterious King, Robur the Conqueror,* and *Master of the World.* We have seen why it is significant that certain characters bear the initials R.C. But why is the name Robur so important? What is behind this frequent reference to the oak? Even if Jules Verne used it to evoke Rennes-le-Château, this cannot be the essential reason. Robur must have another meaning. The symbolism of the oak is of course the key to this name. In *The White Goddess,* Robert Graves tells us that Proteus, a mythological figure who lent his name to one of the secret books of the Rosicrucian Order, was also called the "man-king of the oak." The oak king, Robur, Proteus, the mysterious being who can take on any form before transforming into mist—we seem to be on the right path. Continuing in this direction, we must bear in mind that etymologically, the word *druid* means oak man [63] and comes from the Cymro-Gallic *derw.*[64]

---

63. In argot, it is curious to note that *oak* simply means "man."
64. According to Laurence Talbot, this term would be the origin of *dervish.*

Given the type of hero that appears in these novels, we cannot avoid considering the Carbonari, who seem to have played an important role in the development of French and Italian Freemasonry. In *Les Secrets de la Chevalerie* [The Secrets of Knighthood], Victor-Emile Michelet states: "In tandem with the coronation at Reims, where the king renews the pact concluded between Clovis and Saint Remy in the name of the autonomous communes of the Gauls, there was a secret coronation in which the king had to don garb that was customarily provided by the guilds. Whatever the truth may be, long after the abolition of the Templars, the Beauceant,[65] played a part in this secret coronation displayed by the guilds, calling themselves the 'Frères Charbonniers'.[66] Among these Charbonniers there was a specific group called the Wood Splitters. According to one legend, François I stumbled across one of their initiatory ceremonies. He was made a member, but when he sought to sit down in the master's place, the master objected, saying, "The Charbonnier is the master of his own home." This legend provided another connection between the Charbonnerie and royalty, but a secret royalty that governs in the shadows."

In the eighteenth century, the Chevalier de Beauchesne[67] launched the Order of the Wood Splitters in Paris. The sylvan traditions were more or less adulterated with the erotic sensibilities of that time, but its ceremonial basics remained authentic. They often took on the appearance of an orgiastic banquet, but its festivities served to mask a true Masonic lodge: the Constancy, founded by Beauchesne under the auspices of Charles Edward Stuart—a family that is not unknown to us. Gustave Bed writes: "The lodges of the Chevalier de Beauchesne seem to have formed part of the order of the Emperors of the Orient and Occident."

For Grasset d'Orcet, the Wood Splitters were introduced into Italy under the name Carbonari during the reign of François I. In England, they formed a guild: the Foresters, which was an English translation of

---

65. [Heraldic banner. —*Trans.*]
66. [The coal-burner brothers. —*Trans.*]
67. [Roughly translated, it means "handsome oak." —*Trans.*]

the name of the druids. They had allegedly maintained their traditions from times long past and survived through the Middle Ages, preserving their traditions in the forests of Morvan and Roussillon.[68] Among themselves, they called each other Cousin Duchêne.[69] Grasset d'Orcet informs us that they had preserved denominations more or less reminiscent of the two major divisions of the druidic order, bards and ovates, as Bardaches and Sarons. He also indicates a curious link between the druids and the Merovingian kings. In his opinion, the Fendeurs,[70] whom he also calls the Minstrels of Morvan, were the origin of all modern forms of Freemasonry. They were often in conflict, he says, with the Minstrels of Murcia, who were more strongly attached to Visigoth traditions.[71] The brothers of the oak, or the Wood Splitters, still existed in eighteenth-century France, but primarily in the form of an "aristocratic and literary grade that was bestowed only on masters." The Wood Splitters were specialists in the use of grimoires in which the names of trees were abundantly employed, and one of their principal identifying signs was that of the lamb holding a banner. Grasset d'Orcet adds that one of the names they adopted was Loups[72] or Lupins. Could this explain Maurice Leblanc's choice of a name for his main hero?[73] Couldn't Arsène Lupin be the king of the Wood Splitters, the king of the oak, he who rules in the shadows, and—Arsène . . . in Ren(n)es?

The fact is that the power of the Wood Splitters was great, and even in the nineteenth century, their front order—if we may call it that—the Carbonari numbered no less than twelve thousand members in Paris. It seems they had some ties with Bolshevism. These men who maintained

---

68. Legend tells us that the first troubadour found the "leys d'amor" (the laws of love) in the branches of a sacred oak.

69. ["Cousin of the oak." —*Trans.*]

70. [Wood Splitters. —*Trans.*]

71. These two orientations precisely correspond to those of the Guelphs and the Ghibellines.

72. ["Wolves." —*Trans.*]

73. I should add that one of the characters in *Dorothy the Tightrope Walker* is named Saint Quentin, which the Wood Splitters saw as signifying the quintessence about which Rabelais speaks.

that their order was born in Scotland[74] founded a *vente,*[75] or lodge, in the Montségur region: the Companions of Sabarthez. Their director, Adolphe Garrigou, spent his life investigating traces of the Cathars throughout the land, most particularly in the caves of the Ariége region. The torch was then passed to Antonin Gadal, who belonged to the Rosicrucian Order of Holland.[76] It was he who inspired the German scholar Otto Rahn, author of *Crusade Against the Grail* and *Lucifer's Court.*

Pierre Neuville asks:[77] "Can it be suggested that the old oak, the Foresters, and the Forest are a resurgence of the authentic Rosicrucians, those who wielded such great influence over political events from the seventeenth to the beginning of the nineteenth century?" This is the kind of question that answers itself. Robur is there to show this link, for it corresponds both to Rosicrucian teaching and myths of the Foresters or Wood Splitters—myths connected to Robin Hood.[78]

If we need further proof, we can find it in two novels written by George Sand, *Consuelo* and *The Countess of Rudolstadt,* in which part of the plot revolves around a stone of horror and the great oak of Schreckenstein near the castle of the giants, which sits over an underground world accessed by a cistern. For Albert de Rudolstadt, this oak is a veritable "genealogical tree on which our dark and glorious history has been written in letters of blood." This tree has a connection to Johan Zizka of the Chalice, leader of the Taborites and nicknamed the Hussite. We must not forget that Taborites and Hussites were two sects

---

74. It can be asked if a connection can be seen between the Carbonari and *The Underground City.*

75. [A "fellable stand of wood." —*Trans.*]

76. The Rosicrucian Order of Holland erected a very unusual monument in front of the cathedral of Lombrives: the Galahad Rosicrucian Center.

77. Pierre Neuville, *Les dessous ténébreux de l'histoire* [The Murky Underside of History] (Paris: Albin Michel, 1976).

78. In his indispensable book *The White Goddess,* Robert Graves has demonstrated how Robur the rouvre, just like Robin, was connected to the Christmas period of the calendar: "For at this point in the year, in British folklore, the Robin Red Breast, as the spirit of the New Year, sets out with a birch rod to kill his predecessor, the Gold Crest Wren of the old year, whom he finds hiding in an ivy bush."

quite close to the Cathars. Further, the name Consuelo means "consolation," recalling the Cathar consolamentum. She, the Pure Lady, the Repanse de Joye,[79] Esclarmonde[80] ceaselessly imparts a love that suffused Catharism: "Consolation!" shouted the perspicacious Amélie, "she used this word? You know, aunt, how much it means when my cousin says it." We cannot be surprised to find that these two novels include Count de Saint-Germain and the Rosicrucian Order, the sect of the Invisibles.

Finally, in the prologue of George Sand's book *Jeanne* the author writes: "The prophetic oaks have vanished forever from our land and the druidesses will no longer find there a branch of the sacred mistletoe with which to adorn the altar of Hésus." Sand also included several verses from songs in this novel.

> *Little shepherdess*
> *to war you are bound . . .*
> *She carries the golden cross*
> *And an armful of lilies,*
> *Her like is not to be found there . . .*

Also, and most important, she gives the first verse of three songs:

1. "It's Been Now Six Months since Spring" . . .
2. "There Were Three Small Wood Splitters" . . .
3. "Sing, Nightingale, Sing". . .

Curiosity prompted me to hunt down the full texts of these songs, and I was not disappointed. Here are the first two lines from the song of the wood splitters (number 2 in the list):

---

79. [Respanse de Joye or Repanse de Schoye was the name of the Grail Maiden in Wolfram von Eschenbach's *Parzifal*. —*Trans.*]
80. [Esclarmonde de Foix was a Cathar Perfect and sister to the count of Foix. — *Trans.*]

There were three handsome wood splitters
from the pretty forest.
The youngest held
A flowering rose . . .

And here is a verse from the third song on the list, "Sing Nightingale Sing;"

. . . I cast myself down to rest by a fountain
And the water was so clear I washed myself.
With an oak leaf, I dried myself.
I looked at the end of the bough, I saw the nightingale singing
And sing, nightingale, sing, my mistress has left me
For a bouquet of roses, which I refused . . .

There is a quote from Verne's *Around the World in Eighty Days* concerning Passepartout, whose name, in slang, means "nightingale": "This fine lad now had, concerning his master, the faith of the coal burner."[81]

---

81. [*La foi du charbonnier,* the faith of a coal burner, is a French expression for naïve faith or trust. —*Trans.*]

JULES VERNE
AND THE SECRETS
OF ARSÈNE LUPIN

THE COUNTESS OF CAGLIOSTRO
AND THE MYSTERY OF
RENNES-LE-CHÂTEAU

We have now seen enough evidence to show that Jules Verne was no doubt a member of a Rosicrucian society and that his writings found strange echoes in those of Gaston Leroux and Maurice Leblanc. But there are still more surprises. There are more to be found in the character of Arsène Lupin.

Let's first investigate one of the best-known adventures of the gentleman thief: *The Countess of Cagliostro*. The action starts in Bénouville in the Caux region. There Arsène Lupin finds a group of men putting on trial a woman of enthralling beauty.[1] He cannot abandon her to be condemned to death, so he saves her and thus triggers a series of strange adventures in which he discovers both love and cruelty with the

---

1. This battle is quite reminiscent of the one waged between the Rosicrucians and the Jesuits. One of the noble accusers of the countess holds an important position in the Company of Jesus, moreover, and he plans to deliver to it the treasure protected by the seven-branched candelabra.

beautiful Josephine Balsamo, descendant of the count of Cagliostro.[2]

But most important, this novel provides the opportunity to solve a mystery. As Cagliostro says, he who finds the key will be "king of kings." Should we compare this to the symbol that the beautiful countess wears on her shoulder like the Merovingian king? The Merovingians allegedly had birthmarks on their shoulders shaped like a red cross. This novel certainly does hold a key, and Maurice Leblanc provides us with it almost from the very beginning.

Complications ensue, however, when Lupin must track down the "seven-branched candelabra," which brings to mind Rennes-le-Château. Lupin finds it one branch at a time, and he discovers the first one wrapped in spider webs. He ultimately discovers the secret of the seven abbeys of the Caux region, which are set out in such a way as to be a mirror of the Big Dipper. These abbeys are named Fécamp (on the crypt door of which the signature of the Rosicrucian Order can be seen and which owns its own Grail, a relic of precious blood that was carried there miraculously by a floating tree, similar to Solomon's vessel), Montvilliers, Valmont, Cruchet la Valasse, Saint Wandrille,[3] Jumièges, and Saint Georges de Boscherville.

Arsène Lupin discovers the actual site of the treasure by looking for the projection of a star whose name is obtained by taking the first letter of each of the words carved at the bottom of a mysterious chest, "*Ad Lapidem Currebat Olim Regina*"—Alcor. Some say that

---

2. Take note that the count of Cagliostro had relations with the Rosicrucian Order (see the works of Doctor Marc Haven).

Josephine Balsamo is described as wearing her hair half undone and falling in a thick mass held back by a gold comb. Above her forehead, two coils with tawny highlights are divided equally on either side of her head, and some curls fall over her temples. We might think the author had used for the model of this description one of the stained-glass Mary Magdalenes in the church in Rennes-le-Château. Leblanc tells us she is reminiscent of "those women of Leonardo or rather Bernardino Luini"—a quick wink that speaks volumes insofar as the nickname given to Bernadino Luini was Lupino.

3. St. Wandrille was count of the palace of Dagobert.

on Serbaïrou Hill in Rennes-les-Bains there was a stone that bore this inscription:

LAPID
EMCUR
REBAT
OLIMR
EGINA

This information has not been verified, however. It comes from a book by J. L. Chaumeil, which is not an altogether serious text. Further, even if this stone exists, the engraving would need to be dated. According to J. L. Chaumeil, this stone was first noted in 1892 by Father Vannier, priest of the Rennes-les-Bains mission. Chaumeil obtained his information from Philippe de Cherisey. A translation of the words might be: "Toward the stone once ran the queen." In Maurice Leblanc's novel, the translation of *"Ad Lapidem Currebat Olim Regina"* Leblanc is using some of the same occult material that Verne uses, but locates it in the Norman-Breton region of France, hence the use of real landmarks, whose names will echo the hidden material Sorel-[or-sel] might be "the stone of Agnes Sorel"[4] or "the queen's dolmen" at Mesnil-sous-Jumièges.

Francis Lacassin has good reason to speak of Arsène Lupin as practicing "the art of burglarizing the history of France."[5] He writes:[6] "Many of his interventions take place in the historical dimension: the emptying of the Château de Thibermesnil, the candelabra with seven branches in *The Countess of Cagliostro,* the secret of *The Hollow Needle,* the gold of France in *The Golden Triangle,* the recovery of Alsace in *813,* the

4. Sorel, or [gold]-sel [salt].
5. In *Europe Revue.*
6. Francis Lacassin, *Mythologie du Roman Policier* [The Mythology of the Detective Novel] (Paris: Christian Bourgeois, Second Edition. 1993).

remnants of Roman civilization in *The Maiden with Green Eyes,* and so forth.

ARSÈNE LUPIN, THE MAN WITH THE GOLDEN KEYS

But this novel is not alone in its link to fabulous treasures, for we can read in Leblanc's *La Cagliostro se venge* [Cagliostro's Revenge] "Almost everywhere throughout France, in safe hiding places, river beds, forgotten caverns, holes in inaccessible cliffs, there are gold ingots and sacks of precious stones."

We must also note "La Barre y va" [The Tide comes in there] and the Aurelle River that transports gold dust coming from Roman Butte. We are of course reminded again of Rennes-le-Château, where the River of Colors behaves the same way after periods of high water—specks of gold have even been found in the bodies of ducks that have drunk there. There are similar coincidences with regard to the characters' names. There is Pierre de Basmes ("Baume is a cave"); Mother Vauchel, who says *chaule* for *saule,*[7] which is akin to Vaussel, or Valley of Salt; the place name "oak at the cistern"; *bec-salé;*[8] a tumulus used as a chest *(arca).*[9] Could these all be coincidences?

Here is another significant detail: In the Leblanc's collection of short stories, *Arsène Lupin, gentleman cambrioleur* [Arsène Lupin, Gentleman Thief] the story entitled "Herlock Sholmes Arrives Too Late," gives us the secret of the Thibermesnil Château for which two French kings had the key. Could this again be the work of chance? The secret is expressed by a phrase: "La hache tournoie dans l'air qui frémit, mail l'aile s'ouvre, et l'on va jusqu'a Dieu."[10] This means that we should focus our attention on letters that appear in relief on a chimney.

---

7. [That is, "white washing" for "willow." —*Trans.*]

8. ["Salty river." —*Trans.*]

9. [*Arca* is an old term for clothes chest and also is the name for a certain kind of megalithic construction. —*Trans.*]

10. [The ax spins in the vibrating air, but the wing opens, and one proceeds in that direction to God. —*Trans.*]

Turn the *H* toward the right a quarter circle (la hache tournoie), shift the *R* several times (l'air qui frémit), and open the *L* like a hatch (l'aile s'ouvre) to uncover the entrance to an underground tunnel that leads to a chapel (aller jusqu'a Dieu). Compare this to the words spoken by Jules Verne's Robur: "Doctor Marey had not suspected that the penna (or *pènes*)[11] would partially open during the raising of the wing *(L)*[12] in order to let the air *(R)* pass through."[13]

It is curious that Lupin sets off on an adventure to the South Pole and explores Tibet, but the majority of Arsène Lupin's important adventures takes place in the triangle formed by Le Havre, Rouen, and Dieppe. This is undoubtedly not by chance. Of course, Maurice Leblanc, who was born in Rouen, knew the region very well, and at the beginning of the 1920s he even bought a property in Etretat that he called Le clos Lupin.[14] Nonetheless, the choice of this region was likely not tied solely to his knowledge of the terrain. A number of sites testify to the same toponymy as is found in the Razès. We need only look at Arques and Varennes. This region, too, is home to historical enigmas, a place where treasure abounds. Indeed, an eleventh-century ritual cited in the Rouen Library collection (*Rituale ecclesiasticum et monasticum ad usem ecclesiae gemmeticensism*, no. 93, Rouen Library manuscripts), for use by the monks of Jumièges, includes a prayer concerning the discovery of ancient treasures and the purification of pagan-crafted objects. We can only conclude that such finds were not rare if a prayer regarding them existed. Madame de Grazia, author of historical novels connected to the Templars, has hunted for such treasures at Saint Wandrille. In addition, some Boy Scouts discovered here some two hundred gold pieces bearing the effigy of Louis XV.

Along with being a site of lost treasures, this region is also of inter-

---

11. [Bolts. —*Trans.*]

12. [In French, "wing" is *aile,* which sounds like *L.* —*Trans.*]

13. While we are making comparisons with Robur, note that Lupin shares his tendency to think of himself as the master of the world. In *813* he says: "The Master, the one who wishes and who is able . . . the one who acts. . . . There are no boundaries to my will or power. I am richer than the richest man alive, because his fortune belongs to me. . . . I am stronger than the strongest because their strength is at my service."

14. [A *clos* is a "garden," usually one directly adjoining the house. —*Trans.*]

est to the families whose names are quite familiar to historians of the Rennes affair. For example, among the abbots of Fécamp there are several representatives of the house of Lorraine: the thirtieth degree of Freemasonry—Jean of Lorraine, then Charles of Lorraine, then Louis of Lorrain; the thirty-second and the thirty-fifth degrees of Freemasonry— Henri of Lorraine, but the thirty-fourth abbot was François de Joyeuse, from the family of the lords of Couiza.

It would be hard to resist the temptation to see this region as evoking Rennes-le-Château, just as Leblanc evokes it using the pseudonyms of Arsène Lupin: Prince Rénine (*Les Huit Coups de l'Horloge*, The Clock Stikes Eight), Prince Sernine *(813),* or Baron d'Enneris (*Le Cabochon d'Emeraude,* The Emerald Cabochon; and *La Demeure mystérieuse,* The Mysterious Dwelling). How many times has the theme of the lost son been used seemingly to recall the offshoot of the Merovingians (such as in *Le bouchon de crystal,* The Crystal Stopper; *L'Ile aux trente cercueils,* The Island of Thirty Coffins; *L'Anneau Nuptial,* The Wedding Ring; and many others)? Another of Maurice Leblanc's winks is demonstrated by the fact that his inspiration for creating the character of the hero was a novel by Raban, whose hero bears the name Victor Plantard, a sort of anarchist who steals the "national treasury" in order to redistribute it to the proletariat.[15]

Lupin the anarchist, "heir to the kings of France," brushes upon the secrets of immortality with the countess of Cagliostro, and duplicates key sites: There are two hollow needles, two mysterious dwellings, as if Maurice Leblanc is explaining Rennes-le-Château through an exact copy.

WHERE EMMA CALVÉ REAPPEARS

How would Maurice Leblanc have gleaned all the information he translates in his books? How was it that he was part of the same mysterious

---

15. Raban's 1833 novel is entitled *La baronne et le bandit* [The Baroness and the Bandit]. [Pierre Plantard played a large and ambiguous role in the Rennes-le-Château affair and the Priory of Sion mystery. —*Trans.*]

society as Jules Verne? No doubt the connection exists through his sister. She, an actress, was a close friend to many Rosicrucians: Sar Peladan, Elémir Bourges, and Emma Calvé. In fact, she advanced quite far along the path of esoterism and knew Gurdjieff, about whom she writes:

> He is not consoling, he is better. What he brings is as hard as Jesus, if one goes back to his source. There are no complacent truths. I think that the first requirement for approaching Gurdjieff is to be in full health. One must be capable of tolerating the initial shocks, especially the inconceivable torture of feeling like earth on which something is starting to work. All at once, our forces are employed in an unknown, impossible task. The more one sees it, the more one thinks, "I cannot." But are these really our forces that are being called upon? No, we have never made use of them; we did not know they existed. They are the energies that have been awakened by a new necessity, toward a new purpose.[16]

Georgette spent the greater part of her time with Maurice Maeterlinck, who had great interest in symbolism and esoteric teachings. In *Le Trésor des Humbles* [The Treasure of the Meek], he devoted a passage to Louis-Claude de Saint-Martin and another to Cagliostro, whom he defended. He was also the author of the libretto of *Pelléas et Mélisande*, Debussy's only opera.[17] Now, here is a strange coincidence: It was no doubt in Debussy's home that the meeting of the soprano Emma Calvé and Béranger Saunière took place, and it was Debussy who made possible Emma Calvé's triumph in *Pelléas et Mélisande*.

It should be no surprise, then, to learn that Maurice Leblanc's work was partially oriented toward the greatest enigma of French history, which was connected to the mystery of Rennes-le-Château. We should

---

16. Georgette Leblanc, *La Machine à Courage* [The Courage Machine] (Paris: Ed. J. B. Janin, 1947).

17. Debussy started another opera based on a text by Maeterlinck, *Princess Maleine,* but never finished it. He also began an opera based on the Rosicrucian work of Villiers de l'Isle-Adam, *Axel,* and a project with Toulet involving Shakespeare's *As You Like It.*

not be surprised at the mystery of the royal blood evoked in *The Island of Thirty Coffins,* that isle of Sarek,[18] which holds in its heart the stone of the kings of Bohemia, an enigma that George Sand knew well. We should not be surprised to find mentioned in *The Golden Triangle* places that correspond to sites in Rennes, or to find that one of the names of a main character of this adventure, if slightly altered, (the character is the villainous Essares-Bey) gives us the clue *BS-Razes.* Nor should we be astonished to see that *L'éclat d'obus* [The Bomb Burst] is in fact linked to the history of Stenay[19] and the Abbey of Orval on the Belgium frontier, again a comparison to the Rennes affair and the Great Monarch.

Interestingly, the story goes that a treasure exists at the abbey of Orval and that eight canals bearing the name of an apostle irrigated this site and fed eight ponds. We can also note in connection with this matter of a hidden treasure that in 1916, on the orders of General von Bissing, German soldiers invested the collegiate church of Molhain (in the Ardennes just about two hundred yards from the Belgian border), forbidding anyone from approaching. They excavated for several months and brought to light a tenth-century crypt and underground passage. Following this, they carried away documents and carved stones that the allied governments futilely demanded be returned after the Armistice.

In another book of Leblanc, we are reminded that in prehistoric times, the site of Rennes-les-Bains was covered by the lukewarm, salty waters of a lake[20] and was inhabited by shellfish, some specimens of which can be found in the mountain peaks surrounding the area. A ground collapse that took place 8,500 years ago between the peaks of Cardou and Black Rock emptied the lake and left the fissure in which

---

18. Sarek, we are told, comes from the word *sarcophagus,* just like, I would add, Arques comes from *chest* or *coffer.* In this story, one of the characters of royal blood is named Raynold—the old Rennes, the Rennes of the Aude.

19. In 1917 the crown prince Frederic William stayed at the château of Tilleuls in Stenay for reasons that are related to the subject at hand and which also interested Nostradamus and Louis XVI. For more on Stenay, see Gérard de Sède, *La Race fabuleuse* [The Fabulous Race] (Paris: J'ai Lu, 1973).

20. Until the Revolution, the domain of Quillan belonged to the family of Chevalier de Juvis.

the Sals River now flows. According to Philippe de Cherisey, the three or four pockets of water that still exist beneath the village of Rennes-les-Bains some 4,600 to 5,500 feet down are the source of the hot springs there.

THE SECRET OF THE NEEDLE AND THE TREASURE OF THE KINGS OF FRANCE

The best-known adventure of Arsène Lupin is *The Hollow Needle,* in which the gentleman bandit makes himself master of the treasure of the kings of France. The fortune of France, which is to say its power and destiny in the hands of a man who in some way establishes himself as a legitimate heir, once again brings us back to the hot-blooded offspring of the Merovingians. Maurice Leblanc himself said: "An entire portion of the history of France and the royal house is explained by the needle, just as is the entire history of Lupin." He went on: "Without *The Hollow Needle,* Lupin is incomprehensible," demonstrating that his opus involved a riddle to be solved. Leblanc said in this regard, "the enigmatic coupling of these two words, hollow and needle, has challenged countless Oedipi." The secret of the kings of France and others known by the names of Caesar, Rollo, and William the Conqueror, the alleged secret of the Iron Mask—this is the one Arsène Lupin discovers in the Hollow Needle of Etretat, thereby becoming, in some way, the successor to these French kings. It certainly seems as if this novel conceals a mystery connected to Etretat which is not a hoard to be uncovered[21] and which was well known to Henri IV.

Maurice Leblanc fixes the reader's attention on Manneporte and its well with ninety-seven steps; on the Aval Gate framed by the Hollow Needle and the Maidens' Chamber; on the Amont Gate; on Etretat, a place where the treasure of the state is located.[22] He focuses on a

---

21. See the book by Valère Catogan.
22. [Etretat = *Est* le *tre*sor d'*etat*, or the secret of the state. —*Trans.*]

secret place where a considerable treasure owned by the kings has been hidden and has continued to grow over the centuries in order to alert us and to catch the attention of all those who are easily tempted by gold. He then spares no thought speculating on the presence of Saint-Clair in these sites. The Saint-Clairs have a very close connection to the Merovingian succession and the family's crest is quite obvious to the wise, for it emphasizes the water of the fountain that opens the eyes of the adept.[23]

Someone whose lust for gold will shut his eyes to all else will also not think to ask about another needle quite close by, the needle of Belval.[24] This needle is close by Saint-Anne's Bank, where the marquis of Créqui's ship went down in 1766. Now, the wise person would try to find out why one Leblanc character is named Isidore Beautrelet and why another is named Daval, why Raymond de Saint-Mundi is so similar to *rex mundi* or king of the world. He would discover that a needle describes not only a pointed rock, but also a canal that has been dug to both fill and empty saltwater marshes—in other words a place through which saltwater flows.[25] Interestingly, the Arques region near Etretat is a land of salt marshes.[26] This brings us back to Rennes-le-Château. It should be noted that on one occasion, according to legend, St. Enimie, Dagobert's sister, immobilized the demon Asmodeus and held him down with a 225-foot-tall lock of stone: a needle. Pursuing this further, we find that Asmodeus, who holds up the baptismal font in the church in Rennes-le-Château, was thought to be the first to forge iron and bronze. Asmodeus failed in his attempt to dethrone King Solomon, to whom he had offered a manuscript that was supposedly the

---

23. [Saint-Clair is the French name of the Sinclair family in Scotland, holders of Rosslyn Chapel, who have long been said to be involved in these kinds of esoteric mysteries. —*Trans.*]

24. [The name of an important hero who appears in two of Maurice Leblanc's novels. —*Trans.*]

25. In nineteenth-century argot, *aiguille* ["needle"] also meant "key." Shepherd's needle is a kind of medicinal herb also known as Venus comb. This term could sometimes signify the existence of a tumulus in a place.

26. The largest are located in the communes of Arques and Bouteiller.

source of the mysterious *Necronomicon* (which became so dear to H. P. Lovecraft). Asmodeus slew the first seven husbands of the wife of Tobias and served as a counterpart to Osiris's murderer Seth. He was driven away by the magic fish of immortality and was finally compelled to help King Solomon build the Temple of Jerusalem without the aid of hammer, ax, or any other metal instrument and with the use of only a special stone that cut through other stones like a diamond cuts through glass.

The secret of Etretat is related to the energy that moves the world and lives, that it is connected to alchemy and the hunt for immortality—and it puts in mortal danger all who chase after it.

CAPTAIN ANTIFER AND THE TREASURE OF ARSÈNE LUPIN

Jules Verne is also connected to Etretat. In his novel *The Miraculous Adventures of Captain Antifer,* the title character travels the globe in search of a treasure, which he learned of through his father, who, for services rendered, received a clue concerning the latitude of an islet where the treasure was said to be buried. After learning the longitude from another character, the hero discovers the first island, which provides only a document indicating the longitude of a second island, which forces a search for a new latitude. The second island surrenders only the longitude for a third island whose latitude is discovered in Scotland. When the third island is reached, however, the quest ends with the discovery of an almost completely faded document that does not reveal the discovery of the treasure's exact location but only contains the words "the geometric law . . . pole . . ." The last island is eventually discovered, but too late: Julia Island is swallowed by the waves.

It so happens that there is a Cape Antifer southwest of Etretat.[27] Could this be another coincidence? No more than the fact that the

---

27. Chapter 14 of *The Hollow Needle* opens within sight of the Antifer lighthouse.

captain's voyage follows a diagram[28] well known to Rennes-le-Château specialists.

As Daniel Compère tells us, the center of the tale, the place to which everything returns, is Saint Malo. Further, the narrator explicitly states that Saint Malo was once an island. For him, it is the true treasure island, the one where Juhel marries his beloved Enogate.[29] We might see in her name the gate to the underground, infernal world opened by Aeneas.[30] Why does Verne choose Saint Malo? As we've learned, the author includes nothing by chance. He is giving us a valuable clue. Captain Antifer's name is actually Pierre-Servan-Malo—Verne is obvious in stating the significance of the place. If we go to Saint Malo, or, more precisely, right next to it, at Saint Servan-sur-Mer, we find a Corbières Park and the corniche of Aleth,[31] which is perfect for transporting us back to the Razès (not the least because the fort there was built in 1759 on the orders of Duke d'Aiguillon). It is thus no cause for surprise to see Captain Antifer and his friend Gildas Tregomain, "sons of the Widow," presented as a gentle freshwater sailor and the saltiest of saltwater mariners, respectively.[32]

We should also note these details: the quais of Sillon-Sion; the recommendations given to descend down the Paris Meridian; the Captain Cip, whose name represents a *pic;*[33] a story of treasure "having too far-fetched a mien"[34] and being connected to a tomb, a rock, or a "coffer of

28. See Daniel Compère, *Approche de l'île chez Jules Verne* [Jules Verne's Approach of the Island] (Paris: Lettres Modernes-Minard, 1977).

29. Enogate was the name of one of the first bishops of Saint Servan.

30. [Aeneas is Enée in French. —*Trans.*]

31. [Or Alet. —*Trans.*]

32. [The wordplay in this last sentence resists translation. "Freshwater" in French is *eau douce. Douce* also means "sweet" and "gentle." In additon to "salty," *salé* can mean risqué or dirty. —*Trans.*]

33. [Peak. —*Trans.*]

34. [Mine. —*Trans.*]

stone." There is also the character of "haute mine,"[35] who is not at all of base extraction. Indeed, his "noble origin" (no doubt Merovingian) is quite visible, given his abundant head of hair[36] and his carpet with its flowers "à haute lisse."[37] Captain Antifer has good reason to dream in his house on the rue des Hautes-Salles of the treasure of Kamylk Pasha in three hooped casks sitting beneath three hundred feet of water, while Gildas Tregomain keeps his eye on "this large gold ball, hoisted to the top of the spire of the Paris Observatory and whose fall indicates the precise moment the sun crosses the meridian of the capital."

This chapter has in no way exhausted all the connections between Jules Verne and Maurice Leblanc. Arsène Lupin undoubtedly has much more to teach us.

---

35. [This term has double meaning: "fine bearing" and a "mine at a high altitude." —*Trans.*]

36. [The Merovingians were known as the "hairy" kings because of their long hair. —*Trans.*]

37. [This is another term with double meaning. *Haute lisse* refers to a high-warp loom, but in connection with flowers it brings to mind the Fleur-de-lis, the symbol of French royalty, certainly a high or *haute* lily. —*Trans.*]

JULES VERNE AND
THE GOLDEN DAWN

THE BROTHERS OF THE GOLDEN DAWN

Given a kinship existing between Jules Verne's writings and those of the Rosicrucians, let's explore whether he maintained privileged relations with any particular denomination. Once again, we can find answers in his work. Of course, we might follow his trail to Stanislas de Guaïta or Peladan, but we can aim much higher.

At the time of Jules Verne's writing, the elite of the Rosicrucian movement was represented by the Golden Dawn. This society was born from the Societas Rosicruciana in Anglia (SRIA) founded in London in 1865 by Robert Wentworth Little and claimed to have one hundred forty-four members. Divided into "circles," this Rosicrucian group included nine grades modeled on those of the Gold Rosicrucian Order that existed in Germany at the beginning of the eighteenth century. In order to enter the SRIA, it was necessary to have already attained the grade of master in Freemasonry. At the side of R. W. Little, who was the magus-director, there was a diplomat, Edward Bulwer-Lytton (1803–1870), about whom we will learn more. Following Little's death, the direction of the SRIA was entrusted to a triumvirate consisting of William R. Woodman, W. Wynn Westcott, and Samuel L. Mathers. After a brother discovered an encrypted document, the directors of the SRIA entered into a relationship with a mysterious adept living in Berlin, Anna Sprengel. As a result of these contacts, the directors were authorized to establish an English branch of the mysterious society of which Anna Sprengel was a member. Thus was born the Hermetic Brotherhood of the Golden Dawn in Outer. The Mother Lodge remained located in Germany and was called *Lichte, Liebe, Leben* (Light, Life, Love). Six other lodges were founded, one in Holland (Hermanubis), one in France (Ahator in Paris on rue Mozart), and four in the British Isles (Isis Urania in London, Hermes in Bristol, Amon Ra in Edinburgh, and Horus in Bradford).[1]

The Golden Dawn was organized around eleven initiatory grades and, according to Samuel L. Mathers, was placed under the protection of Secret Chiefs. It also taught the pansophy (universal knowledge) dear to the German lodges. The Golden Dawn also declared that it alone knew the secret of the ever-mysterious Enochian language, which was endowed with magic powers for all those who understood it and mastered its pronunciation. For example, the phrase "Vaorsay goho iad balt, Iansh calz von vo. Sobra z-ol ror l ya nazps" would enable an individual to become invisible. This detail seems almost Lovecraftian. As for the famous Secret Chiefs, Mathers said he rarely saw them in their physical forms:

> For my part, I believe they are human beings living on this Earth, but possessed of terrible and superhuman powers. My physical encounters with them have shown me how difficult it is for a mortal, however "advanced," to support their presence. I do not mean that during my rare meetings with them I experienced the same feelings of intense physical depression that accompany the

---

1. Here is one more coincidence: The Ahator lodge included as a member Jules Bois, a journalist who was, as we have learned, the lover of Emma Calvé. It should be noted that he took a keen interest in vampirism. Another coincidence lies in the fact that Anna Sprengel was supposed to have been the countess of Landsfeld and a bastard daughter of King Louis I of Bavaria (a contested association). Mathers claimed descent from King James IV of Scotland.

loss of magnetism. On the contrary, I felt I was in contact with a force so terrible that I can compare it only to the shock one would receive from being near a flash of lightning during a great thunderstorm, experiencing at the same time great difficulty in breathing. . . . The nervous prostration I spoke of was accompanied by cold sweats and bleeding from the nose, mouth, and sometimes the ears.

It is worth noting that all the members of the Golden Dawn were highly intellectual: They were great writers, doctors, mathematicians, military experts, physicians. Among them were Florence Farr (a friend of George Bernard Shaw), Arthur Machen,[2] Sax Rohmer, W. B. Yeats,[3] Talbot Mundy, Algernon Blackwood, the astronomer Peck, the engineer Allan Bennet, Sir Gerard Kelly (president of the Royal Academy), and Aleister Crowley.[4]

DRACULA OR THE WAY
OF BLOOD

One of the more surprising figures in the Golden Dawn was Bram Stoker. Born in 1847 in Dublin, this Irishman settled in London, where he died in April 1912, after an illness that lasted six years. He was the author of a novel that would enjoy a distinctive fortune with regard to movie adaptations: *Dracula*. Knowing that Stoker was a member of the Order of the Golden Dawn raises the question of whether Dracula may contain revealing passages about the teaching or rituals of this

---

2. Author of, among other books, *The Great God Pan*. After it was translated into French by P. J. Toulet, Maeterlinck wrote to Toulet: "All my thanks for the revelation of this beautiful and singular work."

3. A future Nobel Prize winner.

4. It seems that Crowley, a figure who has inspired much ink, was initiated in Mexico into certain rituals of a blood cult within an order bearing the name Lamp of the Invisible Light. According to Crowley, this order possessed a method for invisibility that was quite close to that of Jules Verne's *Wilhelm Storitz*.

secret society.⁵ What is certain is that Stoker, like other members of the order, studied *The Magic of Abramelin the Mage,* but perhaps only after he wrote *Dracula.* In any event, he obtained valuable information from Professor Arminius Vambery of the University of Budapest, who stayed in London in 1890 and provided him with numerous details concerning the Carpathians and the historical framework used in the novel.

What most people know of *Dracula* has been distorted by the various film versions that are often caricatures of Stoker's novel. The story is about Count Dracula, who became a vampire in order to achieve immortality. This quest for immortality has a black (or rather, red) shade, for it is pursued through sucking the blood of innocent victims. The power thus acquired over time becomes almost the opposite of the immortality pursued by Rosicrucians such as Count de Saint-Germain, who, it is worth noting, was a native of Transylvania, just like Dracula.⁶ It is important to understand that the figure of Count Dracula was not purely and simply a creation of Bram Stoker's imagination. He was a member of an ancient race, and Stoker has him explain:

> We Szekelys have a right to be proud, for in our veins flows the blood of many brave races who fought as the lion fights, for lordship. Here, in the whirlpool of European races, the Ugric tribe bore down from Iceland the fighting spirit which Thor and Wodin gave them, which the Berserkers displayed to such fell intent on the seaboards of Europe, ay, and of Asia and Africa, too, till the people thought that the wolves themselves had come. Here, too, when they came, they found the Huns, whose warlike frenzy had swept the earth like

5. Bram Stoker entered the Golden Dawn in 1890, the same year he wrote *Dracula.*
6. Count de Saint-Germain was allegedly born in 1696 and was the eldest son of François II Rackoczi, descendent of the sovereigns of Transylvania. He married the princess Charlotte-Amélie von Hesse-Rheinfels on September 26, 1694. Constant contact existed between the Rosicrucian Order and Transylvania, and Jacques Duchaussoy views even Jean Corvin, voïvode of Transylvania (1388–1456) as a precursor of the Rosicrucians.

a living flame, till the dying peoples held that in their veins ran the blood of those old witches, who, expelled from Scythia, had mated with the devils in the desert. Fools, fools! What devil or what witch was ever so great as Attila, whose blood is in these veins. . . . Is it a wonder that we were a conquering race; that we were proud; that when the Magyar, the Lombard, the Avar, the Bulgur, or the Turk poured his thousands on our frontiers, we drove them back? Is it strange that when Arpad and his legions swept through the Hungarian fatherland, he found us here when he reached the frontier; that the Honfogalas was completed here? And when the Hungarian flood swept eastward, the Szekelys were claimed as kindred by the victorious Magyars, and to us for centuries was trusted the guarding of the frontier of Turkey-land.

These are the Draculas "of royal blood," summoned to "create a new and ever growing race of demi-demons who would rule over humanity."

We can turn to the novel's historical model. There is a portrait of the count at the castle of Ambras in the Tyrol. It is labeled Vlad III, voïvode of Walachia between 1448 and 1476, known as Vlad Tepes (meaning Vlad the Impaler, or even Dracula, "son of Dracula" or "son of the Dragon"). Born around 1430, then held hostage by the Turks, he attempted to seize power in 1448 and subsequently lived in the entourage of the governors of Hungary. Winning an important victory in Belgrade he regained power from 1456 to 1462. It was during this era that he became known as "the Impaler" because of his somewhat expeditious methods of dealing justice. After falling into the hands of the king of Hungary, Mathias Corvin, he was held prisoner for twelve years in the fortress of Visegrad, near Buda. He was released in 1475 to take part in the battle against the Turks. On November 26, 1476, he was reelected prince of Walachia, but less than a month later, he was murdered by his own men during a battle against the Turks. He was forty-five.

Courageous, putting his own life on the line, a hero of the independence of his country, The most sympathetic side of Dracula paints him as courageous and self-sacrificing and as a hero of the independence of his country, but there is a flip side to this military mettle. Vlad the Impaler certainly earned his nickname, for he managed to impale twenty thousand Turkish prisoners. Chillingly, he would dine while watching his victims being pierced. Modrussa, the legate of Pope Pius II, stated that in 1464, Vlad had slain forty thousand people in a single massacre, including numerous women and children. It is also said that he planted a stake between a mother's breasts, then impaled her baby on it. Even given that exaggeration may play in these accounts, it does not seem that Count Dracula was a very comforting individual.

According to the archives, after his death, his men stretched him over a large shield, following "ancient pagan custom." Through mists and forest, to the sound of drums, they returned him to the (perhaps legendary) castle of Torberg. This was when the tradition was born that made him a "lost king" who would one day return, repossess all that he had owned, and rule forever. In 1931, the Romanian commission of historical monuments sent historian Georges Florescu and archaeologist Dinu Rosetti to the monastery of Snagov. This was where Dracula had in fact been buried, beneath a stone bearing no inscription. The tomb was opened in the chapel—and was discovered to be empty! Was Dracula an immortal? In truth, his remains had been moved during the eighteenth century on the orders of Archbishop Philaretes. Some believed that monks had thrown his coffin into the lake and that ever since that time, its waters had been cursed. Nonetheless, his remains were discovered right next to the porch of the chapel. Fragments of the princely purple still adhered to the skeleton. Under his hand was a casket, covered by a violet cloth that held a gold crown and a necklace bearing a dragon. These remains were transported to a museum in Bucharest, and from there they have since disappeared.

THE DRAGON AND
MAGIC IMMORTALITY

The Dragon found in Dracula's tomb is quite noteworthy. The father of Vlad Tepes was in fact a member of the Order of the Overturned Dragon, founded in 1418 by Emperor Sigismond of Hungary.[7] It was under the banner of this order that Vlad fought the Turks. It should be recalled that the Dragon, in all civilizations, is the guardian of the eternal blood. This story is quite reminiscent of the neopagan philosophy of the Golden Dawn and Count Dracula embodies the inhuman morality highly valued by Aleister Crowley, the morality of a caste that sees itself as an elite, recruiting by cooption and pursuing without weakness or sensitivity a fabulous quest beyond good and evil. The end of *Dracula* is quite significant, with the hero saying: "Seven years ago we all went through the flames; and the happiness of some of us since then is, we think, well worth the pain we endured." This brings to mind the terrible ordeals the Rosicrucian must confront by unleashing the forces of evil in order to overcome them.[8] We might also imagine those mysterious Secret Chiefs of which Mathers speaks, who did not truly possess physical bodies. Jean-Paul Bourre[9] does not hesitate to state that Bram Stoker was "an authentic adept of vampirism," and he adds: "His death certificate indicated death by exhaustion. Isn't this reminiscent of something? Isn't this the way the so-called vampire's victims die? Is he truly dead?"

In any case, it is incontestable that the Golden Dawn was connected to the blood cult attached to the symbolism of the Dragon, for the relationship between blood and Dragon is never broken. We can recall the

---

7. This emperor also used the book entitled *The Magic of Abramelin the Mage* in his attempts to resurrect a young girl with whom he was in love, Barbara de Cilly, veritable muse for the Order of the Overturned Dragon. News of his experiments filtered into the Carpathians and later inspired *Carmilla* by Sheridan Le Fanu.

8. See also *Zanoni* by Bulwer-Lytton.

9. Jean-Paul Bourre, *Le culte du vampire aujourd'hui* [The Vampire Cult Today] (Paris: Ed. Alain Lefeuvre, 1978).

myth of Siegfried who, after slaying the Dragon and bathing in its blood, acquires immortality.

Blood—Dragon—Immortality
Vampire—Dracula—Living Dead

These are two equations connected to a magic practice that is based partially on *The Magic of Abramelin the Mage*[10] and partially on the writings of John Dee.

What exactly are vampires? Must we automatically conjure up visions of bizarre beings sucking the blood of innocent victims? It would seem that vampirism has a long history. The priests of high shamanism were the keepers of a millennia-spanning religion whose magic revolved entirely around blood. It has even been claimed that the shamans kept carnivorous birds that had survived an ancient catastrophe in the cave depths of Altai and that they fed them living victims.[11] We should note that traces of a blood cult and human sacrifices can be found almost everywhere in the ancient world, including in the Bible, for example, in the story of Abraham and in Leviticus 17:10–14:

And whatsoever man [there be] of the house of Israel, or of the strangers that sojourn among you, that eateth any manner of blood; I will even set my face against that soul that eateth blood, and will cut him off from among his people. For the life of the flesh [is] in the blood: and I have given it to you upon the altar to make atonement for your souls: for it [is] the blood [that] maketh atonement for the soul. Therefore I said unto the children of Israel, No soul of you shall eat blood, neither shall any stranger that sojourneth among you eat blood. And whatsoever man [there be] of the chil-

---

10. This work, discovered during the eighteenth century in the Marciana Library of Venice, contains rituals that allegedly permit a dead body to be restored to life.
11. The tribes of the Altai long displayed as a totem a bird with powerful jaws and pterodactyl-like membraneous wings.

dren of Israel, or of the strangers that sojourn among you, which hunteth and catcheth any beast or fowl that may be eaten; he shall even pour out the blood thereof, and cover it with dust. For [it is] the life of all flesh; the blood of it [is] for the life thereof: therefore I said unto the children of Israel, Ye shall eat the blood of no manner of flesh: for the life of all flesh [is] the blood thereof: whosoever eateth it shall be cut off.

In ancient societies, the blood and pain caused by torture were supposed to establish a connection with the gods, or at least with the invisible forces accessible to men. It seems that this cult was perpetuated in Europe itself, in the region that rules all others when it comes to vampirism: the Carpathians. Hungary, Bulgaria, Romania, and Albania are the four countries where it is most prevalent historically[12] and which were home to famous vampires such as Count Peter Plogowitz in Hungary and the son of King Simeon of Bulgaria. According to current information that remains to be confirmed, it would seem a veritable occult church that has adopted vampiric rites has been brought back together in Albania. But vampires have also immigrated to new homelands. The tomb of one of these practitioners can be found in Pere-Lachaise Cemetery in Paris. Near Gilly in Belgium in the hamlet of Tergnée, excavations beneath the choir of a chapel have unearthed five wooden coffins that were pierced through by large nails at what would be the location of the buried individual's chest. These coffins belonged to the lords of Farciennes, who were buried in the middle of the eighteenth century. They included Count Charles Joseph de Betthyany; his wife, Anne de Waldstein (daughter of the Landgrave of Bohemia); and their children, who had all died at a young age—of a wasting disease.[13] They were natives of Transylvania and claimed descent from Vlad of Walachia: Dracula.

---

12. To be fair, it would in fact be necessary to add Lorraine, Venice, and Edinburgh to this list.

13. See Paul de Saint-Hilaire's fascinating work, *Liège et Meuse mystérieux* [Mysterious Liège and Meuse] (Paris: Editions Rossel, 1980).

These nobles, who were impaled in death in a way intended to prevent them from becoming vampires, are not the only ones to have pursued this form of worship.

The vampire can in fact be divided into two species: the living vampire and the undead vampire. The first is a man who seeks to remain young and triumph over death by looking for the vital fluid and soul of individuals in their blood, for the blood is the vehicle of the soul, according to ancient beliefs. François Ribadeau-Dumas believes he has detected certain silimarities between vampirism and the rejuvenation ritual advocated by Cagliostro. Adrien Cremene[14] says of the *strigoi* (the Romanian name for vampire):

> It is generally a creature that is half man, half demon and shares in the double nature of man and the devil. Because of his human aspect, he can travel the earth and soar through the air, ride the clouds and bring hail, things forbidden to demons, because the strigoi is born of baptized parents. With his demon aspect he represents an antiworld, a universe contrary to that of life in which feelings are transformed into their opposites and where beauty becomes monstrosity. Thus it is his family, parents, and children that the strigoi seeks to destroy first because they are the ones he loved most while still alive.[15]

In addition to the human vampire, there is the undead vampire whose body survives after death without decomposing as long as he possesses enough strength not to disappear. The vital force that permits him to appear to the living is something he obtains from the living, drawing it from them until they waste away. To borrow a quote that

---

14. Adrien Cremene, *Mythologie du vampire en Roumanie* [Mythology of the Romanian Vampire] (Monaco: Editions du Rocher, 1981).

15. In fact, on close examination of recorded Romanian traditions on the topic of different forms of vampirism, strigois, *pryccolichs,* and *vercolacs* are not far from the sylphs and other elementals described in *Le Comte de Gabalis* [The Count of Gabalis].

appears in Robert Amberlain's book devoted to this subject, *Vampirism, de la légende au reel* [Vampirism: From Legend to Reality] (Paris: Robert Laffont, 1971): "He will live! He will live henceforth on that strange gangway where life begins or ends and death begins or ends." In fact, a vampire's physical body does not manifest; it is its double that is visible, its astral body, and this is why, according to tradition, its reflection does not appear in a mirror and why it casts no shadow. Vampires' victims lose their appetites and wither away and die without any other symptoms. Most victims can recall seeing a white specter that follows them like their own shadow.

This "double" aspect of vampirism was thoroughly studied by the Rosicrusians of the Grand Rosary, whose birthplace was Prague. But the double will lose energy and wither away (without dying) if it does not feed on blood. During its lifetime, the vampire accustoms its consciousness to leaving its envelope in order to inhabit its double. After death, the double will continue to roam, but it will be a double possessing consciousness. When a normal individual dies, his or her double survives a short time afterward but is not truly inhabited by the soul. The soul generally escapes and the double will wither away after a period of forty days. The initiate of red magic, however, inhabits his double after death and his soul does not return to God. Freed of the body, it is now held prisoner by the double. If the soul dissolves into the whole and loses its identity, then the vampire has made the choice for immortality and that is the end of his wager—a horrible wager from which love is absent, a wager to force matter to endure, a wager that is the reverse of God's wager.

The vampire belongs to the reverse world. It is a phantom, a shadow that feeds on blood. It forms a kind of astral entity that, surviving the mortal husk, delays molecular decomposition indefinitely. It remains connected to the corpse by an invisible bond that extends to infinity, a kind of extendable umbilical cord. A prince of the night, it cannot appear during the day as it belongs to the reverse world. On the other hand, its status as a double permits it to cross through closed doors and windows.

JULES VERNE ON DRACULA'S TRAIL IN
A CASTLE IN THE CARPATHIANS

Dracula seems to have carried us quite far from Jules Verne and yet, the region of Dracula's castle is also that of Alexandre Dumas's castle of Brankowen and Jules Verne's castle in the Carpathians. Here, the Dacians worshipped their supreme deity, Zalmoxis, and the better to establish contact with her they chose their brothers who were most advanced in magic and sacrificed them by piercing them with their javelins. Seven days later, it was said, their transfixed bodies would emerge from their tombs and retake their places among the living as intermediary immortals between the goddess and humanity. Dracula's castle was called Mountain of the Most Distant Midnight.[16] According to prophecy, this was where Lucifer should appear and gather his disciples at the end of time. This mountain is actually located in Cuerta de Arges,[17] where the ruins of the fortress can still be seen.

So what does Jules Verne tell us in his novel *Castle of the Carpathians*? He speaks of "Transylvania whose Carpathian context naturally lends itself to all kinds of psychological evocations." Placed in the comitat of Kolosvar, the Verne castle is quite close to that of Dracula. He writes: "The castle occupied an isolated shoulder on the Orgall Plateau near the Vulkan Pass . . . .[18] Eight or nine hundred feet behind the Vulkan Pass, was a curtain wall, the color of sandstone, paneled with a jumble of lapidary plants." The castle of the Carpathians dated back to the twelfth or thirteenth century. "What architect built it upon this plateau at this height? No one knows and this audacious artist is unknown, unless it was Roumain Manoli, so gloriously celebrated in Walachian legend and who built the famous castle of Rodolphe the Black in Curte d'Argis." But why does Verne emphasize this place

---

16. Refer to this text, the last paragraph of the section entitled Robur, the Rosicrucian Master, chapter 7, page 147.

17. A very interesting place name.

18. Vulkan brings us back to Vulcan and the infernal realm. Orgall is *or* [gold] of the Galls.

name unless it is to lead us to wonder about this castle, which is, of course, Dracula's.

Likewise, it could not be chance that causes Jules Verne, on several occasions in *The Castle of the Carpathians* to stress the Dacian people, who were undoubtedly at the origin of the vampiric customs in this region. Nor could it be chance that the demon flies over the castle in the frontispiece or that the vignette accompanying the title depicts a dragon with a crocodile head[19] (see figure 8, p. 112c). The "dragon" in the Carpathians is believed to be the mount of the Salomonaires, sorcerers and mages in Romanian folk tales, and a name that would be a perfect fit for Dracula, son of the Dragon. This treasure guardian also bears the name of Balaur or Valaur and brings to mind many valleys of gold (see figure 9, p. 112c).

Everything seems to revolve around vampires in *The Castle of the Carpathians*, still speaking of a shepherd, Verne tells us: "Frik was regarded as a sorceror, a summoner of fantastic apparitions. If you could believe what you heard, the vampires and stryga obeyed him." We cannot take this story as a joke, for from the very beginning Jules Verne has warned us: "This story is not a fantasy, nor is it merely fiction. Should one conclude that it is not true because of its improbability? That would be a mistake." In addition, it seems that Jules Verne wants us to see Frik the shepherd as a shaman, a priest of the vampiric cult (see figure 10, p. 112d). He provides this character as a guide, as is revealed by the author's description of how the character likes to be addressed: "By greeting him with the name Pastor, which he preferred." The bond with the reversed, Saturnian world is emphasized on several occasions, if only by these "people apart, of somewhat Hoffmannesque appearance," who are peddlers. They could be better described as "the traveling salesmen of the Saturn and Company Trading House under the sign of the Golden Hourglass."

---

19. For more on this subject, read the passages concerning vampirism in Venice in J. P. Bourre's book, *Le culte du vampire aujourd'hui* [The Vampire Cult Today] (Paris: Editions A. Lefeuvre, 1978).

Long passages in the book are devoted to the weird and otherworldly and demonic creatures and monsters that roamed the countryside.

> With proof to back them up, they declared that werewolves still roamed the countryside, that the vampires known as the strigois, because they cried like screech owls, drank human blood, and that the staffli wandered through ruins and would become dangerous if they were not brought food and drink. There are fairies; the babas whom one must avoid encountering on Tuesdays or Fridays, the most evil days of the week . . . enchanted forests where hide the balaure, a race of giant dragons whose jaws reach the sky; the Zmei, with excessively large wings, who kidnap girls of royal blood and even those of lesser lineage if they are pretty! There are a large number of dreadful monsters, and what kind spirit does folk imagination elect to confront them? None other than the *serpi de casa*, the serpent of the domestic hearth, who commonly lives at the bottom of the hearth and whose positive influence peasants purchase by providing it with the choicest milk.

All these strange creatures are linked to the Carpathian castle. According to the region's inhabitants, "there was no doubt that it [the castle] housed dragons, strigois, and perhaps a few ghosts from the family of the barons von Gortz." So we have ended up with ghosts! Interestingly, the name Gortz has an odd connotation. It is reminiscent of a Luciferian monastery in Palestine that still existed in the eighteenth century and was home to a snake cult: the monastery of El Ghor. But what do we know of the Gortz family? Jules Verne tells us: "While there may be doubts as to the architect, there are none about the family that owned this bourg. The barons von Gortz had been lords of this land since time immemorial. They had been mixed up in all the wars that had bloodied the Transylvanian provinces." This might also be an accurate description of Dracula.

Verne goes on:

> They fought against the Hungarians, the Saxons, and the Sze-
> kelys and their name appears in the cantices and doines,[20] where
> the memory of these disastrous periods is perpetuated. They
> had taken as their motto the famous Walachian proverb *Da Pe
> Maorte,* "give unto death," and did they give! *They spilled their
> blood* for the cause of independence—*this blood that came from
> the Romanians,* their ancestors. . . . These are the words on which
> all their aspirations were concentrated: *Roman on Pere!* Romania
> cannot perish.

Here is yet another example of Verne covertly showing the reader
that the real subject here is immortality through blood. It is truly Vlad
the Impaler we are dealing with here, and if we still have any doubts
about this, Verne's descriptions dispel them. For example, Verne writes,
of nearing the castle: "At the far end of the bank stood a granite post,
the remains of an ancient cross, whose arms were represented on the
upright post by only a groove that was half worn away." In other words,
the cross, which has lost its arms, has become a stake, an article for
impalement.

Of course, as is his way, Jules Verne makes a joke of customs and
legends and offers a scientific and rational solution to the mystery. In
fact, however, he speaks in veiled words about a very real phenomenon,
even if it is habitually confined to the realm of fantasy. His approach is
basically the same as Bram Stoker's.

Before going further, let's take a look at the main subject of this
novel.

---

20. [These are the ballads and national legends of Romania. —*Trans.*]

A STORY OF IMMORTALITY

La Stilla is a singer endowed with great talent. She triumphs in every opera in which she performs and the public loves her. She is also beautiful: "Her long hair of a golden tint, her deep, black eyes in which flames danced, the purity of her features, her warm complexion, and her waist that the chisel of Praxiteles could not have sculpted more perfectly" have earned her more than one admirer. One of these is particularly assiduous. He never misses a single performance in which La Stilla appears and he follows her like a shadow, from city to city, from opera to opera. La Stilla begins to be frightened by this mysterious figure, who is none other than Baron von Gortz.

Traveling to Naples, the young and attractive count Franz von Telek falls madly in love with La Stilla and asks her to marry him. She accepts, though we aren't sure if she truly loves Franz von Telek or is using him to escape the fascination of Baron von Gortz. Regardless, La Stilla decides to leave the stage, and a goodbye party is planned in her honor. The baron is mad with rage. The great night arrives and La Stilla's voice is more moving than ever, but La Stilla can hardly tear her eyes from von Gortz's box; she feels a mixture of hate and a strange fascination for him. Deeply disturbed by this, she begins the great finale of *Orlando*[21] but cannot finish it. Hardly have the words *"Innamorata, mio cuore tremane voglio morire"* left her throat when she collapses on the stage, dead from a burst vein in her chest. Meanwhile von Gortz leaves after threatening Franz von Telek: "It is you who killed her! Woe to you!"

The young count returns to his family castle with only grief as his companion. After several weeks, during which his pain has not diminished, he takes a trip that brings him to the village of Werst and an inn in the Carpathian Mountains under the sign of King Mathias.[22]

---

21. This *Orlando*, written by Maestro Arconati, is a nonexistent opera. Arconati is in fact the name of a count who owned some of Leonardo DaVinci's manuscripts. Orlando is reminiscent of Ariosto's *Orlando Furioso*.

22. This is Verne's indication that this novel has important ties to *Mathias Sandorf*. In addition, he makes von Gortz the companion in arms of a hero of national independence, a former bandit named Sandor.

The population of this village lives in terror: The castle seems to be haunted and strange phenomena occur. This castle also has a legend attached to it. It seems the old beech tree near it loses one limb a year and, the story goes, when it loses its last branch, it will spell the end of the castle. This is somewhat reminiscent of the horror tree of another Carpathian castle, that of the giants of Albert von Rudolstadt, descendent of the kings of Bohemia, in George Sand's *Consuelo*. We should also note that Jules Verne's La Stilla was also inspired by *Consuelo*. Sand writes, for example:

> He was readying himself to congratulate La Porporina at the end of her cavatina, for he had the good fortune of being able to do it personally and still judiciously, when by an inexplicable twist of fate and in the middle of a brilliant trill at which she had never failed, La Porporina, stopped short, directed her haggard eyes at a corner of the room and, joining her hands together, screamed, "O my God!" and fainted to the floor. Porporino hastened to help her up. It was necessary to carry her backstage and a buzzing of questions, thoughts, and opinions rose in the hall.

We can compare this to what Verne wrote about La Stilla's death: "An inexplicable terror paralyzed her. . . . She suddenly brought her hand to her mouth, which reddened with blood. . . . She staggered . . . she fell. . . . Panicked, the audience rose, trembling and at the height of anxiety." Returning to Sand: "There was a first row of boxes that bordered the stage, and all at once, in that of M. Golowkin, I could see a pale figure stand out in the background and lean irresistibly forward as if to look at me. This figure was Albert." And Verne: "At that moment the grill of Baron von Gortz's box was lowered. A strange head with long greyish hair and blazing eyes revealed itself. His ecstatic face was terrifyingly pale."

The plot advances with Franz von Telek deciding to reassure the villagers by paying a personal visit to the castle to see what is going on. He then learns that it is the dwelling of his former rival, Baron von Gortz, who had disappeared from the area many years before. He hesitates, but La Stilla's voice bizarrely seems to fill the air before disappearing. Moved, Franz von Telek then discusses mounting an expedition with the "forester" Nic Deck. When he and his servant Rotzko reach the plateau before the castle, they spot a silhouette there—that of La Stilla. They manage to gain entry into the castle, whereupon an eminently initiatic transition takes place. Franz finally manages to see La Stilla, but she is only the projection of an image on a mirror. All the phenomena witnessed by the villagers were the result of a character's understanding of electricity, from the conduction of sounds by wire to the recording of the voice on wax rollers by Baron von Gortz's companion, the brilliant Orfanik.[23] The castle eventually explodes. Franz, who has gone mad, ceaselessly murmurs the final words of the last song of *Orlando*. Because Orfanik has surrendered the recordings of La Stilla to him, he eventually recovers his reason by hearing the voice of his beloved.

If we examine this story more closely, we can see that it is entirely connected to vampirism. When Franz von Telek of the Romanian race visits Italy, he travels first to Venice, the vampiric city par excellence,[24] and it serves as his home base. Jules Verne perfectly ties together the different elements of vampirism: the dragon (one of his details tells of "some Tarrasque whose jaw emerges from the entrails of the earth") and the concept of vampires as the undead. How does he portray La Stilla after her collapse? Verne writes: "Thus, she who Franz had seen fall dead upon the stage had survived!" La Stilla is one of the undead. Further, we can consider the young forester as a victim of vampirism when we see him thus: "His limbs [were] stiff and his face bloodless. His breathing barely caused his chest to move." We can also take note of the young forester's fiancée, Mioriota, who suggests to us that in the

---

23. This name, through its similarity to that of Orpheus, recalls a descent into hell. It can also be compared to Orsik, which was the name of one of Elsabet Bathory's sons [the infamous Bloody Countess —*Trans.*].

24. See J. P. Bourre, *Le culte des vampire aujourd'hui* [The Vampire Cult Today] (Ed. Alain Lefeuvre, 1978).

Carpathians the most marvelous wedding is considered to be the one in which the deceased is joined to a living individual—a wedding that thereby contains the notion of undeath. All of this, of course, remains connected with the Rosicrucian immortals and their mysterious crypts and perpetual lamps, for at one point our attention is directed to "a glass bulb full of a yellowish light in a crypt."[25] It seems that Jules Verne did not owe all his information to Eliseus Reclus's *Travels to the Mining Regions of Western Transylvania.*

The theme of the undead is present not only in *The Castle of the Carpathians,* although this book was, by Verne's own admission, one of his favorite novels. In *The Eternal Adam,* the teacher has one of the characters present a theory close to old Mexican cosmology. When the cataclysm of the end of time is imminent, the sole chance of delaying the end is to feed the sun so that it will not go out. The vital energy to feed the sun is held in the "precious water" *(chalchinatle),* or, in other words, human blood. To obtain this, it is necessary to perform human sacrifices. In *The Secret of Wilhelm Storitz,* invisibility is linked to blood.[26] The theme of the living dead is also present in *Mathias Sandorf, The Will of an Eccentric, Mrs. Branican,* and *Le Sphynx des Glaces* [The Sphinx of the Ice Fields], not to mention in the character of Phileas Fogg, who, in a certain way, transcends time.

MATHIAS SANDORF AND THE BLOODY COUNTESS

Can we say that the work of Jules Verne was directly inspired by Bram Stoker's *Dracula* or the teachings of the Golden Dawn? I do not believe

---

25. See also *The Chemical Wedding of Christian Rosenkreuz, The Strife of Love in a Dream of Poliphilus,* and the *Fifth Book of Rabelais.* With respect to the Rosicrucians, it should be noted that Proteus ruled a sacred island between Crete and Rhodes named Carpathus.

26. We may wonder why the description of the city of Ragz, where this story takes place, corresponds perfectly to Amiens, and why Doctor Roderich's house is identical to that of Jules Verne.

this to be the case, although *Dracula* and *The Castle of the Carpathians* were both written in 1890. As for the Golden Dawn, Jules Verne was undoubtedly not an adept of the order, but he used information so close to that possessed by the English Rosicrucians that it can raise the question.

As we saw earlier, Verne's Mathias Sandorf possesses the characteristics of the typical Rosicruscian, and there are more telling details:

> Count Mathias Sandorf lived in a feudal era castle in the Fagaras district in one of the comitats of Transylvania. Built upon one of the southern spurs of the eastern Carpathians which forms the frontier between Transylvania and Walachia, this castle rose up in all its savage splendor aboved this precipitous mountain range like some superb stronghold in which conspirators could hold out to the last. . . . Neighboring mines rich in iron and copper that had been industriously exploited formed a considerable fortune for the owner of Artenak Castle.

The details in this passage suggest that we are once more dealing with the castle of Count Dracula. We can also recall these words of Count Mathias Sandorf: "Death does not destroy; it only makes one invisible." Mathias Sandorf's banner, which is green with a red cross on the upper corner, combines the two hues of vampirism: the red of blood and the green grass to which we all return. Pierre Bathory, the young hero whose guardian is Mathias Sandorf, actually appears dead, and we even witness his burial—yet he is not truly dead; he will be reborn. Jules Verne lets us know that Sandorf hypnotized him, placing him in a cataleptic stupor.

Pierre's father, Etienne Bathory, was a Magyar of high birth. Jules Verne informs us that he "belonged, albeit distantly, but authentically, to the lineage of Magyar princes who held the throne of Transylvania in the sixteenth century. The family had split apart since that time and become lost in countless situations and it may no doubt seem surprising to find one of its last descendents in a simple professorship at the Academy of Presburg."

This choice of the name Bathory, a name about which Verne has nothing but good to say, is actually an odd one. We can examine its history as Jules Verne records it. There is, of course, the legendary figure of Erzebeth Bathory, lady of Csejthe. Before her birth, under the reign of Ladislav IV, a Magyar knight by the name of Andrew Briccins displayed exceptional bravery and acquired the nickname of Bator, the Courageous One. This was the origin for the name Bathory. Erzebeth was born in 1560 to a house that included several rulers, among whom was her uncle Etienne, prince of Transylvania (and, in additon, Georgy Thuzzo, paladin of Hungary, as well as a cardinal, governors, and military leaders). It was an illustrious family and Jules Verne's high regard was well-founded.

Nevertheless, these figures concealed quite a few bizarre mysteries, not to mention diseases such as epilepsy and even madness, which are often a consequence of marriage between blood relations. Jules Verne could not have been unaware of the fact that a good number of the Bathory family "displayed a wealth of perversities that defy the imagination. These are the ones that fascinated Erzebeth: Sigismond the mystic; Istvan the Mad; Gabor the incestuous; and, above all, Erzebeth's aunt Klara, the demon worshipper, whose company she sought and whose sadistic games she sometimes shared."[27] Her uncle Istvan had a reputation for being cruel and deceitful and subject to fits of madness. He imprisoned men in the cellars of his castle and forced them to perform magical operations on his behalf. Gabor, Erzebeth's uncle, was a casual pillager and killer, caused an ongoing scandal with his incestuous love affair with his sister, and was eventually assassinated by his people in 1613. He also terrorized his servants, spoke an incomprehensible language, slobbered, rolled on the ground screaming, and tried to strangle anyone who got near him. Her cousin Andras was murdered under mysterious circumstances; he was decapitated by an ax.

We can see, then, that this was truly a bizarre family, and Erzebeth

27. Maurice Périsset, *La comtesse de sang* [The Blood Countess] (Paris: Presses-Pocket, 1979).

was undoubtedly the worst of the lot. She had the idea of bathing in blood for the purposes of rejuvenation and maintenance of her eternal youth. To accomplish this, she ordered that the throats of dozens of young virgin girls be slit. Denounced by one her prisoners who managed to escape; she was the subject of an investigation. Count Gyorgyi Thurzo later wrote, "Let it suffice to say that what was discovered in her cellars was the greatest abomination possible for man to invent." Iron cages were found with mechanisms that tore apart the victim and collected their blood. The countess was imprisoned in her own castle inside a walled-off octagonal room. She died there in 1614 at the same time as the arrival of a violent storm that was long remembered by local inhabitants. An interesting coincidence: One of Erzebeth Bathory's sorcerous advisors was named Dravula.

We cannot attribute to mere perversity the Bloody Countess's desire to bathe in blood. She was simply following old magic recipes. After all, her coat of arms bore three wolf fangs and a dragon, just like that of Vlad the Impaler. Interestingly, a Bathory was at the head of the expedition intended to restore to the throne Vlad III (known as Vlad the Impaler or Dracula). The castle of Fagaras, a fief of Dracula, subsequently passed into Bathory hands. It should also be pointed out that in the cellars of the house Erzebeth owned in Vienna, numerous carved signs and symbols were found connected to the worship of the three-headed lunar goddess Triple Hecate, an infernal avatar of the moon.

Because of all this, there is no doubt that chance is not at work here. As can be verified in other novels he wrote, I have no doubt that Jules Verne's work holds the teachings of the Golden Dawn, even if the author was never an actual member of this order.

JULES VERNE AND THE HOLLOW EARTH

THE SECRETS OF THE GREEN RAY

We have seen that Bram Stoker, author of *Dracula,* was exposed to the same inspiration as Jules Verne, the history and legends of vampirism, the mystic teachings that were honored by the Golden Dawn, and other secret societies. Bram Stoker was also the author of a novel entitled *The Jewel of Seven Stars,* whose meaning was completely distorted in a recent film that transformed it into a mediocre thriller.

The entire story revolves around a mysterious sarcophagus brought back from Egypt by an archaeologist named Trelawney. This treasure is accompanied by "a low table of green stone with red veins in it, like bloodstone. The feet were fashioned like the paws of a jackal, and round each leg was twined a full-throated snake wrought exquisitely in pure gold." Trelawney also brings back a coffer of green stone, a mummified hand with seven fingers, and several other objects, including seven lamps on each of which appears a depiction of one of the seven forms of the Egyptian goddess Hathor.

All these objects came from a lost vale known as the Valley of the Sorcerer and had been collected from a tomb carved into a cliff where the mummy of Queen Tera had been discovered. It seems her double remains linked to the mummy and apparently feeds on blood. Also connected to this adventure is a blood-red ruby carved in the form of a scarab and glittering with seven seven-pointed stars corresponding to the seven stars of the Big Dipper. The Ka mentioned in Egyptian religion is nothing other than the double we have been discussing, the abstract personality imbued with all the characteristics of the individual and endowed with an independent existence. The Ka is inhabited by the Ba, or soul, which animates it. The Ka can leave the tomb, find the inidividual's body, and reanimate it. Connected to the Ka are the Khu, spiritual intelligence or mind (it takes the form of a luminous, intangible, radiant body), and the Sekhen, or "power" of a man (his vital force or energy personified). All these elements—together with the Khaibit, or shadow; the Ren, or name; the Khat, or physical body; and the Ab, the heart, which is the seat of life—form the different components of the body.

In the story, the "vampire" of Queen Tera eventually takes possession of the archaeologist's body and the tale comes to a close within a strange, greenish radiance. This truly provides a nice finishing touch to my theories about vampirism. It also invites us to take a closer look at Egypt, for the emphasis on green radiance in *The Jewel of Seven Stars* is reminiscent of the Green Lion of the alchemists, which is said to fix the volatile blood. Jean-Louis Bernard, specialist on Egypt, tells us that "the Green Ray" turns red when materialized in the blood.[1]

Just what is this mysterious ray connected to the specter, to the green face of Osiris? Jean-Louis Bernard writes:[2]

The phosphorescent power about which Greek mythology speaks is the mysterious green radiance, which is the mystery of both life and death. This green ray was one of the secrets of the Egyptian temples, as a legacy of Osiris, the god with the green face. It had the effect of stimulating healthy cells to transform, but it also accelerated the decomposition of unhealthy cells. The green goddess

1. J. L. Bernard, *Les Archives de l'Insolite* [Archives of the Unusual] (Paris: Livres de Poche, n.d.).

2. J. L. Bernard, *Aux origines de l'Egypte* [At the Origins of Egypt] (Paris: Robert Laffont, 1976).

Hathor concentrates the divine force into a "green ray" that is the essence of biological life in all nature's kingdoms.[3]

Jean-Louis Bernard notes that in its raw and highly intensified and concentrated state, the green ray is intolerable. We can recall that green is the traditional color of dragons, guardians of the threshold, and is the symbol of eternal youth. Jean-Pierre Bayard writes:[4]

The neophyte who dies to profane life in order to be reborn in a higher form is transfigured. This inner light illuminates him and we can consider the causes for his physical rejuvenation. The body is merely the mirror of the soul. The restoration of the inner being therefore becomes a fountain of youth, but this green color is the corollary to the individual's resurrection on a human or on a cosmic plane.

This should be enough evidence to persuade us of the consistency in Bram Stoker's work. We should also be able to find mention of the green ray in the work of Verne. In *The Castle of the Carpathians* one passage discussing "a large ray" commands our attention in this regard:

What hearth produced this powerful light, whose radiations traveled in large sheets across the surface of the Orgal Plateau? What furnace released this photogenic source, which seemed to set the rocks ablaze and at the same time, bathed them in a strange livid grayness?. . . He and the forester have taken on a cadaverous aspect, pale face, dead eyes, hollow sockets, greenish jaws, with a speckled hue, hair ressembling the moss, which according to legend, is said to grow on the skulls of hanged men. . . . Having reached the final degree of fright, Doctor Patek's muscles retracted, his hair standing

---

3. According to legend, the Grail chalice, which contained the blood of Christ, was green and carved from an emerald that fell from Lucifer's forehead.
4. Jean-Pierre Bayard, *La symbolique du feu* [The Symbolism of Fire] (Paris: Payot, 1973).

on end, his pupils dilated, his body caught in a tetanus-like stiffness. As the poet of *Contemplations* said, he breathed horror.

This subject, however, was so dear to Jules Verne that he devoted an entire novel to it: *The Green Ray*. Even if Jules Verne depicted it as a natural phenomenon, truly it is our vital ray, another element that can be found in Rosicrucian tradition. In the beginning of the novel Verne says of two of the main characters: "By doing good, they had continued the generous traditions of their ancestors. Also, both the picture of health and nary an irregularity in their lives to cause them regret, they were destined to age without growing old, neither in mind nor body."

I leave the reader to discover more about Oliver Sinclair (a very interesting name), the novel's hero, but for our discussion here, I cite this passage from the novel:

Have you sometimes observed the sun setting over the horizon of the sea? Yes, of course! Have you followed its descent to just that moment when, the upper part of its disk touching the water line, it is on the verge of disappearing? That's also quite likely. But have you noted the phenomenon that occurs at the precise moment this radiant star gives off its last ray, if the sky, clear of mists, is thus of a perfect purity?. . . [I]t will not be, as one might think, a red ray that will strike the retina of your eye, it will be a "green" ray, but a mysterious green, a green that no painter could reproduce on his palette, a green that nature, with all the varied shades of its plants or seas, no matter how limpid, could ever hope to equal! If there is green in Paradise, it can only be this shade, which is no doubt the true green of Hope!"

And finally, in this book Verne writes: "This green ray is the subject of an old legend. . . . The virtue of this ray is such that he who has seen it will never again be fooled in affairs of the heart, and that he who has been fortunate to see it just once, sees clearly into his own heart and that of others."

BULWER-LYTTON,
THE ROSICRUCIAN MASTER

The green ray is present in a work by another member of the Golden Dawn: Bulwer-Lytton. An extraordinary individual, Edward Charles Bulwer-Lytton (1803–1873) was minister of the colonies under Queen Victoria. He was a descendent of the seventeenth-century alchemist Doctor John Bulwer, who invented, among secret languages, a language for deaf-mutes. Historian Andrew Lang states that Bulwer-Lytton allegedly met Count de Saint-Germain in Paris in 1860. He was the author of a very well-known novel called *The Last Days of Pompei,* but also wrote *Zanoni, a Rosicrucian Tale,* in which a true Rosicrucian sacrifices his physical immortality out of love. This novel takes place in Italy and Paris at the end of the eighteenth century. The sage Zanoni has succeeded in vanquishing death and knows the secret of eternal youth, but he sacrifices himself to save Viola, the woman he loves. The following short passage establishes a relationship to what we have discussed up to now:

> There may be forms of matter as invisible and impalpable to us as the animalculae in the air we breathe—in the water that plays in yonder basin. Such beings may have passions and powers like our own, as the animalculae to which I have compared them. The monster that lives and dies in a drop of water—carnivorous, insatiable, subsisting on the creatures more minute than himself—is not less deadly in his wrath, less ferocious in his nature than the tiger of the desert. There may be things around us that would be dangerous and hostile to men if providence had not placed a wall between them and us, merely by different modifications of matter.

It is curious to note that the heroine of *Zanoni* is Italian, just like Consuela and La Stilla, and is connected to the music world.

There is another novel of Bulwer-Lytton that is of particular interest with respect to Jules Verne: *The Coming Race.* This work describes a race of beings who live beneath the surface of the earth and are superior to humans, both intellectually and technically. The Ana (the name of this race) have long since gone beyond the problem of social struggle and no longer know war. As an energy source, they use a natural power they have developed: Vril,[5] which is nothing other than the green ray. Their world is accessible through a mine,[6] and they claim descent from a Celtic race. Their power is somewhat alarming: They are a subterranean civilization superior to our own and they possess weapons based on vril that are more powerful than our atomic bombs and are capable of instantly reducing to ashes a city two times the size of London. The Ana are served by robots. One day, they will return to the surface, perhaps through an opening located in Iceland, and they will take over the world.

JULES VERNE AND THE JOURNEY TO THE CENTER OF THE EARTH

Exactly how should we interpret all this? It is hard to avoid recalling a subject dear to both Edgar Allen Poe and Jules Verne. According to Lovecraft, Poe's documentation came from "forbidden and unsuspected sources." What appears certain, as Jacques Bergier wrote in his preface to the French edition of *The Coming Race,* is that these sources were included in the documentation of certain secret societies such as the Golden Dawn.

Poe wrote a novel that would serve as great inspiration to Jules Verne, *The Adventures of Arthur Gordon Pym,* which follows an initiatory outline linked to the internal or infernal world. The story is set in motion by the clandestine departure of a young man who stows away on a vessel as it prepares to weigh anchor. This scenario would have been a vivid reminder to Verne of his similar experience as a youth. Part of this novel takes place underground, and the reversed symbolism of the

---

5. Originally, the idea of Vril was found in the work of a little-known French writer, Louis Jacolliot, who was born in 1837 in Charolles and died in 1890.
6. The entrance was made through a mine connected to "a chasm jagged and seemingly charred at the sides, as if burst asunder at some distant period by volcanic fires."

colors there is representative of this inner world. It should be noted that the word *blood* is a key to the novel. After numerous adventures Pym experiences on an Antarctic island, where everything is black and where a maze of caves and corridors is discovered in a world populated by savages whose chief is named Tselemoun,[7] the novel ends at the South Pole, where Pym dissolves into a kind of gigantic, veiled figure that's white as snow. Jules Verne names this figure (and also one of his novels) *The Sphinx of the Ice Fields*. Verne actually conceived a sequel to Arthur Gordon Pym's adventures. On September 1, 1896, he wrote Hetzel: "No need to tell you that I am going infinitely farther than Poe."

This theme of an inner earth is markedly present in Verne's *Journey to the Center of the Earth*. As we discovered earlier, it is true that Jules Verne was inspired by (some might say that he plagiarized) one of George Sand's novels: *Laura or Journey in the Crystal*.[8] It also seems that he may have used a work that was published in 1721 (and recently been reissued by Verdier Editions): *Passage du pole arctique au pole antarctique par les center du Monde* [Passage from the Arctic Pole to the Antarctic Pole through the center of the Earth]. In the 1721 work, the regions traversed by the heroes belong to a topsy-turvy world: fish swim backward and birds make their nests beneath the ground. At the Pole there is an island with three points and its environment is characterized by a zone where the snow gives way to foliage. A lake there is connected to a system of underground canals. Roads form a labyrinth that is quite comparable to the one discovered by Arthur Gordon Pym. The final episode portrays a dead man's ressurection as found in Jules Verne's stories. In this work we see the hero following a stream back to its source, which turns out to be a very beautiful spring in a cavern hollowed out in one of the mountains bordering the valley. Inside the cave there is a round and very deep hole that is a good span in width, and it gives off a warm vapor.

In *Journey to the Center of the Earth*, the main hero, Axel, is a young

---

7. A kind of Solomon.

8. He also borrowed from a novel by Alexandre Dumas, *Isaac Laquédam*, which also features a journey to the center of the earth.

man of as yet unformed character who has no desire to go on an expedition. It is his fiancée who urges him to join the adventure, saying to him: "When you return, Axel, you will be a man." What follows is an extraordinary initiatory journey. As indicated at the start of the third chapter, Marcel Brion, who devoted long passages to this novel in his book *L'Allemagne Romantique et le Voyage Initiatique* [The Romantics' Germany: The Initiatory Voyage],[9] clearly grasped this aspect of Verne's story.

THE HOLLOW EARTH

Axel's initiatory journey aside, what we are most interested in here is the theme of the hollow earth. Axel gives us the source of this depiction of the terrestrial globe by recalling, "that theory of an English captain who compared the earth to a hollow sphere inside of which the air remained luminous because of its pressure, while two planetary bodies, Pluto and Proserpine, followed their mysterious orbits."

Through the words of Doctor Clawbonny in *The Adventures of Captain Hatteras,* Jules Verne gives us details about an English captain, "Captain Symmes, who proposed to attempt this voyage to Humphrey Davy, Humboldt, and Arago, but these scientists refused." Doctor Clawbonny also recalls a legend claiming, "that an immense opening exists at the poles from which the aurora borealis escapes, and through which one can enter the interior of the globe." Amused smiles generally accompany such theories, yet during the sixteenth century the brilliant William Postel stated in his *Compendium Cosmographicum,* "Paradise sits below the arctic pole," a theory that played a role in his arrest and death in an Inquisition prison. Victor Hugo viewed this spot as the entrance to hell in his *La fin de Satan* [The End of Satan]. Buffon imagined the existence of lakes and wide expanses of water beneath the plains and large valleys of that region. Jacques Casanova de Seingalt placed Paradise at the center of the earth. This is the reason behind his work entitled *Icosameron ou*

---

9. Marcel Brion, *L'Allemagne romantique: Le voyage initiatique* [The Romantics' Germany: The Initiatory Voyage] (Paris: Albin Michel, 1977–1978).

histoire d'Edouard et Elisabeth qui passèrent quatre-vignt-un ans chez les Mégamics, habitants aborigines du Protocosme dans l'intérieur de notre globe, traduit de l'anglais par Jacques Casanova, À Prague, s.d., 1788. [Icosameron, or the Story of Edward and Elizabeth Who Spent Eighty-one Years with the Mégamics, Aboriginal Inhabitants of the Protocosmos inside Our Globe].[10]

Returning once again to Verne's novel, on April 10, 1818, all the major universities of the United States and the military and political authorities receive a strange message from the captain mentioned by Doctor Clawbonny: "To the whole world, I declare the earth is hollow and habitable within, containing a number of solid concentric spheres, one within the other, and that it is open at the poles twelve or sixteen degrees. I pledge my life in support of this truth, and am ready to explore the hollow, if the world will support and aid me in the undertaking."

Symmes declares to his friends: "All is hollow on this earth—hair, the stalks of plants, and even our bones. Why would the earth escape this universal law? Various esoteric schools teach that the polar entrances lead toward cities of the underground world." Another American, Cyrus Read Teed, picked up the idea of the hollow earth, but he squarely believed that we once lived inside the world, flattened against the inside wall of the globe. In 1894 he even founded a sect, Koreshism that numbered some four thousand adepts. The hollow earth theory was introduced into Germany by a young aviator, Bender, founder of the Hohlweltlehre (Hollow Earth) Movement. He believed that the sun and moon were located at the very center of the earth. Some Nazi scientists and several writers later adopted these theories.[11]

---

10. [Translated by Jacques Casanova in Prague in 1788.] These Mégamics emerged from bottomless pits and, wearing red capes, gathered in their temples. Their gods are reptiles with sharp teeth and a hypnotic gaze. It is true Lovecraft material. But Casanova also mentions a region of Transylvania near Lake Zirchnitz, a realm of caves and darkness that gives access to the underground kingdom of the Mégamics. See also J. P. Bourre, *Le culte du vampire aujourd'hui* [The Vampire Cult Today].

11. Edgar Rice Burroughs wrote *Tarzan at the Center of the Earth,* and Lovecraft touched on these issues in the story "A Shadow Out of Time." Shaver believed the land within the earth was the country of the UFOs.

All of this has the flavor of folklore, and we might think that the center of the earth must be subject to intolerable heat and pressure. In fact, though, this might not be true. We do know that pressure does not increase with depth, as the animals that dwell on the sea floor prove. Two recent hypotheses have been released on this subject. One was proposed by Canadian geologist Frank D. Adams and mathematician Louis V. King. According to these men, quite sizeable cavities could exist inside the earth at depths ranging between 75,000 and 130,000 feet, a hypothesis confirmed by Doctor Adam's research on melted granite. Another theory was proposed by John Wheeler, the eminent physicist who collaborated with Niels Bohr on the theory of uranium fission. According to him, the earth could have been formed from a *geon,* a region in space of intense curvature where cosmic dust has been deposited and which could contain a veritable universe.

Individuals as eminent as Admiral Byrd, the great polar explorer, believed in the possibility of a hollow earth whose center would be accessible at the pole. Indeed, when he was racing to the pole, he declared: "It is Jules Verne who is bringing me." Extraordinarily, we can see a dark zone that looks like an opening on some of the photos taken by NASA of the geographical North Pole. Could this be the entrance to hollow earth?[12] William Reed had no hesitation writing: "The earth is hollow. The poles, so long sought, are phantoms. There are openings at the northern and southern extremities. In the interior are vast continents, oceans, mountains, and rivers. Vegetable and animal life are evident in this New World and it is probably peopled by races unknown to dwellers on the earth's surface."

Traditions across the globe, from Central Asia to the Americas, state something similar. This idea can be found at all times[13] and in all places. Why couldn't there be a particle of truth in it? And should we

---

12. In reality, these "holes" are due to the fact that a part of the pole was not lit by sunlight when the photos were taken.

13. When Gilgamesh, hero of the Babylonian epic, visited his ancestor Utnapishtim, he entered the entrails of the earth. There are countless similar examples in antiquity. The Greeks, for example, placed the entrance of the underground realm in Arcadia.

deduce that Jules Verne adhered to such theories? Perhaps we should, for this idea was also predominant in *Laura, or the Journey into the Crystal* by George Sand, one of Verne's inspirations. In Sand's book, Nasias says:

> This world we call the underground is the true world of splendor. Now, there certainly exists a vast portion of the surface still unknown to man, where some rent or deep declivity would permit him to descend to the region of gems and to contemplate under the open sky wonders you have seen in dream. . . . I am convinced that this volcanic rift, or rather, crevasse, exists at the poles, that it is regular and appears in the form of a crater of several hundred leagues in diameter and several dozen leagues deep, and that in short the glow of the piles of gems visible at the bottom of this basin is the sole cause of the aurora borealis.

Jules Verne maintained similar theories in other novels beside *Journey to the Center of the Earth* and *The Adventures of Captain Hatteras*. In *The Will of an Eccentric* Jules Verne, speaking of the Mammoth Caves in Kentucky, writes, "Such are the incomparable wonders of these caves that have surrendered only a portion of their secrets. Who knows what they may be holding in reserve for universal curiosity, and will we not one day discover an entirely extraordinary world in the entrails of the terrestrial globe?" In *The Underground City*, certain passages cannot help but bring to mind ancient legends that touch upon elder races that burrowed into the ground and never resurfaced: "It was toward this time that Simon Ford's ancestors entered the entrails of Caledonian ground never to reemerge, from father to son." Other passages are even more extraordinary: "Let's burrow to the center of the globe, if we must. In the same novel, Jack says: "These beings who live in the abysses . . . are not made like we are!" (Interestingly, Nell upon seeing the sun for the first time, believes in fire and perceives the "green ray.")

THE KING OF THE WORLD AND THE BLACK POWERS

Any discussion of these theories of the underground must include Agarttha (or Agartha) and the king of the world. In fact, the posthumous work by Saint-Yves d'Alveydre published in 1910 and entitled *Mission de l'Inde* [Mission of India] contains the description of a mysterious underground kingdom: Agarttha.[14] Ruling the mysterious people living in the cavities of the earth is a mysterious king of the world[15] whose envoys, the secret chiefs, are acting on the governments of the lands on the earth's surface.

The best source concerning the enigmatic Agarttha is the book by Fernand Ossendowski *Bête, hommes et dieux* [Animal, Men, and Gods]. A Buddhist prince declared to Ossendowski:

> This kingdom is Agarti. It extends through every underground tunnel in the entire world. I heard a Chinese lama scholar tell Bogdo Khan that ancient peoples who disappeared under the earth inhabit all the subterranean caverns of America. Traces of them can still be discovered on the world's surface. These subterranean peoples and races recognize the sovereignty of the king of the world. There is no great cause for wonder in all this. Once, two continents could be found in the two largest oceans of the east and west. They vanished beneath the waves, but their inhabitants moved into the underground kingdom.

For Jean-Louis Bernard, this king of the world could well be connected to black magic. In this regard, he mentions the writings of Alexandra David-Neel that report the existence of pseudolamas, a form of living dead who practice vampirism in remote lamaseries. These are old men who are dead but who live in a state of artificial survival. They

---

14. François Jacolliot, already referred to here with regard to Vril, mentions Agarttha.
15. *Robur the Conqueror* and *Master of the World* are also connected to certain alleged entryways to this kingdom.

use their magic to attract lost travelers and persuade these visitors to allow themselves to be ritually slain so that the old men can obtain their vitality through osmosis "during the course of a scientifically-lengthened death agony." This places us somewhere between Dracula and Erzebeth Bathory. This king of the world is thus only king of the marouts, or the living dead. Bernard adds that the Marxist world could have fallen under the domination of such marouts, which would explain the heavy sadness and atony of the lands of the East.[16] This opinion is shared by Jean-Paul Bourre, who wrote:[17]

> Still existing in the Transylvanian mountains is a lost Shambala[18] of vampirism which is inaccessible to humans but which is connected to the Shambala of light by long underground passageways. This is no cause of surprise for initiates: It is connected in the same way that "evil" is tied to "good," by a network of correspondences that give wisdom its true face. Good and evil are one and the same. They share the same splendor, for truth destroys dualism.[19]

The fact remains that Ossendowski linked Agarttha to the question of immortality. In his view: "The deep caverns are lit by a distinctive luminescence that permits the growth of grains and plants, and gives

---

16. It should be noted that after World War II, the Russians launched a vast inquiry into vampirism in Hungary.

17. Jean-Paul Bourre, "L'Agartha, la quête du Graal souterrain" [Agartha: Quest for the Subterranean Grail] (*L'Autre Monde*, no. 26).

18. Shambala is the name of the dark equivalent to Agarttha or sometimes Agarttha itself.

19. Machen writes in "The White People" from *The House of Souls* (New York: Knopf, 1906) that it is stupid to confine the spiritual world to the supremely good. The supremely wicked, necessarily, have their portion in it. The merely carnal, sensual man can no more be a great sinner than a great saint. Most of us are just indifferent, mixed-up characters; we muddle through the world without realizing the meaning and the inner sense of things and, consequently, our wickedness and goodness are alike, second-rate, unimportant. . . . Great people of all kinds forsake imperfect copies and go to the perfect originals. I have no doubt but that many of the very highest among the saints have never done a "good action" (using these words in their ordinary sense). On the other hand, there have been those who have sounded the very depths of sin, who in all their lives have never done an "ill deed."

people long and disease-free lives." And if we can trust the legends, the entrances to Agarttha are not only to be found in Asia. Mont-Saint-Michel and Brocéliande Forest have also been suggested as likely spots where passages to this underground realm might be found.

It would be no surprise to find that Gaston Leroux follows the same trail as Jules Verne. In *Rouletabille and the Gypsies,* he alludes to the hollow earth in connection with Walachia. Interestingly, information imparted to us by René Guénon is that the Bohemians once lived in Agarttha. According to Gaston Leroux: "It is the king of the world who makes the king of the earth." Of course, all of this remains linked to vampirism: "There cannot be a good celebration in the depths of the crypt if there is no blood."

RENNES-LE-CHÂTEAU: ONE ENTRANCE TO THE HOLLOW EARTH

The elements of the equation have become increasingly clear: Rosi-crucianism—Immortality—Vampirism—Agarttha—king of the world. More important, with each of these elements we find Jules Verne, as if his complete opus has a perfect esoteric nature.

But where does Rennes-le-Château fit in here? There are in fact several connections to the Rennes affair. Boudet defined Rennes-les-Bains as an island of Isis, which is the very name a Rosicrucian manuscript gives to a region of Shambala. There also seems to have been a connection between the Grail and Rennes—and between the Grail and the hollow earth. One of the first known texts concerning the Grail dates from the tenth century. In this work, its author, Nommé Menius, spoke of a war against an unbreechable underground fortress where miracles took place. We can recall that the Grail was also connected to the elixir of immortality and thus forms part of the equation.

Starting with Dionysian worship, this elixir was replaced by wine. René Guénon[20] demonstrates how the Grail is linked to the "eucharis-

---

20. René Guénon, *Le Roi du Monde* [The King of the World] (Paris: Gallimard, 1927).

tic" sacrifice of Melchizedek. He goes on to say: "The name of Melchize-dek, or, more exactly, Melki-Tsedeq, is none other than the title used in Judeo-Christian tradition to denote the function of the king of the world." According to the Bible, Melki-Tsedeq, king of Salem, had bread and wine brought forth with which he blessed Abraham. Melki-Tsedeq is both king and priest and his name means "king of justice." At the same time, he is also king of Salem and thus of peace. Justice and peace, according to René Guénon, are the two fundamental aspects of the king of the world, and Salem would hide the name of Agarttha. (Salem is a disguise for the name Agarttha.)[21]

René Guénon also speaks of a figure whom we already came across when looking at the Rennes-le-Château affair: Jacob. As everyone knows, Jacob had a dream in a place named Luz,[22] which he called a new Bethel, the "house of the Lord." Of Luz, Guénon says: "It is said that the Angel of Death cannot enter this town or have any power there; and some claim that through a fairly singular but significant compari-son, its location is near Alborj, which is also the abode of immortality for the Persians." Bethel—the House of God! We can recall the phrase appearing on the portal of the church of Mary Magdalene in Rennes-le-Château: *Terribilis est locus iste,* or "This place is terrible." In Genesis, this text is followed by: "This is none other than the house of God and this is the gate of heaven"[23]—a phrase spoken by Jacob in Bethel.[24] It is the fact that Asmodeus is the first thing you see at the church after reading the phrase from Jacob on the lintel of the church door. Guénon

---

21. Solomon is also a name derived from Salem.
22. Among other things, Luz designates an indestructible physical particle, symbolically depicted as an extremely hard bone, to which the soul remains connected after death and until resurrection.
23. Genesis: "How dreadful is this place! This is none other than the house of God and this is the gate of heaven. And Jacob rose up early in the morning and took the stone that he had used for his pillow, and set it up for a pillar, and poured oil upon the top of it. And he called the name of that place Bethel: but the name of that city was called Luz at first." It seems it is not chance, then, that Jesus was born in Bethlehem, the "house of bread."
24. In the church, near the door, the demon Asmodeus sits in the work of heaven. This guardian of the threshold can be seen as an allusion to the infernal world.

tells us that near Luz-Bethel there is an almond tree (also called Luz in Hebrew) that is hollow at its base.[25] It is through this hole that a person can enter an underground passage leading to the underground city. An old legend of the Razès region tells that underground tunnels lying deep below the castle of Rennes lead to caves where a troglodyte people have been living since the dawn of time. This race has no experience of the passing of time and the light of day and is therefore immortal.[26]

We may ask if the white queen that haunts all the local legends in this region that marries the white and black, Blanchefort and Roco Negro, is not simply the white goddess of ancient times, the one who ruled over the underground world, the goddess of the transition to elsewhere, the lady of the mists. It is quite instructive to refer to the names under which she has been worshipped: Albina (similar to the name of an ancient Visigoth fortress located on the Rennes Plateau, which was Albedunum), and Cardea, for the Romans who regarded her as the mistress of Janus and the queen of "hinges," *cardo* in Latin (similar to Cardou, the name of the mountain overlooking the entrance of the cromlech of Rennes-les-Bains). Ovid said of Cardea: "Her power is to open what is shut, to shut what is open." The white goddess has also been incorporated with Isis[27] by some, according to Lucius, but it is especially important to recall the nickname she was given: the Spider.

This is all well and good, but it is not everything. Now we must find the beginning of these tunnels buried deep beneath the earth that eventually reach the sovereign kingdom of the "master of the hollow hills," as he

---

25. In North American traditions, there is mention of a tree through which humans originally living inside the earth made their way to the surface. Julius Evola (in *The Mystery of the Grail* and his idea of the imperial Gibeline) feels that the withered tree is associated with a depiction of the residence of the king of the world and it will grow green again at the return of this lost king. We cannot help but recall George Sand's novel *Consuelo* and the laurel tree of the Sabarthes that should grow green again as well as the legend of the lost king connected to the Great Monarch that is a feature of the Rennes region. [This theme is also key to J. R. R. Tolkien's book *The Return of the King.* —Trans.]

26. Louis Fédié, "Etude historique sur les Haut Razès" [Historic Study of the High Razès], in *Mémoires de la Société des Arts et Sciences de Carcassonne* [Records of the Society of Arts and Sciences of Carcassonne] (vol. 4, 1879–84).

27. A statue of Isis was found in Rennes-les-Bains.

is known to the Celts. At this moment we can recall that the former name of the peak of Bugarach, near Rennes-les-Bains, was Tauze Peak, with *tauze* meaning "hollow." It is known that a vast network of subterranean galleries exists beneath this peak through which the water of the region's aquifers circulate. The existence of this hydrological system was demonstrated by the research of C. Chanel in *Le séisme aquifère des Pyrénées-Orientales en octobre 1940, son rattachement aux eaux thermals de la region et au système orogénique du Canigou, 1941* [The Aquiferic Earthquake of the Eastern Pyrenees in October 1940, Its Connection to the Thermal Springs in the Region and the Orogenic System of the Canigou].

It is now easy to understand why Jules Verne chose the Bugarach for the family name of the captain in *Clovis Dardentor,* which recalls the Bugarach that is the source of the Sals and the Blanque Rivers—once again an allusion to the color of the white queen and the White Island, which, according to legend, was the destination of Joseph of Arimathea carrying the Grail. Of course, in order to reach it, tradition says that you must "cross the waters."

Andrew Thomas tells us that in Russia,[28] "among the Old Believers of Starovery, there is a strange story that declares that those who follow the path of the Tartar conquerors back to Mongolia will find Belovodye, the land of white waters, where holy men live in seclusion far from the turpitudes of the world." We might say that Bugarach, at whose foot the Blanque River is born, is a kind of land of white waters. Andrew Thomas pursued this notion by citing Nicolas Roerich's report of his discussions with the Old Believers of the Altaï Mountains concerning access to this land. He writes: "After a hard journey, if you have not become lost, you will find the salt water lakes. This passage is quite dangerous. You will then reach the mountains of Bogogorch. Here an even more perilous path awaits you."

Sel and Sals, Bogogorch and Bugarach: Certainly these similarities are not mere coincidences. We are on the right trail, and it is up to the reader to follow it.

---

28. Andrew Thomas, *Shambhala, oasis de lumière* [Shambhala, Oasis of Light] (Paris: Robert Laffont, 1976).

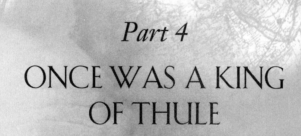

Part 4

ONCE WAS A KING
OF THULE

JULES VERNE AND THE BAVARIAN ILLUMINATI

A SEEMINGLY INCONSISTENT POLITICAL PHILOSOPHY

We have seen the ties connecting the work of Jules Verne to Rosicrucian thought particularly through its avatar, the Order of the Golden Dawn. It goes without saying that all this, in order to be consistent, should have had an influence on the political and social thought of Jules Verne. Everyone has tried to claim Verne for their own: socialists, communists, bourgeois liberals, and so on. This is not so very surprising given that his political position seems uncertain.

One telling piece of information was the Jules Verne's presence on a list of leftist candidates to the municipal council of Amiens in 1888. It was often said at that time and has been said since that he held socialist-communist convictions. In this regard it should be noted that his works, along with those of Jonathan Swift and Daniel Defoe, were selected by the soviet communist party in 1933 as those whose translation was a priority.

It is necessary to be cautious, however. The leftist orthodoxy of Jules Verne has in fact been subject to strong reservations. Even at the time his name was inscribed on the list, Robert Godefroy, municipal councilor of Amiens, wrote to the head of the list, Frédéric Petit: "Jules Verne desires to enter the council on a list sponsored by the citizen Frédéric Petit. Ten years ago this would have appeared quite bizarre, for the pleasant writer, while remaining at a distance from politics, hardly passed for a ferocious Republican. To the contrary, I knew of his Orleanist sentiments."

Be that as it may, on May 13, 1888, Jules Verne was elected on the left slate of the Amiens municipal council, which provoked a bit of a scandal among the high society there. He was even obliged to provide a clarification of his position to some of his friends. He wrote to one of them after the results were in:

> Why do people always mix politics and Christianity with administrative issues? You know me well enough to know that on the essential points I have never fallen under the influence of anyone or anything. In sociology my taste is order; in politics my aspiration is as follows: to create, in the current government, a reasonable and balanced party, respectful of justice, that holds high beliefs and is a friend of men, of art, and of life.

His political positions are not at all obvious. Five years before this election he wrote the Count of Paris on February 27, 1883:

> Milord,
>
> In remembrance of the sentiments that me and mine have always professed for the family of Orleans, in remembrance of the warm welcome that Your Highness has deigned to give me personally, please allow me to join with all men of heart and good intention who have but one duty and one hope today: the duty to protest against the illegal action, doubled by an infamy, with which your family was just attacked, and the hope that a day will come when all these insults will be avenged.
>
> In the meantime, Milord, please accept with all my regrets the assurance of my deepest respect and undying devotion to Your Highness by his very humble and respectful servant.
>
> Jules Verne

So what is Verne, Marxist or Conservative, Royalist or Republican? Contradictions abound in Verne's life. On the one hand, we see him frequenting the company of Nadar, whose anarchist opinions are common knowledge, and on the other hand, he attends the royal family. It is true that on the request of Hetzel, he performed a favor for Paschal Grousset, the exiled Communard, by "rewriting" his *Héritage de Langevol* [Langevol's Inheritiance] under the name of *Bégum's Millions*. Incidentally, speaking of the Communard movement, Verne said, "Well, it's over. It will be defeated, and while the Republican government displayed terrible energy repressing it, as was its duty and its right, Republican France has fifty years of internal peace—that's what I think."

Verne enthusiastically defended minorities such as the Irish and French Canadians. He defended the memory of the Vendéens, the Breton counter-revolutionaries. He ceaselessly displayed a certain kind of anti-colonial sentiment, but elsewhere showed signs of racism. In *La Mission Barsac* [The Barsac Mission] (one example of many), he writes of blacks: "there is no question of consulting one no more than one would consult an ill child about the appropriate remedy to give him." His racism targeted Jews in particular. We have only to look at the figure of Isaac Hakhabut in *Hector Servadec* as proof of such an extreme hatred that it prompted a complaint from the high rabbi of Paris to Verne's publisher, Hetzel, who wrote to his son about the matter: "I warned Jules Verne, I softened more than one passage, but he was so bitter toward this wretched figure that these attempts to soften his descriptions were quite difficult." Indeed, if a Jew in one of his novels appeared almost sympathetic, Verne hastened to let the reader know that this character was an exception.

Verne's ambiguity extended to religion. Raised a Catholic, it appears that he experienced a kind of mystical crisis around 1853. Its culmination can be detected in a fairly extraordinary text entitled *Maître Zacharius* [Master Zacharius]. In 1862 he met Hetzel, who lived in a milieu composed of anticlerical individuals such as Jean Macé and Freemason deists. In his texts though he often refers to God as Providence or the Creator, he never mentions Christ, and though he imagines certain scenes that take place in churches, he never mentions the Church. Simone Vierne notes that the character of Nemo echoes Verne's thought like Nietzsche's shout that God is dead. Nevertheless, it should also be underscored that the philosophies of Verne's heroes are essentially religious.

JULES VERNE OR ARISTOCRATIC ANARCHY

The ambiguity of Jules Verne's political positions are clearly shown by one of the chapter titles in Gilbert Prouteau's book, *Le grand roman de Jules Verne, sa vie* [The Great Book of Jules Verne, His Life]: "A Conservative Anarchist." This same ambiguity can be also found in *Chemin de France* [Path of France] in which Jules Verne writes: "Sometimes it is reported that I am on the right when I am on the left. Sometimes the left when I am on the right."

To untangle this web, we must explore how idealism and realism both laid claim to his character. Realism made him a man of law and order. Idealism made him an anarchist, but not a bitter advocate of revenge so much as an aristocratic anarchist, one prompted by ideals. His sympathy for Promethean heroes who reject society is quite evident, men such as Robur and Nemo. Jules Verne was also in contact with important anarchists such as Elisée Reclus,[1] no doubt thanks to Hetzel.

To a certain extent it is possible to see a revolutionary in Jules Verne. Pierre Louys, who did a handwriting analysis of him,[2] highlighted the fact that he was an "underground revolutionary." We may consider him a revolutionary, but on condition that we do not force on him the masks that accompany this term today. First of all, I can say that Jules Verne was no Marxist, with all due respect to those seeking to enlist him to that cause. We can find proof of this in the novel *The Survivors of the Jonathan*, which seems to be quite representative of his political philosophy. In

---

1. This anarchist geographer was also a Freemason and member of the lodge known as The Renaissance.

2. This handwriting analysis was published in *Broutilles* [Trifles] (Le Roche-sur-Yon, 1938) and was cited by Marie-Hélène Huet in *L'histoire des voyages extraordinaires* [The History of the Extraordinary Voyages] (Paris: Lettres Modernes, 1973).

this book, the victims of a shipwreck, poor folk who had been traveling to the ends of the earth in search of their fortune, find themselves at Tierra del Fuego, where they are forced to work together to survive. Some individuals seek to take over the group, which gives Verne the opportunity to portray communists and socialists and to depict their attempts to form a government.

He describes one of the "communists" this way: "Dorick preached equality in such a way that made it detestable. He did not look at things from the bottom up but from the top down. Thought of the miserable fate reserved for the immense majority of humans did not cause his heart to beat with any emotion, but the idea that a small number of them held a social rank higher than his sent him into fits of rage." With regard to socialism, he settled his score with it just as lucidly: "Socialism, this doctine whose claim is nothing less than the remaking of society from its very foundations, in fact does not have the merit of being innovative. Following many others now lost in the depths of time, Saint-Simon, Charles Fourier, and Proudhon and "tutti quanti" are the precursors to collectivism. More modern ideologues such as Lassale, Karl Marx, and Guesde, have done nothing but refloat their ideas with varying degrees of modification." He adds:

> If the socialist movement as it has declared during the second half of the century has not been useless, if it has had the beneficial consequence of stimulating a general sympathy by calling attention to human misery, of directing the mind to seek out means of alleviating it, of prompting generous initiatives and inspiring laws that are not all bad, this result has been obtained only by preserving intact the social order it claims to be destroying.

In other words, socialism either is a form of reforming liberalism or it is dedicated to catastrophe. In the face of a communist and a socialist, whose behaviors are far from praiseworthy, Jules Verne offers his model of an anarchist, Kaw-Djer. This character who had found a haven on this island for a long time is a former prince who had abandoned everything out of political conviction. He is an enemy of every system and an adversary of any organization that restricts the freedom of individuals. "I am the irreconcilable enemy of every government of any kind. I have employed my entire life considering this matter and I do not think that there is any possible circumstance that gives anyone the right to violate the liberty of his peers." Behind this anarchist who abdicated out of respect for his ideals there may be a real prince: Jean Orth, the Hapsburg archduke. But Kaw-Djer's anarchist sentiments are shaken. He is the sole "strong man" on this island, the only one capable of organizing the survivors and preventing their lack of preparation for the coming winter from carrying them off causing them to descend into a wide variety of vices. He is the only one who is capable of preventing the island from being ruled by the law of the most brutish lout. In order for the colony to succeed, this anarchist finds himself obliged, with a heavy heart, to traverse through every stage of despotism, for it seems that only a flawless authority can serve the common good and allow Hoste Island to preserve its independence.

Jules Verne does not use this character and the situation to justify despotism. He is merely trying to show that the majority of humans do not have the courage to be free and need someone to take charge and direct and lead them without care. What do people want? The answer, Jules Verne seems to suggest, is a father figure who will be the keeper of the law to which all can cling. For most people, too much freedom gives birth to a sense of abyssal vertigo that can prove fatal. It is easy to see, then, why Jules Verne had a soft spot for characters who appeared to be, to some extent, aristocratic anarchists.[3]

SPARTACUS AND HIS SLAVES

This anarchistic sentiment displayed by Jules Verne is important because it was more or less championed by the Rosicrucians (or at least some of them) during the nineteenth century, through the lineage of the secret

---

3. The same characteristic can be observed on another scale in Maurice Leblanc's work about the adventures of Arsène Lupin.

societies that influenced the French Revolution under the influence of the Bavarian Illuminati. It seems that the Golden Dawn experienced the influence of Illuminati teachings through the intermediary of the Ordo Templis Orientis (O.T.O.).

The Illuminati was largely the work of one man: Adam Weishaupt. Born on February 6, 1748, in Ingolstadt, he graduated with a doctorate in law at the age of twenty-five and became dean of the law school two years later. Despite his brilliant career, Weishaupt felt he did not receive sufficient recognition for his merits and blamed the Church, specifically the Jesuits.

His advanced ideas led his colleagues to consider him a dangerous innovator. Weishaupt, believing that strength lay in union, conceived the idea of creating an organization capable of acting as a counter balance to the influence of the Jesuits, which lead, in 1776, to the birth of the Order of the Perfectibilists. Weishaupt had decided to gather the best young minds in this society in order to instruct them in the Enlightenment philosophy that had been banned from the university curriculum. For a long time the group consisted of only five members. In order to structure his order, Adam Weishaupt became a member of the Freemasons. In fact, he was turned down first by the Gold Rosicrucians, but in 1781, Adolf von Knigge, a penniless baron of the empire, came to his aid and provided the Order of the Perfectibilists real organization by giving it a large encyclopedic library, historical archives, and scientific displays so that they could battle the ignorance maintained by those he viewed as the "enemies of the future and humanity"—in other words, the Jesuits.

The order then adopted the name Order of the Illuminati and structured itself along the grades of Novice, Minerval, Illuminatus, and so forth. The members took names borrowed from Greek antiquity, which is how Weishaupt became Spartacus. The cities were also designated under code names, and Ingolstadt became Eleusis. To teach wisdom and virtue, Weishaupt, under the influence of von Knigge,[4] borrowed the

---

4. Von Knigge was initiated in Cassel into the Templar Strict Observance and maintained a diligent correspondence with Rosicrucian groups. He was C.B.C.S. in Rectified Scottish Freemasonry and, as a deist, eventually broke with Weishaupt.

methods of his enemies, the Jesuits. He advocated informing and spying among members and advised the practice of "the art of dissimulating, observing, and spying on others."

The society did not accept monks, women, or Jews as members. It taught that every king was the usurper of the rights of the people, and that liberty and equality were the essential rights of mankind. To restore his natural rights to man, religion had to be destroyed and property abolished. Once the initiate had learned all this, he was worthy of wearing the Phrygian cap. The Illuminati professed that all religions were based on imposture and chimeras and rendered man cowardly and superstitious. Some suspect that the Count de Saint-Germain, Cagliostro, and even the Duke of Orleans—the future Philippe Egalité—were members of the order.

What is certain is that the ideas of the Bavarian Illuminati had a considerable influence not only on the French Revolution,[5] but also on a good number of the esoteric societies of the nineteenth century. Karl Marx drew some of his doctrine from these philosophical stores.

Louis Blanc (*Histoire de la Révolution*) [History of the Revolution] writes of the aim of the philosophy of the Illuminati:

> With only the attraction of mystery and the power of association, subjecting to one will and animating with the same breath thousands of men in every country in the world, but first and foremost in Germany and France, it will make of these men, by means of a slow and gradual education, entirely new individuals. It will make them obedient to the point of madness, until death, to invisible and unknown chiefs. It will with such a legion weigh secretly on hearts, encircle the sovereigns, direct as it pleases the governments and even Europe to the point that all superstition is annihilated, every monarchy toppled, all birth privilege declared unjust, and the very right of property abolished. Such was the gigantic scheme of Illuminism!

---

5. In 1797–1798, Abbot Barruel brought out a four-volume work; *Mémoires pour servir à l'histoire du Jacobinisme* [Memoirs Illustrating the History of Jacobinism], in which he denounces the role played by the Bavarian Illuminati in the fall of the monarchy.

Louis Blanc finds this cause for celebration, but while creating a fanatic band is one thing, knowing the purposes to which it will be put is another, and this opens the door to totalitarianism. For all practical purposes, Weishaupt can be considered the true father of Marxism. Bakunin was a disciple of Weishaupt, and in the notes of the founders of the Bavarian Illuminati a phrase can be found that can be read textually in Bakunin: "We must destroy everything, blindly, with but one single thought: as much as possible and as quickly as possible." Werner Gerson writes in *Le Nazisme Société Secrète* [The Secret Society of Nazism]: "Weishaupt sowed the seed that would later give us Babeuf, Buonarroti, Elisée Reclus,[6] Bakunin, Kropotkin, Jean Grave, and also, but indirectly, Blanqui, Trotsky, and Lenin. These are no coincidences."

JULES VERNE, SPIRITUAL HEIR OF THE ILLUMINATI?

Is it a coincidence that the spirit of the Bavarian Illuminati can be found, at least partially, in the work of Jules Verne? Kaw-Djer, hero of *The Survivors of the Jonathan* is a pure emanation of Adam Weishaupt in his basic principles. The very fact that the image of the circle forms a permanent presence in Verne's work, from the circular journeys to the circles that meet, can be interpreted in connection with the Illuminati. For example, the Reform Club is a circle, as we can deduce after reading, in the words of Marquis de Luchet in *Essai sur la secte des Illuminés* [Trial of the Illuminati Sect], a work that appeared in 1789:

> The circles are the administrative committees of the sect. There are as many as are felt needed. They are divided up among the different provinces, and each one consists of nine persons. They are initiated by the same powers, have experienced the same trials, are bound by the same oaths, are imbued with the same principles, correspond with one another using hieroglyphys unknown to the rest of the

---

6. He was a friend of Jules Verne.

world, and, despite this obscure language, do not entrust their missives to anyone. They are the keepers of conspiracies in service of the public and they employ means of communication that are as mysterious as their figures. These circles have anonymous travelers. They are ordinarily men of simple appearance, men of letters with a predilection for philanthropy."

It is particularly important to note that the Illuminati took a special interest in literary societies, creating groups of writers and infiltrating Masonic or Rosicrucian lodges. In this way they applied the technique of the Jesuits—not proclaiming their doctrine themselves but having it proclaimed by others—and trained those who had power over the media of the time and even establishing their own bookstores. Orders were given to the adepts to recruit artists and even booksellers to such an extent that an Englishman, Mr. Robison, published a book *Proofs of a Conspiracy Formed by the Freemasons, the Illuminati, and the Literary Societies Against All Religion and All the Governments of Europe.*

We should not assume that Jules Verne was a member of the Bavarian Illuminati in a real sense, but it is very possible that he belonged to one of these literary societies (see the next chapter for their names) and that these societies, like many of the esoteric groups of the nineteenth century, were at least partially subject to the influence of the doctrines and methods of the Illuminati.

With regard to Verne, we can see that, in addition to his noteworthy love of secret writings, an additional clue is provided by the methodic precautions to have esoteric or incriminating papers safeguarded or destroyed in the event of one's death. Similar methods were outlined in the workings of the Illuminati. In fact, the writing or books relating to the Illuminati were given to Novices only in very small numbers—in dribs and drabs, we might say—and on the condition that no one else would have access to them. As adepts advanced in grade, they were allowed to hold on to such writing for longer periods of time, but first had to indicate what precautions they had taken to prevent their discovery, even in the case of sudden death. Weishaupt said of each of his adepts:

> He must draw up his Last Will and Testament wherein he will spe-
> cifically express his final wishes concerning his secret papers that
> may be found at his home, if death arrives unexpectedly. He must
> have provided himself, either from his family or the public magis-
> trate, a legal receipt of the declaration he has made on this portion
> of his will, he must have received a written promise that his inten-
> tions will be honored.

It is clear that Verne consciously carried the ideas advocated by Weishaupt, but revisited these options at the end of his life, a subject we will discuss later. He was not the only one to honor Weishaupt's concepts. George Sand, who repeatedly comes to the fore in any study of Verne's life and work, devoted her most beautiful novel, *Consuelo*, to the development of Weishaupt's doctrines.

THE BAVARIAN ILLUMINATI AND A CASTLE IN BOHEMIA

In *Consuelo* and its sequel *The Countess of Rudolstadt,* George Sand tells of a mysterious sect of the Invisibles. She writes: "They are the instigators of all the revolutions; they are in the courts and manage all business there, decide on war or peace, redeem the wretched, punish the rogues, and cause kings to tremble upon their thrones." Consuelo is inititated by these Invisibles who preach Liberty, Fraternity, and Equal-ity: "These are people who are not seen but who work behind the scenes. They do all manner of evil. We do not know if they have one place in which they reside, but they are everywhere. . . . They are the ones who murder many travelers and who lend powerful assistance to others against robbers, depending on whether they have judged these travelers worthy of receiving punishment or protection."

George Sand invested these Invisibles with all the powers of the

Rosicrucians. Moreover, she was one of the first to demonstrate the ties existing between the Rosicrucians, the secret society of Sainte-Vehme, and the Bavarian Illuminati. The end of the book is entirely devoted to the Invisibles-Illuminati, for the author clearly was fully informed on the inner workings and doctrine of the sect.

On Weishaupt himself, George Sand writes: "Keep moving then, acting and working. Heaven has ordained you as the organizer of destruction: Destroy and dissolve, there is your work. It requires faith to tear down as well as to build." The same might be said of Captain Nemo or Robur the Conqueror. Leaving the floor to Spartacus-Weishaupt, Sand then writes, "I believed that there was nothing left to be hoped for from the official society and no reform would be possible by remaining within it. I placed myself outside of it, and, despairing to see salvation befall the people because of this corruption, I have devoted the last years of my strength to act directly on the people." These words could just as readily have come from the mouth of Kaw-Djer. Sand places these words in the mouth of one of Weishaupt's interlocutors:

"Learn one thing that must be the rule of your soul. Nothing is ever lost. Your name and the shape of your works will disappear; you will work namelessly, like me, so that your labor shall not be lost. The divine balance is mathematics itself, and in the crucible of the divine chemist, all atoms are reckoned at their precise value." This surely brings to mind Nemo.

To sum up what we have deduced so far: Beyond his knowledge of the Rennes-le-Château mystery, Jules Verne was a Freemason and belonged to a group that proclaimed its affiliation to Rosicrucianism. We have seen that his knowledge is connected to the teachings of the Golden Dawn, but also, in a way, to the Bavarian Illuminati. But how exactly is he connected to these? In what group would Verne have acquired such knowledge, and was he commissioned to transmit this teaching? We will go on to explore the answers to these questions.

THE CHALICE IN
THE FOG

The work of Jules Verne follows a certain logic that corresponds to a very specific purpose. The path the author follows leading from Scottish Freemasonry to Rosicrucianism is quite obvious. It is equally easy to follow his trail related to themes of the Golden Dawn, from vampirism to the hollow earth. Yet our investigation is missing some specific information or signature. Verne had certainly been initiated into Freemasonry and surely knew the Rosicrucian doctrines, but this does not tell us precisely to which society or denomination he belonged. His work, entirely dedicated to the transmission of a message, should, from all evidence, be the reflection not of the single philosophy of a man but that of a whole community. The ties connecting Verne's political philosophy—or, more exactly the one emerging from his work—and the fundamental themes of the Bavarian Illuminati lead us, quite logically, to those societies that specifically brought together artists and writers. Parallel research I conducted on Gérard de Nerval aroused my interest in a very rare book that chance (or providence) fortunately placed into my hands, and it provided me with the element my study was still missing. It is to this book and the mysterious society for which it was a breviary that we now turn.

THE CLAW OF THE ANGEL IN THE FOG

The literary coterie called the Angelic Society was founded by the Lyonnaise printer Gryphe during the sixteenth century. Grasset Orcet tells us that this group was placed under the ultra-Masonic protection of Saint-Giles. Its adepts took as their crest an angel head: "chef Angel[1] translated into Goliard language by St. Giles." In reality, the printer Gryphe, named Sebastian Greif, was a native of Reitlingen in Wurtemburg. He had settled in Lyon in 1522 and taken the gryphon as his emblem. He had adopted his pseudonym Gryphe because of the phonetic tie it had to his actual name and because of its connection to the Greek society named Nephes meaning "the mist" or "the fog"—a term that designated the universal principle of the unknown. As R. Mazelier informs us,[2] "It was the thick mist, the cloud that Ixion embraced and which the Greeks called Gryphe, the 'entangled one,' with a bull's head as its hieroglyph." We should not overlook this bull's head, this steer's skull, sign of man's labor upon himself, of his attempt to rid and free himself of the old man. In addition, Nostradamus tells us about the ancients: "When they wished to signify labor, they used the image of a bull's head from which time had stripped the hide, as the laboring men it symbolized were made thin by their labors."

In any case, the angel appears as the messenger of this fog, and the Angelic Society sometimes changed its name to simply the Fog. According to Grasset d'Orcet, this name also reveals "a very important branch of Freemasonry worshipping the sepulchre of a Neapolitan scholar known as Pierre Barlieri."[3] We should recall that the pre-Masonic sects of the Middle Ages often formed attachments to tombs, most popularly

---

1. ["Chief angel" or "angel head." The Goliards were initially a group of the clergy who wrote satirical Latin verse lampooning the Church, the crusades, and so forth in the twelfth and thirteenth centuries. It later became an accepted term for minstrel. —*Trans.*]
2. R. Mazelier, "En lisant Nerval: *Angélique*," in *Cahiers d'Etudes Cathares* [Journal of Cathar Studies].
3. Fans of Nerval can make an easy comparison to another Neapolitan tomb.

to those of Solomon and Hiram. Other popular choices were those of Virgil, Pierre Brouillard, and Pierre Abelard.

As for the fog or the mist used in this way, as we've seen, it does represent the unknown and presides over Aristophanes's *Clouds* as well as the *Niebelungen*. There is something equivocal about this unknown, however. Is it God, the demiurge, Lucifer? Can it be compared to the cloud that pervaded in the Temple of Jerusalem when God was allegedly present? Can we connect it to those mysterious fogs that prevail at the appearance of the bizarre and disturbing beings in the novels of H. P. Lovecraft and A. Merritt?

The fog is not only a symbol of the indeterminate; it also represents chaos, the confusion of the time of origins generally linked to that era the Greeks attributed to the rule of Chronos, known to the Romans as Saturn, king of the Golden Age. This age has been forgotten and is a kind of paradise lost because of the fall into matter. Man has emerged from the clouds and incarnated, and by losing his nebulosity has thereby lost paradise. He can regain this aspect of himself only on the other side of death, through his astral body.

The ancient Irish texts evoke the mist in connection to the music of the Sidh (in the beyond) or to the Sidh themselves. Similarly, the Sanskrit word *ghana* (cloud) is used in reference to the primordial embryo, and the cloud (al'amâ) in Islamic esoterism is the unknowable state of Allah before manifestation. More recently, Louis-Claude de Saint-Martin maintained that nebulosity always surrounds the bursts of light that sometimes carve through human darkness because our senses could not support the full resplendence of this light. Thus as the symbol of the undifferentiated, the fog can also be the symbol of a state that the initiate must reconquer in order to separate from the material world. It is certainly not by chance that Bram Stoker ended his novel *The Jewel of the Seven Stars* with these words:

I saw something white rising up from the open sarcophagus. Something that appeared to my tortured eyes to be filmy, like a white mist. In the heart of this mist, which was cloudy and opaque, like an opal, there was something like a hand holding a fiery jewel flaming with many lights. As the fierce glow of the coffer met this new living light, the green vapor floating between them seemed like a cascade of brilliant points—a miracle of light! . . . Black smoke began to pour out. This grew thicker and thicker with frightful rapidity, in volumes of ever-increasing density till the whole cavern began to become obscure, and its outlines were lost.[4]

The ambivalent aspect of the fog is worth underscoring: It is either luminous mist or a foretaste of the darkness. This dual aspect is well illustrated by Grasset d'Orcet's words: "The fog wishes the sun (the solar seed) to rise and move into the blood of man, to make young the body of the son, into which the Fog can then enter so that he can be reborn and topple the fog."

A very strange book by Willis George Emerson that appeared in 1908 recounts the tale of Olaf Jansen, a Norwegian who became an American citizen. Interestingly, Jansen stated that he had visited the inhabited subterranean world and returned.[5] The book is entitled *The Misty God,* a name designating a sun within the earth.

THE DREAM OF POLIPHILUS

The Angelic Society, or the Fog, possessed a breviary book known as *The Dream of Poliphilus.* The Jesuit Tiraboschi described it as follows: "Fortunate are those who succeed, I will not say to understand it, but only to grasp what language it is written in, as it is such a confused blend of fables, history, architecture, antiquities, mathematics, and a thousand other things, with the strangest piling of Greek, Latin, Hebrew, Arab, Chaldean, Lombard, and Italian words."

---

4. In Bram Stoker's novel *Dracula,* the fog is mentioned no less than fifty times. It is worth noting that there are numerous links between vampires, dragons, and fog.
5. Legends consistently state that the entrances to the underground world are protected by a fog, just as a perpetual mist covered the land of Thule.

This work is attributed to Francesco Colonna, and interestingly, if we put together the initial letters of each of its eighteen chapters, this is the Latin phrase that results: *Poliam frater Franciscus Colonna Peramavit,* which means "Brother Francis Colona loved Polia madly." The assumed author of the work was a Dominican monk who, according to some analysts, was in love with a beautiful Trevisana woman named Polita or Ippolita. To hide the trail of this love, however, he would have recounted its stories in masked names, using various languages. This is quite a barebones explanation for this work and is one that makes the author both complicated and incredibly puerile.

In fact, this analysis of the text is merely superficial. The book, a magnificent quarto volume illustrated with wood engravings, which was published in Venice by Alde Manucce in 1499 under the title *Hypnerotomachia Poliphili,*[6] was probably the work of a coterie, and Brother Francesco Colonna was only a pen name. As Emanuela Kretzulesco-Quaranta has shown in an admirable work,[7] the love story that gives orientation to the events in Poliphilus's Dream was inspired in large part by the life of Lorenzo di Medici, known as the Magnificent, and his love for the beautiful and pure Lucrezia Donati.[8] Kretzulesco-Quaranta has grasped this completely and fully demonstrates that the *Hypnerotomachia Poliphili* was actually written to transmit a message on behalf of a group of Platonic scholars who had been persecuted around 1468, the date of the trial of Rome and the Camaldoli Congress that brought together the Florentine Academicians."The ideas and theories of Leon Baptiste Alberti, protégé of Nicholas V and Cardinal Colonna, coming from the research of the Cardinal of Cusa synthesized in his 'Hunt of

---

6. In the 1546 reprinting, the title was expanded to *La Hypnerotomachia di Poliphilo, cioè pugna d'amore in sogno,* which can be translated as *The Strife of Love in Poliphilus's Dream* or, more exactly, *The Battle that Poliphilus Waged in Dream against Love.*

7. Emanuela Kretzulesco-Quaranta, *Les jardins du songe* [The Gardens of Dream] (Paris: Les Belle Lettres, 1986).

8. Lorenzo the Magnificent also partly served as a model for Shakespeare's Romeo. Prospero's character in Shakespeare's *The Tempest* was inspired by Prospero Colonna. As an additional curiosity, Lorenzo's motto was "Time Returns."

Wisdom,' are reconizeable throughout 'Poliphilo's strife.'" It is therefore Alberti whom we recognize beneath the pseudonym of Poliphilus, the first father of the *Hypnerotomachia*. It is to him that we owe the resurrection of the art of Vitruvius and the spread of the ideas that guided the Renaissance humanists. As Kretzulesco-Quaranta says in *Les jardins du songe,* it was he who was the protagonist of *The Strife of Love in Poliphilus's Dream.*

The coterie that presided over this writing believed the best access to knowledge of God was the study of nature and its laws, a point of view quite close to that of the gnostics and, much later, the Rosicrucians. We can also compare this philosophy with that of Virgil: Love, divine Eros, is the motor force of All.[9] Moreover, it is not by accident that Poliphilo's itinerary mirrors that of Aeneas. The first part of the book is connected directly to Alberti's conceptions and leads to the conquest of the mystical fountain of divine love that gives life. The second part, more inspired by the loves of Lorenzo the Magnificent, goes further in the search for true love. Following the persecutions that began in 1466, Leon Baptiste Alberti was forced to seek refuge in Florence with the Medicis. Shortly afterward, both Nicholas de Cusa and Prospero Colonna died, no doubt by poisoning. The papacy seems clearly to have decided to eliminate what was sometimes called the Church of the Enlightenment or the Church of the Fog.

DEI MATER OR THE HERALDIC LANGUAGE

The Strife of Love in Poliphilus's Dream is primarily an encrypted work. Leonardo Crasso, who printed the text, alerted the readers in his introduction: "These matters are not to be exposed to the vulgar or proclaimed at the crossroads, but brought forth from the sanctuary of philosophy and drawn from the Muses' springs with a novel refinement of speech, deserving thanks from all superior men." This

---

9. *"Amor che move il sole et l'altre stele"* is the verse that Dante uses to end *The Divine Comedy* in which he declares himself a disciple of Virgil.

is heraldic language, the language of the blazon. Grasset d'Orcet advises us in no uncertain terms: "The word blazon certainly has nothing to do with the German *blasen* (to blow). Like grimoire, it comes from the Greek. The stonecutters took as their patron St. Blaise, whose name in Greek means *bléser*[10]—in other words, talk like the people of Auvergne, whose gutturals are hushed, not sibilant. To speak in blazons is to speak like St. Blaise—to lisp."[11] Plato refers to this manner of disguising one's thought as "the language of the gods."

Four languages are required for understanding *The Strife of Love in Poliphilus's Dream*: Greek, Latin, Tuscan, and the common tongue, which, in heraldic language, always means French. It is for interpreting the rebuses formed by the engravings illustrating the book that French is essential.

The book itself indicates the path to follow. In the beginning, Poliphilus decodes one of the rebuses and gives us the meaning that it is necessary to apply to this collection of images. If we compare this interpretation of the symbols to the system proposed by the *Hieroglyphs of the Orus Apollo*, it is possible to reconstruct the system used to decrypt the text. Helpful to the reader are Rabelais's words on this account as well as the works of Grasset d'Orcet on this subject. In order to grasp the very pith of the text, it is also beneficial to read carefully Nostradamus's little-known work *Interpretation of the Hieroglyphs of the Orus Apollo*, a book its author dedicated to Jeanne d'Albret, mother of King Henri IV and a member of the Angelic Society. I cannot stress too strongly the importance of *The Hieroglyphs of the Orus Apollo* about which Nostradamus himself wrote:

> I have not rendered these two books in vain,
> But to show those who labor hard to know

---

10. [To lisp. —*Trans.*]

11. In the Limoux church, not far from Rennes-le-Château, the chapel dedicated to St. Blaise is decorated with Masonic symbols.

That to good books they should more studious go.

Of secrets thus they'll know the usefulness

Whose notes, once noted, do the truth confess,

For when the learnèd shall my prologue see

Of hidden lore philologists they'll be,

And capable to marvel quite a whit

How nature works somewhat as it befit,

And know those facts no man can understand

Which Epaphus writ clearly in his hand,

Having of Memphis found each sacred sign

Whose inventory they did first define

This book is important not only for revealing the method to follow to decrypt *The Strife of Love in Poliphilus's Dream,* but also for revealing the way in which *The Centuries* (Nostradamus' works) were written. If we are interested in Rennes-le-Château, we are compelled to pay attention to the passage in which Nostradamus says: "How they call the infernal gods they call manes DM," especially when we recall a certain quatrain from *The Centuries* that says:

Quand l'escriture DM trouvée,

Et cave antique à lampe découverte,

Ley, Roy et Prince Ulpian ésprouvée,

Pavillon Royne et Duc sous la couverte.[12]

In returning to *The Strife of Love in Poliphilus's Dream,* we can note its odd rituals, which are sometimes linked to blood magic. We follow the hero to the Temple of Venus, attend a sacrifice, and admire the birth of a tree fed on the blood of victims—a tree whose fruits serve as food to

---

12. [When the writing *DM* shall be discovered, / And by lamp an ancient cavern revealed, / Law, King, Ulpian prince will be proved, / Under the cover of Pavillion of Queen and Duke. —*Trans.*]

hierophants during a kind of Last Supper connected to the mysteries of blood and love. Venus then leads us to Cythera, a place dear to Gérard de Nerval and Watteau.

We might find it surprising that a book like this was not more widely known, but two factors have contributed to its neglect and kept its reading confidential: its reputation as an erotic book[13] due to certain engravings, and its "unreadable" and deadly boring aspect. But what riches await on the other side of the boredom! For Grasset d'Orcet, *The Strife of Love in Poliphilus's Dream,* contains the key to all chivalrous literature. This literature, like the *Dream,* generally portrays at the beginning a figure wandering through a forest, the signature of a brotherhood of foresters (qui en **forêterrent**).[14] In 1881, in the *Revue Britannique* Grasset d'Orcet wrote:

> There are literary names that never vanish from the great human signboard. These are the artists whose works combine a rather deep knowledge and a form that is moving enough to compel the interest, at least by one side of their compositions, of all social classes. In modern times this list would include Dante, Rabelais, Cervantes, and Goethe. My comparison of these four geniuses who are otherwise so different is not unintentional. Each surrendered only a part of his secret to the public, reserving for an infinitely more restrained circle of associates the complete understanding of his work. Goethe was the last of these four, and he died at the height of the nineteenth century. A host of distinctive signs indicate that he belonged to the same mysterious society as his illustrious predecessors.

This society was the Angelic Society, and to the list established by Grasset d'Orcet, which stops at the beginning of the nineteenth century,

---

13. This cannot help but bring to mind some of Jules Verne's allusions that mask his most important passages.

14. ["Who in the Forest wander"—the bolded letters spell *frère,* meaning "brother" in French. —*Trans.*]

we should add Dumas, Nerval, George Sand, Jules Verne, and several others, as well as numerous painters and artists of diverse origin. It is surprising that Grasset d'Orcet did not allude to Shakespeare[15] or to painters such as Nicholas Poussin, Eustache Lesseur, Le Guerchin, Claude Gelée, Leonardo Da Vinci, Watteau, Delacroix, and a host of others.

AND TRINK, THE HOLY BOTTLE

The case of Rabelais is particularly significant, for he had a close interest in *The Strife of Love in Poliphilus's Dream* and wrote:

> The sages of Egypt followed a very different course when they wrote in letters that they called hieroglyphs—which none understood who did not understand, and which everyone understood who did understand, the virtue, property, and nature of things thereby described. On this subject Orus Apollo has composed two books in Greek; and Polyphilus has gone further into the matter in his *Dream of Love*.

Rabelais used comparable methods to write his own books.[16] In *Gargantua* he wrote: "For here you will find an individual savor and abstruse teaching which will initiate you into very high sacraments and dread mysteries concerning not only our religion but also our public and

---

15. Do not forget that Jules Verne was crazy about Shakespeare. In his youth he fasted for six days to save enough money to buy Shakespeare's complete works. On several occasions Verne alluded to his plays, most particularly *The Tempest*. To get an idea of the ties existing among the works of Dante, Rabelais, Shakespeare, and Cervantes, it is helpful to read the book Victor Hugo devoted to Shakespeare (which was published by Hetzel).

16. A typical example: Rabelais tells us how Pantagruel "received from a Parisian lady a letter addressed in the following manner: 'To the best beloved of the Fair and the least faithful of the brave P.N.T.G.R.L.'" On opening the letter he finds nothing inside except a gold ring "with a flat-cut diamond." The ring has carved upon it: *Lamah Saabachtani,* "Why hast thou forsaken me?" The diamond, however, is paste and the explanation of the lady's message is: "Say, false lover, why have you abandoned me?"

private life."[17] Just like Verne, he often hid his most important secrets behind apparent vulgarities. There seem to have been ties between Rabelais and the Rosicrucians. Fulcanelli believed he was the hermetic teacher of the Rosicrucian Louis d'Estissac. His most "initiatory" work is no doubt *The Fifth Book,* which was largely inspired by *The Strife of Love in Poliphilus's Dream.* Therefore, the passage Rabelais devotes to the episode on the Temple of Bacbuc and the oracle of the Holy Bottle, whose watchword is Trink, is quite important. It is not surprising that Father Boudet used it with regard to Rennes-les-Bains by giving a stream there the name Trinque-Bouteille—especially if we consider that the Temple of Bacbuc lies underground and some phrases Rabelais uses to describe suggest it is connected to the hollow earth. The description of this temple is largely borrowed from that of the temple of Venus in *The Strife of Love in Poliphilus's Dream.* Rabelais was reputed to be a member of the Agla Society, whose emblem was the numeral 4[18] above an interlacing Marian A and M. It seems clear that this was merely an assumed name for the Angelic Society. Of note is the fact that making the numeral 4 on paper is similar to drawing a cross without lifting the pen from the paper. This mysterious sign, just like the interlaced A and M, is connected to the Rennes' affair. As for the word Agla, it consists of the initials for the words Atha, Gibor, Leolan, Adonai, meaning, "You are eternally strong, Lord."[19]

IN THE SHADOW OF THE PATTY CROSS, BENEATH THE SIGN OF ST. GILES

The first French translation of *The Strife of Love in Poliphilus's Dream* dates from 1546 and is attributed to a Knight of Malta. Grasset d'Orcet

---

17. We should not overlook *Gargantua* in which Rabelais writes: "That is the reason you must open the book and carefully weigh up its contents. You will discover then that the drug within is far more valuable than the box promised; that is to say, that the subjects here treated are not so foolish as the title on the cover suggested." [François Rabelais, *Gargantua and Pantagruel,* trans. J. M. Cohen (Middlesex, England: Penguin, 1955).]

18. The numeral 4 was sometimes used as an identification sign among the Cathars.

19. For those who knew how to read it, the Van Eyck brothers left a message in their painting indicating a link between the Templar Order and the Agla Society.

does not fail to see this as a sign concerning a possible Templar affiliation. This does not seem a terribly compelling connection, but Grasset d'Orcet pursued it in his reading of the phrase *Poliam frater Franciscus Columna peramavit*. He believed this Latin phrase should be translated as "Courteous brother Francis the column worships," which would no longer refer to the name of the author but to his grade and could be interpreted as "He is Templar brother Francis Gold Column." I will leave full resposibility for this assertion to its author. D'Orcet adds, furthermore, basing his assertion on a panel in the book serving as the title for the chapter on knights, that "the Italian monk translated the code from the Provençal language, for which the symbol is a periwinkle. This easily explains why a Knight of Malta, heir to the Templars' secrets, has deemed it wise to translate Francesco Colonna for the use of some lodge of the knights of his order." Grasset d'Orcet seeks to confirm his finding by adding: "The secret of *The Strife of Love in Poliphilus's Dream* is entirely in the Greco-Latin title of his book *Hypnerotomachia Poliphili*, which should translate into Greek as *Love Dreams He Fistfights* (*pugnare* means combat) and Latin as *Poliphilus*. All together this gives us the common title in French: *Singilpin Grimoire Affiliated with the Temple*. Grasset d'Orcet also believes that *The Strife of Love in Poliphilus's Dream* reveals the secret statutes of the Templar Order, which is not at all obvious.

OH DEMETER, MOTHER OF THE FOALS, TELL US WHERE THE GOLD LIES HIDDEN

Now let's turn our attention to the name of the heroine of *The Strife of Love in Poliphilus's Dream*, Polia. This name has received a variety of translations, from "white" or "brilliant" to "ancient," or "antique." In Greek it means "having white hair," or old age. This cannot help but bring to mind the ancient white goddess, who is quite often found beneath the symbolism of Demeter.

Let's follow Grasset d'Orcet in his understanding of Polia.

She is one pulley and Poliphilus is another one. The two make a pair, and the pair, joined by a chain or a mesh, form a pulley block or a hoist used to transfer cargo to a ship, stones to a scaffold, or, most simply, the bucket from the bottom of a well to the surface. The majority of the collections of Goliard prints and old paintings depict a girl and a well. The well is Poliphilus. The girl is holding a bucket in one hand—this is Solomon—and in the other she is holding the chain that is rolled around the pulley. . . . The hoist belongs to the Knights of the Temple and Malta, and by extension, the military orders. . . . In fact, every hoist consists of a couple at the very least; that is to say a fixed block and an idler pulley. . . . The same was true of the Knights of the Temple and of Malta, who formed couples, meaning that each knight had his apprentice. The initiatory knight was the fixed block, the initiate was the idler pulley, and together they formed the block-and-tackle pair. . . . One still said, "my old fellow" or "my old branch" to recall the friendship that linked the idler pulley to the fixed block.

Grasset d'Orcet then mentions a certain four-class hierarchy in the Templar Order, stating in passing that the amorous quest was reserved for the "born sires," which will ring a bell with d'Orcet's admirers.

Their Masonic standard, provided by Poliphilus, is one of the most interesting hieroglyphs in his book. It is square, edged with six pales decorated with rains (branches) of periwinkle (Provence),[20] and contains a world (globe) bearing the crescent and the sun (solar cross on the mountain) and an antique vase in which a flame is burning (a fiery vessel), all connected by a branch of periwinkle. This should be read as "Solomon's sepulchre will set Provence free." (See figure 11, p. 112d.)

Grasset d'Orcet then tells us that the Templars "called themselves

---

20. ["Periwinkle" is *pervenche* in French. —*Trans.*]

the lougarous[21] or logres knights, and they, like others, worshipped the rising sun (sol-mont), hence the Solomon of ancient Freemasonry, whose origin is not biblical but Gallic, because the sun is the ancient god Belenus or Pol, Apollo in Greek, represented by a colt. . . . Because the root of his name means round, it is probable that the name of pulley and the name for hoist comes from him as well as all the rest of the legend concerning the pully hooked with the idler pulley."[22]

What is worth noting in all of this is of course the constant appearance of Polia-Pole-Pulley-Pal-Poulain.[23] It is likely that polia, or Dame Cognoissance,[24] is nothing other than the gnosis of the troubadours which the Greeks regarded as divine wisdom and worshipped under the name of Athena Polias. The followers of the Angelic Society pursued a gnostic quest in which the pole—as an axis of creation—played an important symbolic role. The Greek word πολοσ designated the celestial vault, the gnomon,[25] and the pole all at the same time and also applied to "colt."[26] This son of the horse is often considered a son of the night, a child of darkness, but because of this very fact, it also the life that has been born from the darkness, like a form of rebirth or renaissance. In him the kingdom of the night gives birth to light.

The colt necessarily leads us to an affair closely connected to that of Rennes-le-Château—that of the Templar treasure in Gisors. Legend says that there the white queen had a lover named Poulain.[27] We might wager

---

21. ["Werewolf." —*Trans.*]

22. [*Pol* is the root for *poulie* (pulley) and *palan* (hoist). —*Trans.*]

23. [*Pal* means "stake" (or pale) and *poulain* means "colt." —*Trans.*] Recall the importance of the stake in vampirism and its presence in Dracula's coat of arms. In passing we can note that Hungary is the sole country to have on its heraldry a so-called angelic crown, and this is not by chance, especially if we consider that in German the word *angel* means "pole." As a final observation, the rallying cry of the Medicis, founders of the Arcadian Academy, was *Palle! Palle!* [Meaning "ball" in reference to the red balls that appeared on their coat of arms. —*Trans.*]

24. [Lady Knowledge. —*Trans.*]

25. See also the Celtic cromlech of Rennes-les-Bains.

26. [*Poulain.* —*Trans.*]

27. ["Colt." —*Trans.*]

that this white queen is none other than the white goddess who is also called Hel, the Misty One. The fact remains that the king, according to legend, imprisoned Poulain in a part of Gisors castle that since that time has been known as the Prisoner's Tower. Charles Nodier took a close interest in this tower, notable given that he was a great connoisseur of cryptography and Macaronic languages,[28] a great admirer of Rabelais and the *Hypnerotomachia Poliphilia,* and a friend of Nerval and Hetzel. The Prisoner's Tower has numerous sculptures and graffiti, many of which are deeply carved. As their analysis here would lead us too far afield, we can limit ourselves to one detail. The prisoner (a sculpture of whom, now in the Saint Gervais-Saint Protais Church of Gisors[29] and wearing the same mysterious smile as Leonardo da Vinci's Mona Lisa) left behind, among other things, this strange piece of graffiti reported by Gérard de Sède:[30] "O Mater Dei Memento Meo Poulain."

This is how the lovers of Wisdom addressed the Lady, Demeter, and signed Poulain in honor of Polia. The set of myths connected to Demeter can be compared to the ogre stories and the Chronos-Saturn tales. In *The White Goddess,* Robert Graves says:

> That the Mare-Demeter devoured children, like the Sow-Demeter, is proved by the myth of Leucippe (White Mare) the Orchomenan, who, with her two sisters, ran wild and devoured her son, Hippasus (foal); and by the myth, recorded by Pausanias, that when Rhea gave birth to Poseidon, she offered her lover Cronos a foal to eat instead of the child, whom she gave secretly into the charge of the shepherds of Arcadian Arne.

It should be noted in ending this examination of the Polia-Pole-

---

28. [Referring to texts in which lines in Latin alternate with those written in the author's native tongue. —*Trans.*]

29. These are twin saints dear to the Templars. Could they be viewed as a fixed pulley and an idler pulley?

30. Gérard de Sède, *Les Templiers sont parmi nous* [The Templars Are Among Us] (Paris: Julliard, 1962).

Poulain-Templar relationship that it is illustrated not only in Gisors but in a good many other places as well. For example, as Paul de Saint-Hilaire points out in *La Belgique Mysterieuse* [Mysterious Belgium] that in the village of Casteau, the sign of the post inn (which was a meeting place for Masonic officials) included an anomaly which allowed him to discover evidence of an encrypted text—*aastor* and *pollya*—in which can be found both Castor and Pollux, the twins dear to the Templars . . . and Polia, for which, as we saw earlier, the Order of the Temple and its successors held the key. And this is but one sign of many that appear in the same region.[31] At Holy Cross Church in Liège (dated from the twelfth to the fifteenth century), Saint-Hilaire also discovered a mausoleum whose inscription had been coded after *The Strife of Love in Poliphilus's Dream* by Francesco Colonna.[32] He shows that this book served as a breviary for a secret society that met in Liège. The black stone mausoleum was constructed according to the designs and measurements provided by Francesco Colonna on pages eleven and thirteen of the 1553 edition of *The Strife*. Using the same procedure employed by Colonna, the first letters of an inscription, the adepts were able to emphasize the word *rose* placed immediately below a cross. Here we find merging *The Strife of Love in Poliphilus's Dream* and the Rosicrucian Order.

Thus the *Hynerotomachia Poliphilia* truly was a breviary. It also served as a model for the construction of numerous buildings and all the initiatory gardens of the Renaissance, such as the Bomarzo gardens. "A mystery makes its presence known on the threshold of certain gardens," says Emanuela Kretzulesco-Quaranta, "symbols stop the stroller and enlist him to capture a silent message in the gestures of the statues." One of the most famous of these gardens is that of the château of Versailles. Louis XIV knew the *Hynerotomachia Poliphilia* and Mazarin owned

---

31. In Hex, the castle of the bishop prince of Velbruck is decorated with paneling with symbolic designs and steer skulls inspired by *The Strife of Love in Poliphilus's Dream*.
32. Paul de Saint-Hilaire, *Liège et Meuse mystérieux* [Mysterious Liege and Meuse] (Belgium: Ed. Rossel).

not only the French versions published by Jacques Krever in 1546 and later, but also the two printings of the Venetian edition. Mazarin had been raised in the home of the Colonna and during his youth had fought under the command of Palestrina. In the park at Versailles we can find the principle elements of the *Hynerotomachia Poliphilia*.[33] Madame de Scudéry, who visited Versailles in 1699, wrote an account of her visit and added to this a novel entitled *Célanire*. The engraving of the frontispiece, signed P. Lalande, is described thus:

> One sees there a large winged genie sitting on the edge of the base of a double column; with its index finger pressed against its lips it forms the classic Harpocratic gesture, that of silence to be observed. The other index finger is pointing at his bared left knee, which is the rallying sign of the Pythagorians. A group of children and winged spirits press up behind it. One of them points at the sky with his left hand while in his right hand he holds a lit torch turned toward the ground. We know that the upside-down torch signifies death. This symbol should thus be read as: "After death, heaven." Another winged child is making the gesture of prayer and a third, a little to the back, is shaking a tambourine with an air of joyous abandon. The rebus therefore offers the following translation: "The adept of Pythagoras will obtain, through his prayers, heavenly joy after death." In the background of the picture there can be seen the château of Versailles, still limited to its central structure and lacking a roof, as it was at the time of the book's publication.[34]

---

33. It should be pointed out that Louis XVI took a close interest in Rennes-le-Château. Colbert, who owned the original manuscript of Nostradamus's interpretations of the hieroglyphs of Orus Apollo, ordered archaeological digs in the Blanchefort mine next to Rennes-les-Bains, on the advice of Marquis de Créqui. What was he looking for? Why did Louis XVI and Colbert imprison Fouquet, whose relationship with Poussin was rather odd? Why did Colbert invite Swedes to seek gold in the Rennes-les-Bains region in 1678?

34. Emanuela Kretzulesco-Quaranta, *Les jardins du songe* [The Gardens of Dream] (Paris: Les Belle Lettres, 1986).

P.S.

We have seen that a connection exists between the *Hynerotomachia Poliphilia* and the Rosicrucian Order. The fundamental texts of the Rosicrucians appearing in 1616 bear a vignette depicting a serpent twined around an anchor, a drawing that is quite close to the dolphin depicted in *The Strife of Love in Poliphilus's Dream*. In addition, there are almost identical passages in *The Chemical Wedding of Christian Rosenkreutz* and the *Hynerotomachia Poliphilia*. In *The Bible of the Rosicrucians*, Bernard Gorceix tells us:

> The writings attributed to the Swabian Johann Valentin Andreas (1586–1654) are a valuable link of this chain that joins Francesco Colonna's *Hynerotomachia Poliphilia* of 1499, *The Fifth Book* of Rabelais in 1654, and *The Voyage des Princes Fortunés* by Béroalde de Verville in 1610. Through their literary beauty and their spiritual richness, they demonstrate an interest that is not merely scientific in a thorough understanding of a history of occultism.

Grasset d'Orcet informs us that the name Saint-Gilpins, which he associates with the Angelic Society, is, just like the term Goliard, synonymous with the Rosicrucian Order. Furthermore, he connects, as we have done here, the names Wood Splitter and Forester to this same Goliard. He mentions in passing that he believes the institution of the Rosicrucians goes back to Godefroy de Bouillon. It so happens that the secret society that claimed the Templars emerged from their order also claims Godefroy de Bouillon as its founder. This society attracted attention when it found itself mixed up in the affairs at Gisors and Rennes-le-Château. This Priory of Sion, claiming a connection to Solomon, was customarily recognized by the mark of its intials: P.S.[35] The P.S., however, appears in Rennes with a drawing indicating it should

---

35. [Prieuré de Sion. —*Trans.*]

be turned around. P.S. then becomes S.P., and could well be the key to reading the mysteries of Rennes—its grimoire: the *Songe de Poliphile* [The Dream of Poliphilus]. This would seem to be confirmed by Father Boudet's system. Researchers know that the name Lenoncourt is connected to the documents touching on the Rennes affair, and it so happens that a French translation of the *Songe de Poliphile* completed in 1554 and reprinted in 1561 was specifically accompanied by a "Dedicatory Epistle" to Henri de Lenoncourt, who was the true translator of the work. The oldest of the emblazoned cast-iron hearth plates in the Lenoncourt castle in Lorraine bears the Hapsburg coat of arms, for the House of Lenoncourt was presented as a cadet branch of the house of Lorraine.

THE MARK OF THE ANGELS AND THE SECRETS OF ALEXANDRE DUMAS

Given the relation between *The Strife of Love in Poliphilus's Dream,* the Angelic Society, the Rosicrucians, and Rennes-le-Château, it would be quite surprising to find no traces of the Angelic Society among the authors published by Hetzel. Nerval, first of all, devoted a major part of his work to the encrypted secrets of this society,[36] declaring in *Angelique* that the blazon is the key to the history of France. It was also his plan to stage with Hippolyte Lucas a musical play entitled *Francesco Colonna* to the music of Mozart's *The Magic Flute.* In addition, according to Serge Hutin, Nerval belonged to the same lodge of which Nadar, friend to Jules Verne, was the elder. This is the legendary Nerval who, when talking too much during his periods of madness, was treated by the discreet (and initiated) Doctor Blanche, to whom Jules Verne turned for advice concerning his son Michel.

We should also note Nerval's Saturnian obsession with the clock, which Jules Verne also incorporated into *Master Zacharias* and *Around the World in Eighty Days* and which we find in Gaston Leroux's *Queen*

---

36. Refer to Jean Richer, *Nerval, experience et creation.* [Nerval, Experience and Creation] (Paris: Hachette, 1963).

of the Sabbath. Indeed, Master Zacharius is a veritable personification of Saturn-Satan. We know of an odd letter written by Gérard de Nerval to Hetzel:

> My dear Hetzel,
>
> Houssaye[37] has asked me to ask you if you could go see him tomorrow; he will be home all day. It is very important. He has seen Cavé—you know about what—you know why.
>
> We should both be extremely reserved—as Don César de Bazan says.
>
> > Adieu then.
> > Your friend,
> > Gérard

This strange letter could quite possibly refer to the activities of the Angelic Society, especially if we examine the "A" in Adieu, which is adorned with a fairly strange kabbalistic zigzag.

Let us now turn again to George Sand. She referred to "Angels" almost everywhere—in *Spiridion,* first and foremost, with the novice Angel and the first name she chose for Hebronius: Pierre d'Engelwald.[38] In *Consuelo* the daughter of Corilla and Anzoleeto is named Angel, and in some odd passages in *The Countess of Rudolstadt,* Sand links the angel and the bird: the nightingale.[39] Interestingly, the *Hynerotomachio Poliphilia* ends with a mention of the nightingale's song.

Next we turn to Dumas. He often met with Eliphas Levi and was a friend of Papus and he played an important role in the life of both Gérard de Nerval and Jules Verne, who met Dumas through Chevalier d'Arpentigny, a well-known palm reader of the time who Verne had met at the salon of Madame Barrère. To borrow the term of Madame Allotte de

---

37. He was a friend of both Gérard de Nerval and Jules Verne.
38. [Peter Angelfield. —*Trans.*]
39. This can be compared to the myth of Philomeles and the persecutions affecting the Cathar Church. See also George Sand's *Jeanne.*

la Füye, Verne soon became one of Dumas's familiars. "He ate the flaming omelets and divine mayonnaises cooked up by Dumas with his own hands for the young men starving for glory and debilitated by the triturations of the lowest-order taverns." It was Dumas who gave Verne his chance by allowing him to stage a play written in his youth: *Les pailles rompues* [The Broken Straws]. It was also Dumas who introduced him to Hetzel.

It is not surprising to learn that Alexandre Dumas wrote a novel in 1839 that is rarely if ever mentioned. The title *Captain Pamphile* includes the syllable *pam,* which is similar to *pan.* Pamphile, therefore, is none other than Poliphilus. It is a strange novel, which combines the tribulations of the favorite animals of Dumas's Parisian painter friends with the exotic tribulations of the Marseilles adventurer Captain Pamphile. In it there are also two apes named James 1 and James 2 (a reference to the Stuarts) and one of Captain Pamphile's lieutenants is named Policar (Policar = Polia + *CR* = Polia Rosicrucian).[40]

A NIGHTINGALE IN THE FOG, OR THE SECRETS OF *AROUND THE WORLD IN EIGHTY DAYS*

As you may have guessed, Jules Verne was a man who could not help but write his own version of *The Strife of Love in Poliphilus's Dream,* especially as an admirer of Rabelais,[41] Shakespeare, and Leonardo and a friend of Dumas. We find a few echoes of *Poliphilus's Dream* in *The*

---

40. In addition there is a shepherdess carrying roses, the flag of a vessel bearing a green dragon, a parrot that—like Captain Pamphile—speaks only the Oc language of the troubadours, allusions to Virgil and Arcadia, a forest crossing incontestably inspired by the *Hypnerotomachia Poliphilia,* and other related details.

41. He even wrote a "quarter hour of Rabelais." This author appears in Captain Nemo's library. ["A quarter hour of Rabelais" means to undergo a painful moment that cannot be avoided (often this refers to the pain that comes with the bill for a meal). It is allegedly based on a ruse that Rabelais employed to avoid paying an innkeeper in Lyon. He left two packages in his room labeled poison for the king and poison for the queen. When the innkeeper discovered them, he called the authorities, who sent Rabelais to Paris to face royal justice. There his friend, King François I, laughed at the joke played by his friend and released him. —*Trans.*]

Castle of the Carpathians. In this novel, in addition to the distinctive journey through the forest and its Poliphilus-like itinerary, it is primarily La Stilla who shows us what direction to take. She plays a role similar to that of Angelica in Arconati's *Orlando.* In addition, she dies while singing the great aria *Innamorata, mio cuore tremante, voglio morire.*

Professor Mario Turiello wrote in number 7 of the *Bulletin de la Société Jules Verne* that, "because he knew even the most minor composers of his homeland, there had been no need for him to do any research, to know that these two names Arconati and Orland were pure inventions of Jules Verne—useless and inexplicable ones." But it seems there is nothing inexplicable in Jules Verne's work—we need only to know to look and have a little luck. In this way, we can quickly discover that Arconati, while not a muscian, was a count who, in 1636, donated to Ambrosien the Leonardo da Vinci manuscripts that have been housed at the Institute of France since the time of Napoleon. It so happens that Leonardo, a grand master of cryptography and esoteric representation,[42] belonged to the Angelic Society. What Professor Turiello should have noted was the relation that exists between this Orlando and Ariosto's *Orlando Furioso.*[43] Ariosto has also been linked to the Angelic Society, and in *Orlando Furioso* "we see at the side of Prester John a queen . . . [Prester John is the king of a mythical Christian kingdom in Africa, the queen at his side is the queen of Cathais named Angelique] (who Jean d'Armana claimed was in fact a queen of the Cathars). Subject to persecution, she could escape her enemies only by placing in her mouth a magic ring that made her invisible. (We are reminded of how La Stilla herself became invisible.) This is clearly the secret language of a persecuted church that was an offshoot of the Cathars. We might also see an Orlando Furioso in Franz de Telek, who goes mad.

In a significant passage in *Journey to the Center of the Earth,* Jules Verne describes Professor Lidenbrock: "He was an egotistical scientist, a *well*[44] of science whose *pulley* grates when anyone tries to pull something

---

42. See the book Marcel Brion wrote on Leonardo da Vinci, published by Albin Michel.
43. Michel Serres, on the other hand, recognized it perfectly.
44. [*Puits. —Trans.*]

out of it. In other words, he was a greedy individual." If Lidenbrock knew the law of love leading to Polia, his pulley certainly would not have grated. In the same novel, Verne mentions the founding of a literary society in 1818, which might be a covert indication of the reactualization of the Angelic Society.

But the brightest jewel of Verne's heroes in this area is the one we meet in *Around the World in Eighty Days*: Phileas Fogg. His name is his veritable signature: In Greek, *eas* means "overall" (equivalent, therefore, to *pan* or *poly*), which links Phileas to Poliphilus. Fogg relates to the English word *fog*, which is the very name adopted by the Angelic Society at certain times. In the novel Phileas Fogg wins his lady, Aouda, whom he eventually marries with the help of his servant Passepartout. This servant has a simple soul's wholehearted devotion to his master [45] and was preceded in his post by a man named Forester, which brings to minds the wood splitters. [46] Now let's reflect for a minute on the meaning of Passepartout. [47] This is a tool that replaces all keys and can open any lock, equally importantly, its slang name is a *rossignol*. [48]

During Fogg's race around the world, he is followed like a shadow by Inspector Fix, who would arrest our heroes "in the name of the queen." The idler pulley clearly has its fixed pulley here! Fogg goes in the opposite direction of the sun's course, but given by Verne the attributes of a planetary body, he is a kind of black sun, which gives him yet another connection to Saturn. In addition, the engraving of him that illustrates the book is quite revealing: His feet are square, his right hand is placed over his heart, and his left hand is propping up his right. Nearby there is a fabric whose subtle arrangement of folds delineates a scythe. This rebus is not the only one in the book that contains a great deal of wordplay. It should be noted that in the course of the story Phileas Fogg must fight the Thuggees, followers of Kali, who represents the black, voracious, and

---

45. ["The faith of the coal burner is the literal translation. See chapter 7, note 80 for further explanation. —*Trans.*]

46. [*Fendeurs.* —*Trans.*]

47. ["Skeleton key." —*Trans.*]

48. ["Nightingale." —*Trans.*]

bloody aspect of the Hindu doctrine—the vampiric aspect, which the Rosicrucian should fight or, even better, transcend. Transcendence clearly describes what occurs when the apparent corpse springs from the funeral pyre with the anima (Aouda) in his arms. (See figure 12, p. 112d.)

There can be no doubt that Jules Verne belonged to the society called the Fog. He was even kind enough in this book to specify the connections this society had to the Rosicrucian Order, for what could this noble traveler named Phileas Fogg be if not a Rosicrucian? Fogg has not aged—he resembles "a serene Byron who has lived one thousand years without aging." No one knew his past or fortune:

> Had he traveled? It was likely, for no one seemed to own a better map of the world, figuratively speaking. There was no spot so remote that he did not appear to be intimately acquainted with it. With a few clear words, he often corrected the thousand conjectures advanced by members of the club as to lost and unheard-of travelers . . . seeming as if gifted with a sort of second sight, so often did events justify his predictions. He must have traveled everywhere, at least in the spirit.
>
> Was Phileas Fogg rich? Incontestably. But those who knew him best could not imagine how he had made his fortune. . . . In any case, he was not lavish, nor, on the contrary, avaricious; for whenever he knew that money was needed for a noble, useful, or benevolent purpose, he supplied it quietly and sometimes anonymously.

Fogg belonged to the Reform Club, whose initials R.C. indicated the reformational Rosicrucians. This Reform Club stood in Pall Mall, another reminder of Poliphilius and *The Strife of Love in Poliphilus's Dream*. When one enters the club's "entrance hall with its mosaic tiled floor, it leads into a circular whose blue-windowed dome is supported by twenty Ionic columns of red porphyry." This circle is clearly the same as that of the Rosicrucian Order, alias The Fog, and Poliphilus, alias Phileas Fogg, is clearly a master because the gas is burning like an eternal lamp and he is traveling while trying to do good. For example, he gives his gambling winnings to an old woman, even thanking her for the pleasure of her acquaintance. In addition, Jules Verne uses the very motto of the Rosicrucians that can be found on the faked tombs of Rennes-les-Bains ("He has passed through while doing good") when he states that the phrase that should guide every reasonable man is "*Transire benefaciendo.*"

IN THE SHADOW OF THE ILLUMINATI

The Angelic Society or The Fog appears as the crossroads where the Freemason writers following the Rosicrucian doctrine found themselves during the nineteenth century. Now it is well-known that the Illuminati took on as one of their goals, on the recommendation of Adam Weishaupt himself, infiltrating literary societies. When we see Jules Verne defending certain anarchic ideals and appearing on the left slate for election to the Amiens Municipal Council, and when we see George Sand vigorously defending the same ideals, we may ask if they are defending the ideas of the secret society to which they no doubt belonged.[49] Both these authors revolved around the same figure: Hetzel—and this is no coincidence. Some critics have wondered if Verne was not simply an executant of Hetzel's desires when the author wrote his "extraordinary voyages."

We do know that Hetzel sometimes oriented the political aspect of Verne's novels, even restraining his enthusiasm in some cases. Furthermore, following Hetzel's death in 1886, Verne gives an impression of having greater freedom, and this emerges in his style. We should not forget that Hetzel was a politician: He was leader of Cavignac's cabinet, chief of the cabinet of the Marine Ministry, then of Foreign Affairs. His last act in this position was to deliver a letter of recommendation to Nerval, who was leaving for Germany. When Napoleon III assumed power, he lost these posts. He fought like a fanatic for Republican ideas,

---

49. We should keep in mind that the theories of the Illuminati have served in different fashion, both the extreme right and the left, a topic we will revisit. With all due respect to narrow-minded classifiers, it can be said that Illuminism simultaneously inspired Marx, Lenin, and the founders of Nazism.

but was forced to emigrate to Belgium, from where he would not return until the amnesty of 1859. In August 1848 he failed to hire Nadar as a secret agent but eventually retained his services as a caricaturist. In any case, it was according to a well-determined political philosophy that he founded, with the notorious Freemason Jean Macé, the *Magazine d'Education et de Récréation.*

THE MYSTERY IN FULL LIGHT

Before this chapter closes, we must explore another author who belonged to the Angelic Society and took an interest in the Rennes affair: Maurice Barrès. In *La colline inspirée* [The Mystic Hill], the author portrays figures who actually existed: the three Baillard brothers and the mage Vintras, whose attempt to launch a reform of Christianity and rituals more directly inspired by the blood mysteries received financial assistance from the Hapsburg family. In the book, a mysterious ceremony takes place on the mystic hill of Sion-Vaudémont, which is intended to hasten the coming of the Great Monarch.

Setting aside Vintras, who proclaimed that humanity would be saved by the angels, we must dive into Barrès's posthumous work, *Le mystère en plein lumière* [The Mystery in Full Light], with its evocative title and luminous content, which is an anthology of several essays. In one of these studies, "The Testament of Eugene Delacroix," Barrès focuses particularly on the "angelic aspect of his work."[50] He writes:

> For the last twenty years hardly a month has gone by when I have not visited the Chapel of the Angels in Saint Sulpice to see Eugene Delacroix's famous fresco *Jacob Westling with the Angel.* I go there to recharge my forces, tone, and nostalgia. But what force, what nostalgia? And I always wonder, spoiling my pleasure a little, just what is it I find so pleasing in this painting. Is it a music, a solitude, a counsel,

---

50. In *Under the Sign of the Spirit*, he says: "It is the battle with the Angel, from which one can only emerge defeated, but by a defeat that offers its own laurel crown."

a rule of life? Where leads this initiation I find there and this kind of novelesque and virile introduction to the life of superior men? The great artist painted here one of his last works, his testament.

And Barrès mentions the angels, "those great mysterious beings who connect heaven to the earth." In this study, he provides valuable information about Delacroix, writing: "The highest grandeur is overcoming the angel and wresting away his secret. The angel wishes to open the door of the invisible to us; that is his mission. But he will not open it without a fight; he will not open it to the indolent, the lukewarm, but only to those who, in order to carve a path, are not scared to pounce on him."

Other essays are included in this collection.[51] The most interesting in the context that interests us here is no doubt "Autumn in Charmes with Claude Gellée." Describing this painter, who was also known as Le Lorrain,[52] Barrès writes: "Like the most beautiful autumn days in Lorraine, these beautiful destinies born in the *fog* and are surely recognizeable only in the middle of the day, when the noon bells ring over the prairies. . . . Swedenborg was right when he wrote: 'The older the *angels* are, the more beautiful they are.'" Still talking about Gellée, Barrès writes: "One clearly feels he was not born in one fell swoop, that *he was prepared.*[53] If we wish to know Gellée, we should refer to Sandrart's drawing in which he is presented in the most worthy company of his friend *Poussin.*" As if Claude Lorrain was incomprehensible without Poussin! And Barrés goes on to say: "What philosophy is he expressing? I think that of the *nightingale.*"

Regarding Poussin, Barrès tells us: "Poussin completely intellectual.

---

51. The "Letter to Gyp on Spring in Mirabeau" will particularly interest the fans of Frédéric Mistral and the quest for the Star, so dear to Nerval. With respect to the latter, the reader would be wise to examine another posthumous book by Barrès: *N'importe où hors du monde* [No matter where outside the world].

52. [Claude Lorrain. —*Trans.*]

53. One of Claude Gellée's patrons was a prince of Colonna, for whom he produced a landscape with Psyche and the palace of love and several other paintings.

The part of animality has been removed. Therein lies his nobility. . . . How was it possible for Gellée, who was never an educated spirit, to elevate himself to this point? He was *supported, I believe, by an admirable milieu, by a tradition; he knew and understood a certain number of great men. . . .* Claude never gropes in the darkness." Shouldn't all this encourage the belief that Barrès was describing Nicholas Poussin, Delacroix,[54] and Claude Lorrain in this way to hint at their role as painters for the Angelic Society and the bearers of its messages?

If there are any lingering doubts as to these connections, we can simply refer to the following passages by Barrès: "We must always contrive some corner in our work for the tombstone with the famous inscription *Et in arcadia ego.* A genius yells to us from the depths of his tomb, an artist whose talent we have inherited: I, too, have lived in Arcadia, in the bewitching land of the imagination. This splendid reminder inspires reverie. We are all in agreement, are we not, that he[55] painted the figures in his painting quite clumsily if not poorly? I like this, for it is a sign of his amiable purity of heart. He is nothing if the angels are not holding his hand, if he is not in the celestial society, if he strays from what enchants him, supports him, and uplifts him. He knows his poem and outside of that knows nothing."

Here then, as in Rennes-le-Château, Poussin's tombstone marked *Et in Arcadia ego* signals the presence of the Angelic Society,[56] this "celestial society" without which painters such as Poussin and Lorrain would be nothing, this society which, through its artists and writers, surrenders in the language of the birds the secrets of Poliphilus. There can be no

---

54. Delacroix revered Poussin, "a unique painter," and devoted an essay to him. On September 6, 1854, he wrote in his journal: "I confess my predilection to the silent arts, for those mute things that Poussin claims as his profession." He also greatly liked Eustache Lesuer, the painter charged by Richelieu with executing eight subjects taken from *The Strife of Love in Pholiphilus's Dream.* In 1862, Delacroix confided to his journal: "Lesueur, his character, his angelic naiveté."

55. Claude Gellée.

56. In a letter to Gustave Flaubert dated December 17, 1866, George Sand gives a sign of her membership to the Angelic Society by writing: "In any case, today all I am good for is writing my epitaph! You know, *Et in Arcadia ego.*"

doubt that Barrès is returning to the task when he says: "He gathered the confidences of the angels. Why did the angels approach this little shepherd? It was because of his grace and his privilege. He had the inner fire to which celestial beings hasten. And it was their visits that induced his nostalgia. . . . He made a dream of the higher life and communicated it to us. . . . These are my sources; those are his. We have drunk from the same springs." It could not be put any more plainly.

In another posthumous book, *Les Maîtres,* Barrès writes:

> To clearly grasp this blend of technical richness and freshness of feeling that Italy has combined in its painting and loved to deploy in its literary works, let's take Colonna's *Hypnerotomachia Poliphilia.* . . . Had this *Strife of Love in Pholiphilus's Dream* truly exhausted its effectiveness? It is an exceedingly tedious work, that's understood, but is an extraordinary display of the plastic and erotic imagination and of licentious decorative power, which was translated several times into French, lastly by the amateur scholar Claudius Popelin.

In the same article devoted to Dante he continued: "For me, I had only one idea in writing this little speech, reminding the fans of Fog that a beautiful work must have transparency and limpidity at the same time that it contains mysteries."

We have closed the circle: Rennes, Poussin, Delacroix, the Angelic Society, Barrès, Dumas, George Sand, and Jules Verne. Everything holds together; there are no coincidences here. Each author has hinted in his own way of his membership in the Angelic Society, the celestial society, and Jules Verne has not failed to say it in veiled words in *Around the World in Eighty Days.* This is the mysterious society to which he belonged, the one connected to Freemasonry and the Rosicrucian Order; this is the secret society that stands behind the mystery of Rennes-le-Château.

NIGHT AND FOG

If Jules Verne was a link in an initiatory chain that extended beyond him in time, we should be able to find avatars of this society closer to our own time, people who preserved ties with the teaching found in Verne's work. Necessarily, we should find a secret society that is extending this tradition. It so happens, that by pursuing the Rosicrucian-Golden Dawn chain, we cannot help but arrive at the mysterious Thule Society that was at the origins of Nazism. I want to say at the outset that any direct Verne-Nazi connection has no basis whatsoever. Yet we can show how Jules Verne fits into the line of descent that leads to the Thule Society.

RUDOLF VON SEBOTTENDORF
FROM THE ROSICRUCIAN ORDER TO
THE THULE SOCIETY

The Thule Society emerges at the origin of The Order of the Germans founded in 1918. One of its instigators, Rudolf Von Sebottendorf, was entrusted in December 1917 with the leadership of the Bavarian province of the order that, under his impetus, took on the name of Thule Society.

It is interesting to examine the personality of the founder of the Thule Gesellschaft who declared in his work *Bevor Hitler Kam* [Before

Hitler Came] (Munich: 1933), without ever being belied, that he "had sowed what the Führer had made to grow." We cannot fail to think of the declaration of Aleister Crowley, Golden Dawn member: "Before Hitler was, I am."

A Knight of the Imperial Order of Constantine, Rudolf Von Sebottendorf's real name was Rudolf Glauer. He was born in Hoyerswerda in Saxony on November 9, 1875, and spent some time as a gold hunter. He resided in Turkey, in the region of Bursa, starting in 1900. In 1911 he obtained Turkish citizenship and was adopted by the Baron von Sebottendorf. Taken under the wing of a Jewish merchant named Termudi, he was elevated to the mastership of the Rosenkranz Order of the Order of the Rosary. Seriously wounded during the Balkan War, he returned to Breslau in 1913. There he financed the research of an engineer, Friedrich Göbel, who was fine-tuning assault tanks. In 1933, he returned to Turkey, where he exercised the duties of Mexican Honorary Consul. From 1929 to 1931, he visited Mexico and America, negotiating concessions for Turkey. Since 1900, Rudolf Von Sebottendorf diligently frequented Turkish secret societies. In 1911, within the borders of Persia, he was even welcomed among the Druse initiates—the same Druses who gave Christian Rosenkreutz, eponymous hero of the Rosicrucian Order, his clearest knowledge; the same Druses to whom Angelic Society member Gérard de Nerval went in search of secret teachings; and the same Druses who claimed to hold their knowledge from the king of the world. Jean Mabire discovered a novel-like autobiography by Sebottendorf which the baron, who had been initiated by the Druses, entitled *Der Talisman der Rosenkreuzers* [The Testament of the Rosicrucians]. It is not surprising that Sebottendorf gave the groups gravitating around Thule the name *rings* (circles).

The Thule Society gave life to National Socialism and propelled Hitler onto the social stage. At his death in 1923, the Thule Society member Dietrich Eckart told his friends, "Follow Hitler! He will dance, but it is I who wrote the music! I have initiated him into the secret doctrine. I have opened his centers to the vision and have given him the means to communicate with the power. Do not weep for me; I will have influenced history more than any other German." Be that as it may, the Thule Gesellschaft was the Munich center that prepared the advent of National Socialism. Alfred Rosenberg, one of Nazism's principal theoreticians, said in this regard: "The Thule Society? But everything started from there! The secret teaching that we were able to draw from it has served us better than any number of SA and SS divisions. The men who founded this association were true magicians! Their names were Karl Haushofer, Rudolf Von Sebottendorf, and especially Dietrich Eckart!" This last was nicknamed the Pole Star by Hitler, who called him "one of the best" in *Mein Kampf.*

We know furthermore that the Thule Gesellschaft maintained relations with the Golden Dawn—not only with Crowley and his initiatory center Thelema, but also with the whole society. It is interesting to note in this regard that the Gestapo, at war against secret societies, never carried out any searches of the Templum of the Golden Dawn in the very heart of Berlin.

THE GOLDEN CHALICE IN THE FOG

The name Sebottendorf chose for his society, Thule, is not insignificant. Of course, it brings to mind Ultima Thule, the large Nordic mythical (and yet real) island of the Hyperboreans at the spot where an eternal battle is waged between ice and fire.[1] Fabulous Thule, mother of men, was known to the Toltecs, who evoked her as Tula, the white isle. (These same Toltecs said they came from Aztlan).[2] The name Tula means "balance" in Sanskrit, and some researchers have thought to find its origins in the precence of the Pole Star and, for quite a long time, in the sign of Libra.[3] In fact, it is fact Greek grammarians whom we should follow on this subject. According to them, Thule comes from

---

1. It is this same battle that features in Jules Verne's novel *Captain Hatteras,* with its erupting volcano on an island located precisely on the pole.
2. For more on Aztlan, see my book *Histoire Secrète du Pays Basque* [The Secret History of the Basque Country] (Paris: Ed. Albin Michel, 2000).
3. ["Balance" in French. —*Trans.*]

Tholos or Tolos: *fog.* The land beyond the mists, land of the white goddess:[4] Thule is the fog.

It is also interesting to note that Thule is linked to the Grail and to the sanctification of blood, as is suggested by Goethe's ballad of the King of Thule. Laurence Talbot was clearly correct to write:[5] "As concerns Thule, what has survived through the Germanic song is the cult of the golden cup. . . . The use of the sacred chalice was the prerogative of the Celto-Nordic peoples. . . . The king of Thule, beneath whose balcony rumbles the sea, is the replica of King Uther that Merlin mentions, having before him many beautiful gold cups."

The gold cup, sign of the race of the ark—now there is food for thought! The connection between Thule of the fog and the cup is certain and is confirmed by linguistics: the word *talle,* the former French word for *taille* or *coupe,* the *tailloir,* the cup of Thalos, well-known giant of the Argonauts.[6] We can recall the Nazi's relentless search for the Grail cup, most specifically at Montségur, which may well have been Wolfram Von Eschenbach's Montsalvat.[7] We should especially recall the Christian legend that associated the Grail cup with the blood of Christ. It was said that it is this cup that Joseph of Arimathea used to collect the blood of Christ when he suffered on the cross. Other legends associate the Grail and the color green and more specifically relate it to the emerald that fell from Lucifer's forehead, and, by the same occasion, to the green ray.

The Grail's connection to blood reminds us of vampirism. The cup-blood bond is eternal. We can then take a closer look at the blood mythology that fascinated the members of Thule. Jean Mabire writes: "The true secret of Thule is not the creation of a secret society, but the

---

4. In Brittany, a place near Locmariaquer is called Path of Thule because sometimes people see there the masters of Thule, diaphanous silhouettes with white hair who seem to float above the ground.

5. Laurence Talbot, *Les Paladins du Monde Occidental* [The Knights of the Western World] (Centre du Livre L.T. Tangiers: Éd.Marocaineset Internationales, 1965).

6. [*Taille* is "to prune," *coupe* is "to cut" or "cup," and *tailloir* is "abacus." —*Trans.*]

7. The author of *Parsifal* attributed the story he told to a certain "knight Kyot." This is none other than Guyot le Provençal, who signed his name with a swastika enscribed in a rose.

conservation of blood, which means, in the final analysis, of the spirit." It is not by chance that the dagger given to boys belonging to the Hitler Youth bore the inscription *Blut und Ehre* ("Blood and Honor"). The social headquarters of the Thule Society, chosen by Sebottendorf, is also evocative. It was located in Munich, at the Four Seasons Hotel on the Maximilianstrasse, the very same place where Jonathan Harker began his quest for vampirism in *Dracula*. In all the rooms there had been painted swastikas as well as the Thule arms that everyone wore carved on an insignia: a swastika[8] over which were crossed two stakes—the stake so dear to both Vlad the Impaler and the Turkish magic Sebottendorf knew so well. In this regard, there is a coffin in castle Kaznachorka in Hungary that contains a beautiful sleeping maiden. She has been dead for two centuries but her body remains intact. The site has a reputation because of a certain number of vampire stories that center on this maiden. It is said that for two centuries the finger of her corpse has been making a sign of self-identification that is precisely the same one used by adepts of the old Turkish magic familiar to Sebottendorf.[9]

Although the question will make some shrug their shoulders, it is legitimate to ask to what extent the Holocaust of World War II was the fruit of a vampiric cult. It is undeniable that the SS, under the influence of the Thule Society and specifically charged with researching the blood of ancestors, closely studied everything touching on immortality. This sheds light on something Martin Bormann said: "Practically speaking, there is no death; no total extinction of a man. We should posit the principle that every awakened being continues to live indefinitely in his vital manifestations. . . . This is the direction in which we should orient National Socialist philosophy." This is confirmed by Sebottendorf: "Our god is the father of battle and his rune is that of the Eagle . . . which is the symbol

---

8. The oldest swastika found in Europe goes back to the era of the polished stone, and it was discovered in Transylvania. Additionally, in 1925 a large number of Cuna Indians rebelled, killing the Panama police living in their territory, and founded an independent republic of Thule, whose flag was a swastika over an orange background with a red border.

9. See J. P. Bourre, *Dracula et les vampires* [Dracula and the Vampires] (Monaco: Ed. Du Rocher, 1913–1916).

of the Aryans. . . . The red Eagle reminds us we must pass through death in order to live again!" Vampiric techniques figure in the passage through death to renewed life. According to Renée Davis,[10] "the members of the Thule Group promised to die by their own hands if they committed a transgression that broke the pact, and to perform human sacrifices."

The cup not only relates to blood, but also it has a relation to the myths of the hollow earth. George Sand's *Laura* is definitely an extraordinary key for those who desire to penetrate these mysteries, a true nightingale. For good reason Jules Verne used this book as inspiration for *Journey to the Center of the Earth*. In fact, the culmination of the journey through the crystal brings the hero and Nasias to a very distinctive place: "It is clearly a remote island far from any visible continent and hollowed like a cup." In this cup, a very high peak transforms the entire site into a kind of gnomon.[11] The hero tells us of this peak: "It was impossible to distinguish the base, that rested in a misty circle." At its foot was the "gaping mouth of the terrestrial axis," which of course permitted access to the cavities of the hollow earth. Another noteworthy passage: "Do you not see the polar crown, the great obsidian peak and the white vitreous sea surrounding it?"[12] It is not surprising that Nazi scientists, impelled by the Thule Gesellschaft, fine-tuned several theories concerning the hollow earth and performed research in this direction.

In *The Vril*, mouthpiece of the Grand Lodge of the Vril, a neo-Nazi movement of the 1960s, we can read in an article entitled "Thule, Primordial Tradition:" "Certain sequels to the legend attest that following

---

10. Renée Davis, *La croix gamée, cette enigme* [The Mystery of the Swastika] (Paris: Presses de la Cité, 1967).

11. An obsession of the time, this gnomon also appears in *Journey to the Center of the Earth*. It is a reminder of the Celtic cromlech of Rennes-les-Bains. I should mention in this regard an esoteric group that had fraternal relations and a certain number of members in common with the Golden Dawn. After the second grade (Eagle), in which one performed the consecration of the Golden Ark, the adepts were directed toward the Golden Dawn. This group bore the name Temple of the Cromlech, and the white stone, the lamb, and Mary Magdalene played an important symbolic role in its teaching. It was composed in large part by ecclesiastics. This could really shed light on the work of Boudet and Saunière.

12. In the same novel, George Sand speaks of lisping the romance of the willow.

the destruction of the continent Thule, a migration led by one of its last kings . . . Master of Fire and the Forges, would have guided the survivors, still the keepers of archaic secrets, *toward the entrails of the earth*...This allows us to deduce the existence of a Thulian civilization, still alive today in its state of primitive perfection within our world." In the same review, we can read:

> The Greens[13] explore beneath the earth's surface. . . . They reveal the existence of subatomic particles emitted by the incandescent core of the earth, the domain of heavy fire. These particles are capable of resolving the ancient dream of the Greens: mastering time and prolonging indefinitely the life of the physical body. The discovery of an unknown complex with incandescent flora and fauna toward the current Altai Mountains would make the partisans of the right hand, the Greens, the occult arbiters of profane human history. Their leader, the Kara-Kratu, the Immortal, would soon be called Destiny, Chance. This was what gave birth to the underground empire of Khamballah. Thanks to the mastery of vril, the vrilja, those born of vril, could extend the physical life of the same body, which amounts to saying they obtained physical immortality.

WHERE THERE IS A POLE, THE GREEN-BORN WILL BE FOUND

This was the quest of the men who propelled onto the political stage Adolf Hitler, whose signature was adorned with the identification sign of the numeral 4. This entire quest was centered on the pole, which explains the name of a secret society connected to the Thule that pursued the search for the Grail in the Pyrenees: the Polars. They assisted SS member

---

13. All the important members of Nazism and those of the Thule in particular always carried a green pencil as a sign of identification. I should also emphasize the role played among them by the mysterious monk with the green gloves, a reference to Haushofer, who had developed some of his gifts in Japan in the Society of the Green Dragon.

Otto Rahn, who belonged to the Ahnenerbe, in his investigations. Jean-Michel Angebert reminds us that the swastika was first and foremost the sign of the Pole—related to the pole that Verne's hero Captain Hatteras seeks to reach through the fog, no matter what the cost, until he reaches an island-volcano where fire and ice war with each other.[14]

Verne's fascination with the pole is found not only in *The Voyages and Adventures of Captain Hatteras* (1866) but also in *Twenty Thousand Leagues under the Sea* (1869-1870) and *The Sphinx of the Ice Fields* (1897). In this last novel, Verne describes "this indecipherable fog" behind which the hero is searching for "the white giant, the giant of the pole." Marie-Hélène Huet writes about this: "Jeorling's journal is to Pym's journal as the fog is to the landscape of the pole. It hides, it conceals, it envelops with an impenetrable whiteness." To this list of novels we can also add *The Green Ray*, which, although not connected to the pole, offers an extremely interesting passage in this regard. The heroine, Miss Campbell, is described as "one of those noble daughters of Thule, with blue eyes and blonde hair." We can also underscore the interest shown by Verne in the lands near the South Pole—Patagonia and Tierra del Fuego—which was echoed by the SS.

Concerning comparisons between the work of Verne and the Thule Society, we should touch on the issue of racism and anti-Semitism in Verne's work, which we've already discussed to some extent. It is true that a good number of Verne's deliberations reveal that he was racist and especially anti-Semitic—but this in no way means that he would have approved of concentration camps.[15] He considered, though, that some races were superior to others, at least at a given moment in history. As mentioned earlier, this anti-Semitism with respect to *Hector Servadac* did prompt the high rabbi of Paris to lodge a protest.

We can find proof of Verne's opinion on this subject in many of his

---

14. The Nazi scientist Horbiger believed that the cosmos was governed by an eternal war between hot and cold, between ice and fire, between the forces of attraction and repulsion.

15. It should be noted that the plan to exterminate the Jewish race was called "Night and Fog" for a reason.

other novels. In *The Castle of the Carpathians*, in which the Jewish character is Jules Verne's idea of the "good Jew," we find the only sympathetic portrait of a Jew in his entire work. Here is one sentence that begins: "While the majority of the comitat's peasants have been devoured by usury, which will soon make the Israelite lenders the true proprieters of their land." But in speaking of the inn owner, a "good Jew," Jules Verne writes: "Thank heaven if all the Jews settled in Transylvania were as accommodating as the innkeeper of Werst! Unfortunately, this excellent Jonas is an exception." Even taking his prejudice into account, Jules Verne, smitten with freedom,[16] would undoubtedly have detested Nazism. In fact, his novel *Begum's Millions* provides an advance condemnation of it. The least we can say is that he did not arouse the sympathies of Herr Professor Schultze. The November 27, 1935 issue of the *Journal d'Alsace-Lorraine* and the November 11–12, 1935 issue of the *Journal de Strasbourg* found in the Hitlerian Press of that same year phrases that Jules Verne in 1879 had placed in the mouth of his far from likable character.

We have looked at Jules Verne's somewhat anarchic ideas, yet it seems that he always felt these principles to be unrealistic, and in practical matters he always took the side of order. In fact, we must distinguish two separate periods in his life: In the first one, when in the employ of Hetzel, Jules Verne was more or less a reflection of his employer. After Hetzel's death, Verne emancipated himself and both his opinions and his writings evolved. We will see later what the consequences of this liberation were for Verne at the end of his life.

In any case, we can note that, surprising as it may seem, Nazism, just like communism, owed a great deal to the Illuminati of Bavaria. In 1917, Lenin was financed by Germany. In 1918, the Spartacus League, which owed its name to Adam Weishaupt, master of the Bavarian Illuminati, was born in the same country, in Bavaria, just like the Thule Society that would eventually wage war against the communists. Serge Hutin notes:[17] "Behind

---

16. He wrote: "I love naught but freedom, music, and the sea."
17. Serge Hutin, *Gouvernants invisible et sociétés secrètes* [Invisible Leaders and Secret Societies] (Paris: J'ai Lu, 1971).

the Russian Revolution, one could undoubtedly perceive the activity of a very mysterious secret society, that of the Green Dragon." This mysterious Green Dragon, we know full well, was also behind Haushofer and Thule. The rise of communism in the East and Nazism in the West signified two attempts to lead the world in a predetermined direction. Their competition was allegedly meant to stimulate each of the two systems. What the people of the Thule Society perhaps did not foresee was that Hitler wished to escape these systems and govern by himself. When he achieved this, the Führer's first act was to attack communist Russia, which until then had faithfully observed the Germano-Soviet pact. At that moment it was as if Hitler had signed his own death warrant; the Thule Society abandoned him and Russia entered into a conflict that would eventually lead to the defeat of Germany. It was only then that the Western communists, mainly the French, who had until then observed a kind of benevolent neutrality, entered the Resistance, and even then, not all of them participated.[18]

All this may appear odd to the reader, for it is not exactly what official history teaches, but official history has its reasons of state that are hardly observant of the truth. In addition, the secret societies leading the world do not reason in accordance with the Manichean attitudes of common folk. To get a good grasp of this, the best comparison we can make is to a game of chess. Everyone knows that it is sometimes necessary to sacrifice important pieces in order to win the game. It is important not to note how many pawns are still standing on the board at game's end, but whether you have won. Werner Gerson writes in this regard:[19] "These secret societies are created as they are needed. They are separated by distinct bands that are opposed merely in appearance, each respectively professing the most contrary opinions of the day in order to direct separately and with full confidence all religious, economic, political, and literary parties. Yet they are connected to a common center

---

18. With respect to Hitler, we should take note of the great interest he had in the Holy Spear of Longinius that had been discovered in the Holy Land by the count of Toulouse, Raymond de Saint Gilles, and which became part of the Hapsburg treasure.

19. Werner Gerson, *Le Nazisime, secrete société* [Nazism: Secret Society] (Paris: J'ai Lu).

from which they receive a shared direction." René Guénon, meanwhile, writes: "True esotericism lies beyond the oppositions that declare themselves in the external movements that stir up the profane world, and if these movements are sometimes incited or directed invisibly by powerful initiatory organizations, it can be said that these organizations dominate them without mixing with them, in such a way as to exercise their influence equally on each of the opposing parties."[20]

The quest must be carried out beyond good and evil. Arthur Machen writes in his essay, "The Red Hand": "There are sacraments of evil as well as good about us, and we live and move to my belief in an unknown world, a place where there are caves and shadows and dwellers in twilight." If we accept these principles, we begin to see a bit more clearly in the fog and can perceive that Jules Verne was sometimes a tool in the hand of his masters, a pawn on a chessboard. The awareness of this phenomenon darkened the end of his life, and we will see that in his final moments, doubt had put down roots in him.

---

20. René Guénon, *L'Esoterisme de Dante* [The Esotericism of Dante] (Paris: Gallimard, 1958).

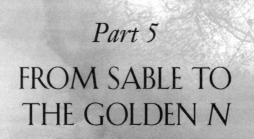

Part 5

FROM SABLE TO
THE GOLDEN *N*

THE SECRETS
OF CAPTAIN NEMO

THE BLACK ANGEL

There is one novel by Jules Verne that, in a certain way, sums up everything we've discovered to this point: *Twenty Thousand Leagues under the Sea*. It is the most famous of all his works because of the subject matter, of course, but no doubt also because every reader has a sense that Jules Verne is present in this novel.

Verne wrote to Hetzel about the theme of the novel, saying: "I have never had a more splendid subject in hand." In fact, he owed the theme to George Sand, who wrote him in 1865: "I hope you will soon lead us into the depths of the sea and that you will have your characters travel in one of those diving machines that your science and your imagination will allow you to perfect." Jules Verne one day admitted to one of his friends this debt he owed to Sand. It seems he also invested a great deal of himself in this novel, to the point of having himself portrayed in one of the engravings that illustrates the book. Professor Aronnax is Jules Verne at the age of forty-one.

We can say of the novel as a whole that it cannot be anything but initiatory, and there is good reason connections have been established between *Twenty Thousand Leagues under the Sea* and Shakespeare's

Tempest.[1] Mireille Coutrix writes: "Nemo is Caliban, no longer taking possession of trinkets of knowledge, but of knowledge itself. Diving to the depth of the sea, he finds the book cast into the waters by Prospero[2] and the booty of the black work: the omnipotent gold of the Spanish galleons that henceforth feeds the revolt of all the world's Calibans. An act of mimetism then makes Caliban a new Prospero." From there we have to take only one small step to the Angelic Society, as confirmed by the saturnine aspect of Captain Nemo. Claude Mettra writes:[3] "There is much imagery connected to smoke, fog, and mist—in other words, all that refers to a space full of what cannot be touched or seen, belongs by privilege to Saturnian characters." He also says:

> Lost in the smoke, Saturn protects himself by hiding inside and locking himself within his own secret. This is how he indicates to future alchemists who, with the subtle design of vapors, will free matter of all that is not divine. But in exploring another path, we could also think that this world of fog with which Saturn is confronted initially is the one where matter still remains indistinct and unformulated. It is an imprisoned light, and it is through a series of tests, which are also tests of matter itself, that Saturn slowly will draw matter from its immature state. Prisoner of the depths of the earth, he will also become its organizing principle. It is the strength he gains from all the spells of smoke that gives him the ability to confront the transparency of space where the celestial ether takes delight.

---

1. Mireille Coutrix, "Verne et Shakespeare, etude comparative de la Tempête, Vingt mille lieues sous les mers et l'Ile mystérieuse" [Verne and Shakespeare, Comparative Study of *The Tempest, Twenty Thousand Leagues under the Sea,* and *The Mysterious Island*] in *Cahiers de l'Herne,* no. 25.
2. In Shakespeare's work, Prospero is modeled on Prospero Colonna, which brings us back to the dream of Poliphilus.
3. Claude Mettra, *Saturne ou l'herbe des âmes* [Saturn or the Herb of Souls] (Paris: Seghers, 1981).

We might think that this speech on Saturn was written with Captain Nemo in mind, most specifically for the Nemo of *The Mysterious Island*.[4] Nemo is Saturn, and like Saturn, he belongs to the "land of the oppressed." Recognizeable in him is the anarchist ideal; he has rejected all outside authority, even divine authority, as he has assumed the right of vengeance, and it is not by chance that he unfurls the black flag on the South Pole. Nemo is a figure of melancholy and the black sun. He is the eternal rebel, the one who says no, the one who dares raise his head before God in defiance—he is the fallen angel, he is Satan-Saturn.[5] His knowledge is the knowledge of disorder, desolation, and dispersion, at least where *Twenty Thousand Leagues under the Sea* is concerned.

First and foremost, this novel is a Saturnian book connected to death and reincarnation. We should not overlook the fact that originally the empire of the dead was believed to be an undersea kingdom for which Capricorn, with its satanic horns and fish tail. is a reminder. Mireille tells us that Nemo "becomes a kind of messiah of destruction, a savior from below." A dark angel of the Apocalypse, he emerges from the bottom of the sea "on whose mane," like the (Byronic) knight Harold, he sets his hand. He shares with Harold the same passion for the storm, thunder, and rough waters. Both dream of a word that might be "a flash of lightning" to burn away all that the human being has erected.

Yes Nemo is truly Saturn, whom Plutarch says dwelled on an island lost in the mists: "Saturn himself is there, inside a large cavern with a rock that gleams as if it were pure gold." This cavern is a maritime cave like the one in *The Mysterious Island,* Captain Nemo's final refuge. Here again, we might think Claude Mettra is speaking of Nemo when he speaks of Saturn, "the banished one whose only dwelling is an ocean grotto found in no atlas."

Under these conditions, it is normal that *Twenty Thousand Leagues under the Sea,* just like *The Mysterious Island,* is connected to death and

---

4. In addition, the island is in the shape of a scorpion, a Saturnian animal.

5. Jules Verne describes Nemo as "this terrible righter of wrongs, a veritable archangel of hatred."

reincarnation. For example, we see Professor Aronnax (avatar of Verne himself) fall in the water and seem to die: "It was the final cry I could utter. My mouth filled with water. I was thrashing, pulled down into the abyss." The "moon appeared . . . that benevolent light revived my strength." It so happens that the moon was regarded by our ancestors as a psychopomp and a kind of magnetic force that drew the soul after death. It is not surprising to note a sort of alliance between Captain Nemo and this moon, an "obliging satellite" on which he can rely to the point of asking it "a favor which I wish to owe to nothing else."

But the assistance provided by the moon seems to be of short duration for Aronnax, who tells us: "My hand no longer provided any support; my mouth opened convulsively, filled with salt water; the cold penetrated my entire body. I lifted my head one last time, then sank." How could the author signify any more clearly that Professor Aronnax is entering the kingdom of the dead, Nemo's kingdom? In this morbid world, the *requin*[6] has its name pulled from the word "requiem," and his dorsal fin takes on the shape of a scythe. But the sea is also a source of life and death that in Jules Verne's novels always assumes a rebirth or even reincarnation. Nemo tells us: "The sea is merely the vehicle of a supernatural prodigious existence; it is only movement and love; it is living infinity, as one of your priests has said. The sea is the vast reservoir of nature. The world started so to speak with the sea and who knows if it might not end in the sea as well!" Here, the sea is clearly connected to the phenomena of birth and life and death. In fact, the fetus is immersed in a salty liquid inside his mother-ocean.[7] And Nemo exults: "Ah! Sir, I tell you live, live at the heart of the seas! Only there is freedom to be found! There I have no masters! There, I am free!"

After death comes rebirth. In fact, while *Twenty Thousand Leagues under the Sea* ends with the disappearance of Captain Nemo and his *Nautilus* in the abyss of the maelstrom, the rebirth is carried out at the beginning of *The Mysterious Island*. This novel begins in the same way

---

6. ["Shark." —*Trans.*]

7. [This is a homonym in French: *mère-mer*. —*Trans.*]

that *Twenty Thousand Leagues under the Sea* ends: with a whirlwind. The *Nautilus* falls from the surface of the sea to the bottom, the balloon falls from the air[8] to the surface of the earth, symbol of souls incarnating. On its own, the balloon confirms this aspect. French argot refers to a pregnant woman as "one carrying a balloon." Furthermore, the souls to be incarnated, the newly born who are the heroes of *The Mysterious Island* are connected to the balloon by an "appendage" that will be broken on landing, mirroring the cutting of the umbilical cord. The island itself is a new bond, an umbilical cord connecting them to Nemo's cavern; it is the original material cause.

A LITTLE BLOOD IN THE NIGHT

Nemo is master of the reversed world in more ways than one. He lives beneath the surface of the waves for a time, then on the surface of the earth for another period. The God of the Christians has no place in his kingdom. "There is not a bit of bread or wine" in the *Nautilus*. Even when playing the piano, Nemo strikes only the black keys—nothing could better describe him than this. But in this world where he is absolute master, the captain appears to have been granted, in some ways, the attributes of the deity and in others, he is a possessor of immortality, something that will change in *The Mysterious Island*. He seems to stand outside time. "This figure was thirty-five or fifty years old, I could not say precisely. And what a gaze! . . . as if he was looking straight through to the soul! How he could pierce those liquid sheets that are so opaque to our eyes, and how he could read the greatest depths of the seas!" Just who is he? How old is he? Is he even truly alive? "I am dead, my good professor, as dead as those friends of yours resting six feet under the ground," he tells Aronnax.

We can see here yet again a connection to the immortality rituals of the Rosicrucian Order: a life that has mastered and gone beyond death. Aronnax says: "So to that question raised some six thousand years ago

---

8. Because they are caught in a waterspout, although they are in the air, they find themselves in an aqueous environment.

by Ecclesiastes: 'Who could ever sound the depths of the human soul?' two men out of all men now have the right to give an answer. Captain Nemo and me!" We should not forget that these immortality rituals are linked to blood. In this regard we turn to Verne's description of Captain Nemo's ancestry in *The Mysterious Island:* "These rulers call themselves the sons of crocodiles[9]—in other words, they are the issue of the highest origin a human being can claim. These scaly ancestors teem on the rivers of the island and are the object of a distinctive worship. They are protected, spoiled, fawned upon, and fed. They are offered young maidens as meals, and woe to the stranger who dares lay a hand on one of these sacred lizards." The burial of Nemo's companions in the sea is also connected with blood. Their tombs are made of coral, which justifies "by its vivid colors its poetic names of blood flowers and blood foam." We might ask whether the coral crosses on these tombs might not be Rosy Crosses. We can also find allusions to Freemasonry. For example Cyrus Smith, whose name fits so well with the idea of infernal forges, attaches the two arms of the compass with an acacia thorn.

Nemo is an odd bird who owns more beautiful shells than those of Saint Sulpice, who reads Rabelais and George Sand, who can do everything and is no one. Nemo is merely an echo of Ulysses' response[10] to the Cyclops Polyphemus when the Cyclops asks him to identify himself: My name is no one. In *The Mysterious Island* Captain Nemo tells Cyrus Smith, "I have no name, sir."

Nemo's submarine, the *Nautilus,* is also of interest. A machine of this name, a kind of diving bell, already existed in Jules Verne's time, and Robert Fulton had baptized the ancestor of the submarine in 1791 with this same name. Jules Verne presents the *Nautilus* as being like a "sacred ark," but it is also the ship of the Argonauts in search of the Golden Fleece. The nautilus is also a mollusk that is quite similar to

---

9. Dracula and other vampires are sons of crocodiles or dragons.
10. There are other allusions to Homer's work: "I thought I could hear the Canadian Homer chanting the *Iliad* of the hyperborean regions," Aronnax says, speaking of Ned Land.

another mollusk known as the argonaut.[11] Mobile in a mobile element, the *Nautilus* bathes in the mother waters of creation.

NEMO THE AVENGER

Nemo, archangel of hatred, himself confirms a number of points we have touched on in this exploration, most particularly to the supposition that Jules Verne belonged to the high grades of Freemasonry and to the connections between his work and the doctrines of the Bavarian Illuminati. For example, in the ritual of the grades of Freemasonry, which we have already explored somewhat with regard to Michael Strogoff, a significant grade was Nekom.[12] It may have been pure chance, yet, in the second novel featuring Captain Nemo, *The Mysterious Island*, Jules Verne gives his hero the name Cyrus Smith. Smith, as in blacksmith, symbolically confirms the meaning of his first name, Cyrus, which is connected to the ritual of the Chevalier of the Orient or of the Sword.[13] The word Nekon, connected to the grades of vengeance, means: "I have removed him from the ranks of the living." This could certainly apply to Nemo's case. The grade instruction contains the following maxims: "All men are equal and none may be the superior to another. Sovereign powers should belong to the many; the people bestow sovereignty as they wish and take it back when they wish. Every religion presented as the work of God is an absurdity—any authority that calls itself spiritual is an injustice and an assassination attempt." It seems the very doctrines of the Illuminati of Bavaria are recognizable here.

It is George Sand to whom we turn for enlightenment again; most specifically we can look at the second volume of *Consuelo*, called *The Countess of Rudolstadt*. Toward the end of the novel, George Sand devotes a chapter to Adam Weishaupt, founder of the Bavarian Illuminati, who, as we have discovered, adopted the name Spartacus. There,

---

11. Jules Verne writes that Nemo would have done better to name his *Nautilus* the *Argonaut*.

12. This grade is linked to the color black and to death.

13. See René le Forestier, *La Franc-Maçonnerie templière et occultière* (La Table

on the paths "sandy with gold,"[14] the young Spartacus meets an old man who gives him the following counsel:

What I felt when listening to you, what you were able to pass on to me of your hope, is a great proof of the reality of your mission. So keep marching forward, taking action and working. *Heaven has made you organizer of destruction, destroying and dissolving, there is your work.* It requires faith to knock down as well as to build. Myself, I would have intentionally left the roads upon which you have launched yourself: I would have deemed them evil.[15] They were no doubt only accidentally so. If true servants of the cause feel tempted to try them still, it is because it has become practical to do so. I believed that nothing was left to be hoped for from official society and that no reformation of it could be made by staying within it. *I took a place outside of it,* and, despairing to see salvation fall upon the people because of its corruption, I have devoted the final years of my life to acting directly on the people. . . . Everything is linked, good and evil, for dashing toward the divine ideal. . . .

To this counsel, Spartacus responds:

Yes . . . I felt I had been given a mission. I have approached those who govern the earth and been struck by their stupidity, their ignorance, and their hardened hearts. Oh! How beautiful are life, Nature, and humanity! But what do they do with this life, Nature, and humanity?

The old man goes on to say:

I was right in saying that you would do naught but destroy! . . . May a secret society be formed in your voice for destroying the current shape of the great iniquity. . . . Know one thing that should

---

14. Compare this later with the features of Captain Nemo's flag.
15. See also *The Survivors of the Jonathan.*

be the rule of your soul. Nothing is lost. Your name and the shape of your works will disappear, *you will work namelessly,* like me, so that your work shall not be lost."

It seems that all of this could just as easily be referring to Captain Nemo.

FROM THE SABLE/SAND TO THE GOLDEN *N*

Nemo, the man who says No, the man of the color black and the night, the man whose hieroglyph is the letter *N*, sums up in a certain way the entire opus of Jules Verne.[16]

In his book *The White Goddess*, Robert Graves has made a valiant attempt to analyze the secret, hieroglyphic meaning of the Celtic alphabets. Among others, he studied the letter *N*. We can link this consonant with a passage that says: "Because he remains in safety in the hollow boat until the winds carry him home;" but Graves also connects it to the numeral 13, which is evocative of death. It is curious to see how this transitional letter is often used as a key to cryptograms, both by Father Boudet in *The True Celtic Language and the Cromlech of Rennes-les-Bains* and Maurice Leblanc: It is the *N* that is the key to the central rose window opening the chest of Essarès Bey in *The Golden Triangle*. According to Valère Catogan, it is the *N* the young Arsène Lupin wears embroidered on his clothing.[17] It should be noted that Nemo has more that one similarity with Lupin, just as his haven on *The Mysterious Island* exhibits attributes in common with the hollow needle. Is it Nemo or Lupin who says, "Infinitely rich, sir, and I could pay without any trouble the ten million France owes in debts"? It is Nemo who says it, but it is Lupin who pays the debts of France.

---

16. Some likely allusions to the Rennes affair can also be detected in *Twenty Thousand Leagues under the Sea.*

17. Valère Catogan, *Le secret des Rois de France ou la veritable identité d'Arsène Lupin* [The Secret of the Kings of France or the True Identity of Arsène Lupin] (Paris: Editions de Minuit, 1955).

It is the *N* that serves as hinge of the famous Sator magic square. It is the *N* that corresponds to the god Enn, whom the ancients considered the unknown god, the one who could not be depicted. Likewise, there is the Ennoë River, the vehicle of knowledge, which Leonardo da Vinci showed repeatedly in the misty backgrounds of his paintings. Yet this *N*, by its design, is also reminiscent of Aleph, the first letter of the Hebrew alphabet and sign of creation. Aleph was the distinctive symbol of the supreme council of the Kabbalistic Order founded in 1888 by Stansilas de Guaïta, which consisted of twelve members, six of whom were known and six unknown. Among the known six, several maintained close relations with Emma Calvé (Papus among them). The double *N* was also the sign appearing on the register of Mauthausen that indicated the extermination of the Jews by the Nazis in the camps. N.N. stands for Nacht und Nebel (night and fog), the name given by the SS to this operation. In this regard, we turn the floor over to H. Vidal Sephilia:[18]

> But what did this N.N. mean originally? That never seems to have been revealed. And yet what a symbol! . . . We need only consult a German dictionary to discover with stupefaction that this sigil was used in Germany long before the Hitler regime. The *Deutsche Wörterbuch* by Jakob and Wilhelm Grimm (1881) defines it as follows: *N. oder N.N., statteines Namens den man nicht weiss (nomen nescio) oder nicht nennen will (notetur nomen).* In English this means "Name N.N. used instead of a name that is not known (Latin: *nomen nescio*) or that cannot be mentioned (Latin: *notetur nomen*)." Thus the first image given by these two fateful letters still used today in Germany is that of Anonymous.

N for Nacht und Nebel, *N* for Nemo-no one. Here is a piece of historical logic that is perfectly coherent with Jules Verne's logic. Nemo is the man of the black flag, the banner of the anarchists but that is also

---

18. In *Europe*, September–October, no. 65.

struck with the silver runes of the SS.[19] His black canvas flag bears a gold N. in each quarter. Here is the quote from *Twenty Thousand Leagues under the Sea*: "Captain Nemo unfurled a black banner, bearing an N in gold quartered on its bunting." The figure of N is not so far in shape from the rune for lightning, the well-known ⚡. All that is necessary is a slight pivoting of the letter. The Verne character closest to Captain Nemo is without a doubt Robur the Conqueror, and he too owns a black flag: a black banner scattered with stars and bearing a gold sun at its center. Like Nemo, he is one of those individuals who say no and is of the world of the dark angel. Unfurling his flag at the South Pole, Nemo addresses the sun. "Goodbye Sun!" he cries. "Vanish radiant body! Go to sleep beneath this free sea and allow a night of six months to extend its shadows over my new domain."

But Nemo is not only Saturn; in a way, he is also Jules Verne, who, instead of the phrase "Neither God nor master," cried out before dying: "God and Country."[20]

Like Verne, Nemo appears besieged by doubts. Like Nerval, Verne abandoned his revolt to hope in the redemption of Christ.

---

19. The black flag also plays a role in *Famille sans Nom* [The Nameless Family]. Meanwhile, the black flag of the pirate Sacratif in *L'Archipel en Feu* [The Archipelago in Flames] bears a fiery red S. We should also make note of the classic black flag of the convict Bob Harvey in *The Mysterious Island*. In addition, Ker Karrage in *Facing the Flag* has a red canvas flag struck with a gold crescent in the corner, which predicts somewhat the flag of the U.S.S.R.

20. In the original text of *The Survivors of the Jonathan*, before Michel Verne altered it, the condemnation of communism and socialism was even more violent and even anarchism appeared insufficient. Verne ended the book by putting in the hero's mouth the name of God instead of the phrase: "Neither God nor Master!"

JULES VERNE FACING GOD

THE ATTEMPTED MURDER

So doubts assailed Jules Verne at the end of his life. Was he the victim of a deception? Did he allow himself to be deceived by a light bearer in the fog? In the first part of his career, Verne seems to have admired and loved Hetzel as if the publisher was a father, a teacher, and a guide. It was Hetzel who Verne told the illustrators to use as their model for Mathias Sandorf. As Verne wrote to Hetzel, "Mathias Sandorf, that's you."

But over the course of the year, his opinion changed, it seems, as did that of George Sand. Verne more or less turned away from Hetzel, and in 1886 he did not participate in the chorus of praises that filled a special edition of the *Magasin d'Education et de Récréation*, published on June 15 in memory of Hetzel. The publisher had given him a leg up, supported him, and led him to fame and glory. How, then, could Verne have been so ungrateful as to not hail Hetzel's memory at his death? It seems inconceivable, unless Jules Verne had serious reasons, unless he was annoyed with Hetzel and had pushed him from his heart.

Jules Verne himself admits this by writing *Begum's Millions*. It is certainly not a simple coincidence that the name of the cursed, inhuman city in which men are reduced to slavery is Stahl-Stadt, the city of Stahl, the very name used by Hetzel in signing his own writings. Additionally,

Verne indicates that this city is located in a "false Switzerland," an allusion to Hetzel's *Swiss Family Robinson*. Finally, we have the tyrant himself, Herr Schultze. Jules Verne seems thus to be accusing Hetzel of having deceived him. He, who believed himself to be defending freedom and the chivalrous spirit at all costs, had perhaps been only playing a game crafted by tyrannical systems. Had he been manipulated? What society was hiding behind Hetzel? We have seen how the doctrines that can be linked to the work of Jules Verne led to both communism and Nazism. *Begum's Millions* is a kind of foreshadowing of Nazism, of a Germany organized for production and destruction, as it was in 1940, in the service of an omnipotent tyrant and megalomaniac who surrounded himself with a black guard. This at least gives us legitimate grounds to ask if, upon realizing the kind of society under whose influence he had fallen—a society whose purposes or means he did not approve, Jules Verne had not tried to escape. And by the same token, we might ask would someone have tried to prevent him?

It is undeniable that there is a troubling evolution visible in Verne's work. As early as 1865, something had happened that affected the author. During this period, notes Marie-Hélène Huet, "Jules Verne's two characters no longer matched. It seems that to his family he remained the joyful joker, the coordinator of Chantenay get-togethers, a coiner of adolescent rhymes for whom everything should be forgiven. Several friends, to the contrary, speak of the coldness of Jules Verne, his cutting manner, and the short voice he used when meeting strangers."

Toward 1878, we can note a new development. "The work written until this time expressed a certain optimism, not unbounded, certainly, but which stored great credit in human possibilities. Around 1878 the English and Americans, who had represented the avant-garde of progress and the accomplished type of future man started appearing in the guise of despicable spoilers, vulgar merchants, pitiless speculators."

Upon the arrival of 1886, the same year in which Hetzel died, Verne seems discouraged. He even sold his yacht, the Saint-Michel, for a ridiculously low price, thereby renouncing the journeys he loved so much. Then a dramatic event took place. On March 9, 1886, Jules Verne was returning home, breathing in the damp aroma of the magnolias. Rue Charles-Dubois was deserted. As he tranquilly pulled the key from his pocket and placed it in the keyhole of the gate, a shadow sprang from a nearby nook. Jules Verne turned around and recognized his nephew, Gaston, son of his brother Paul. The young man looked haggard and was out of breath and did not seem to be in his usual state. He mumbled a few words, alluding to the yacht sold by Jules and the money it must have brought in, and urgently solicited Verne for money to go to England, as if his life depended on it.

Verne reacted in surprise, but Gaston gave him a warning: "You are being pursued. Someone wishes to kill you." Then he added, "There are people who have never forgiven you." Verne did not understand. Gaston then pointed to the trees in the park and yelled: "There they are!" Surprised, then, that Jules refrained from defending himself (but against what?), Gaston panicked, pulled a revolver from his pocket, and fired point blank at his uncle. Jules Verne raised his arm reflexively, knocking away the demented young man's hand and thus saving his own life, but a bullet struck him in his leg. Just as abruptly as he had pulled out the revolver, Gaston put it back and stood there with his arms crossed, watching his uncle, who was pressing on his wound from which blood flowed freely. The detonations had alerted the neighborhood and people rushed to the scene and overpowered the maniac, who spouted odd insults while the author was taken to the hospital.

Two days later, *Le Figaro* announced:

Jules Verne's state remains the same. Yesterday, *Le Progrès de la Somme* tells us Doctor Vernueil, assisted by Doctors Lenoël, Cortis, Froment, and Penlevé, performed an operation to attempt to remove the bullet. He noted that the projectile was lodged in the tibia. With the aid of a hammer, he was able to determine its exact position, but did not think he could extract it. He settled for widening the path taken by the bullet and inserting a tube, with the hope that the projectile would come out on its own. Jules Verne had been chloroformed for this long and painful operation that lasted no less than three fourths of an hour. Doctor Verneuil left favorably impressed with the patient's overall health. As for the author of the attempted murder, he is still undergoing treatment at the Hôtel-Dieu, while waiting for the doctors in charge of examining his mental state to conclude irresponsibility.

And then it was over, and the newspapers said not another word about it. Madame Allote de la Fûye writes: "The press is in an uproar, then abruptly shuts up." The word *abruptly* is interesting. Surprise seems to be a legitimate option, like that of Marcel Moré, who writes: "The newspapers rarely have the habit of keeping quiet if silence is not imposed upon them to avoid a scandal." Yes, but what scandal? Surely not the kind thought of by Mr. Moré, who sees homosexuals everywhere and makes pedophilia an explanation for everything.

Let's go back for a moment to Gaston. He had been a brilliant student and became an attaché to the Ministry of Foreign Affairs. After this act, he was to be declared not responsible for his actions and interned in a mental institution. But if he was crazy, there was certainly something that was driving him, an element however small—jealousy perhaps, we cannot be certain—but something which in his demented logic took on enough importance to compel him to go to his uncle's home and shoot him. His motive has never been explained. The family more or less described it as a question of money or jealousy, were contradicted, and finally never revealed the secret. As for Jules Verne, who could never walk normally again and was forced to use a cane to the end of his days, he never revealed anything either. He always held his silence and imposed it on his entourage, letting his interlocutors quickly know that it was a subject of which he did not like to speak.

It seems legitimate to ask if someone may well have armed Gaston, and if someone may have been trying to warn or eliminate Verne, who was no longer toeing the line. It is not a good idea to try to leave certain societies when you might know too much. I admit that this is only a somewhat adventurous hypothesis and that there is nothing that would allow me to confirm it.

THE BLACK SUN OF MELANCHOLY

Eight days after March 9, 1886, when Gaston attempted to take the life of Jules Verne, Hetzel died. Less than a year later, on February 15, 1887, Verne's mother died. He did not have the strength to attend the funeral. He went to Nantes, but only several weeks later, to sell the family home of Chantenay. Jules Verne seemed more and more discouraged and bitter. He had escaped a brush with death, placed his foot on the edge of the abyss, about which Madame Allotte de la Fûye wrote: "He will always have a nostalgia for abysses, infinite abysses of the air and mysterious abysses of the waters." Now disabled, his lameness made him a man of the topsy-turvy world according to a universal symbolism,[1] an initiate who has achieved his descent into hell and been resurrected like Lazarus. In retrospect, it is curious to note how deeply Verne's work is marked by death. J. P. Picot notes:[2] People die quite frequently in Verne's work, and death lurks everywhere, including in the places and the landscapes themselves." It is not only death that is omnipresent, but also its attributes, and Jean-Claude Vareille noted during a colloquia in Cerisy "that there are numerals in Verne's books that turn up repeatedly, namely 13 and its multiples."

In any case, Jules Verne's sorrow only grew, and it is hard to believe that it was only because he had become lame. In fact, he made a joke of his lameness: "Here I am, condemned to a lameness for which I console myself with thoughts of Mademoiselle de la Vallière, Tallyrand, and Lord Byron." No, his sadness definitely arose from another source. He no longer believed in the values he had defended, he had denied Hetzel in some way and it was too late for him to start over from zero. He was a prisoner of his work and his membership in the Angelic Society.

He continued to write, however, and to follow the clues given him, but without any joy. The more time passed, the more sorrowful he grew.

---

1. For more on this, see my book, *Histoire secrète du Pays Basque* [Secret History of the Pays Basques] (Paris: Albin Michel, 2000).

2. "Prelude to an exploration of death in Jules Verne," in *Bulletin de la société Jules Verne*, no. 56 (1980).

Honorine could feel her husband was dark and melancholy, desperately enamored of solitude, haunted by some incomprehensible mystery that he guarded deep within himself. Verne also explicitly wished that no interest be taken in his personal life. No doubt he deemed it preferable that his secret would never be discovered. He no longer seemed to have any hunger for life. When his brother-in-law, the ship owner Guillon,[3] built a sailboat that he christened *Jules Verne,* the author did not even travel to see its launching—he who would not have missed that for the world a few years earlier. Nor did he make the journey to attend his nephew Maxime's wedding. He explained his reasons in a letter to his brother Paul dated August 1, 1894: "I have far too many serious subjects of sorrow to mingle with the joys of the Nantaise family. All gaiety has become intolerable to me, my nature has changed profoundly and I have received blows from which I will never recover." Speaking of his brother's poems, he added: "I see that you still take delight in flowing your thought into the poetic mold. So much the better! There are only these intellectual distractions that are worth taking."

Things only grew worse. After 1897, Verne's books seem to prove his total lack of enthusiasm, as if a spring had been broken. Did he have the feeling that he had wasted his life? He had been guilty of neglecting his wife and particularly his son, Michel, and it seems quite likely that he realized this and that his late reconciliation with Michel was connected to this realization. Yet beyond this personal aspect, we might ask if he had the feeling that he had been working for the forces of evil. Like Nemo, hadn't he scorned humanity and overlooked love? Hadn't he pursued a Luciferian quest, and hadn't he contributed to the opening of one of those airlocks dear to Lovecraft, which permitted the gods of the antiworld to manifest among us? Hadn't he contributed to hastening the advent of a colossal Walpurgis Night?

This was the kind of agony that tormented him on his deathbed, whereas his tomb, strangely reminiscent of the themes of the Golden Dawn and the Thule Society, portrays him as an immortal. Was his

---

3. The husband of his youngest sister, Marie, nicknamed the Cabbage. [*Chou* is an affectionate nickname in France. —*Trans.*]

return to Catholicism a sign of his remorse? Perhaps it can be viewed as a disavowal of the doctrine and the secret society defending it. Jules Verne was always more or less a deist, and Mario Turiello, in an article devoted to faith and morality in the "extraordinary voyages," noted: "While there are few priests in the 'extraordinary voyages,' the majority of Jules Verne's heroes are religious." For example, one of his characters, Barbicane, declares: "If we die, the result of our journey will be magnificently enlarged. God himself will tell us his secret. In the next life, the soul will have no need of machines and engines to know. It will be identical with eternal wisdom." Madame Allotte de la Fûye tells us of Verne: "He remained a spiritualist and of Catholic spirituality . . . and he thought, as did Cyrus Smith, that all great deeds go up to God, because they come from Him."

Whatever the case may be, the fact remains that the ailing Verne, feeling the approach of the Grim Reaper, told his wife: "The next time, you will bring the priest with the doctor, that's all!" Madame Allotte de la Fûye tells us: "She obeyed—Jules Verne confessed happily, and even told the priest who came to see him every day: 'You've had a good effect on me, I feel regenerated.'" Perhaps this is simply a pious family story with no basis in fact, but it might be completely true. We need only recall Nerval, who also belonged to the Angelic Society, to see how the fallen angel eventually has a need to believe and hope in God.

There is another reason, perhaps, for this return to Catholicism. Grasset d'Orcet tells us in fact that the precept of the Gilpins, who belonged to the Angelic Society, commanded them to have a Christian death.

EN ROUTE TO IMMORTALITY

One of the greatest mysteries of Jules Verne's life resides in his death. We should recall that he respected the precepts of the Illuminati of Bavaria by destroying notebooks of accounts, notes, keys, and means of decrypting his work. Only his son, Michel, perhaps had the right to know part of his secret. Nevertheless, the symbols of his life followed him beyond death, pursuing him to his very tomb. I wonder how many of the people who accompanied him to his final resting place were aware of the irony of fate—or the mark of destiny—in his regard. Perhaps such awareness touched the special ambassador Flotow, delegated specifically by His Majesty William II, emperor of Germany and whose presence greatly amazed the family, for Verne was not always very kind to the Germans.

If you are in Amiens, do not fail to pay a visit to Jules Verne's tomb. After wandering about the labyrinth of the cathedral of Notre Dame and attempting to decode the Gothic riddles covered by the dirt of ages, leave this building, which has a pressing need for cleaning, and make your way to the banks of the Somme, which you will have to cross to reach the spot where Jules Verne lies. Then take a moment to think about *Clovis Dardentor* and Rennes-le-Château, and contemplate Mary Magdalene, who guards, near the sources of the Sals, in a zone that was once swampland, the treasure of the kings of France. Recall the interest Jules Verne held for this history when you start heading in the direction of the former swamp by the path of La Salle, and you will end up in the Magdalene Cemetery. Destiny sometimes winks at great men; we can note similar oddities with regard to Gérard de Nerval, another member of the Angelic Society.

Once you have arrived at Magdalene Cemetery, take a moment simply to enjoy the charm of the location. Wander among the once rich tombs that are now more or less abandoned. Meditate before these marble plaques that no longer seal tombs that have been broken open by roots overflowing with life. Follow the mossy paths that cut through this rather hilly garden of the dead, which has been planted with beeches and plane trees.

Taking a detour from one path, below the butte, you will find Jules Verne's tomb. There is a funerary monument his son, Michel, had built by the sculptor Roze, who topped it with the shadow of a cross. Jules Verne is depicted there as springing forth from his tomb. Pulling himself out of the ground and finding support on a square stone, the writer is emerging from the grave. With his shoulders he is pushing aside the fractured tombstone and, ripping away his shroud, he is gazing straight at heaven with his arm extended and his palm open in greeting. Near the ground, the folds of the shroud fall in complex curves, forming (is this merely by chance?) a strange figure: a vampire, like the one depicted among the gargoyles of the cathedral.

I cannot help but see this as proof that Michel Verne was perfectly aware that his father belonged to a secret society, for the sculptor Roze has translated into stone the mirror image of its doctrines. From the vampire to immortality by way of the greeting, everything seems to agree, as does the inscription with the double meaning, which appears only on the plaster model of the funerary monument: "Toward immortality and eternal youth."

Standing in front of this tomb, you might be inspired to read some passages from *The Will of an Eccentric* and note the words of J. P. Picot:

> And this is the true resurrection, that of the billionaire Hypperbone declared dead by science and scientists and even by all recent X-rays. But here he is rising from his munificent tomb and walking—and he who compelled his presumptive heirs to run along the squares of the noble game of Snakes and Ladders is going to make them walk, moreover, not revealing his return from the beyond and running his own game, as well, until he wins it.[4]

Everything seems mad, but remember what Jules Verne wrote in *Twenty Thousand Leagues under the Sea:* "I am the historian of apparently impossible things, things which are real and incontestable, however." This is how, even after death, Jules Verne continues to generate mystery.

ET IN ARCADIA EGO

Just what is this tomb that simultaneously evokes immortality and infernal vampiric "larva"? Perhaps it is an ark. With regard to the Ark

---

4. J. P. Picot, "Prélude à une exploration de la mort vernienne" [Prelude to an exploration of death as conceived by Verne] (*BSJV*, no. 56) [Bulletin Society Jules Verne].

of Solomon's Temple and the doctrines of the Gilpins, Grasset d'Orcet writes that it was "nothing by a coffin enclosed within a temple built in the shape of a coffin." The motto of the Gilpins, meanwhile, was "Free in the Sepulchre," suggesting precisely what is displayed by the tomb-ark of Jules Verne. Recall the *Nautilus,* which in *The Mysterious Island* serves as tomb and coffin to Captain Nemo and which Jules Verne describes as both a black mass and a "holy ark." This ark is a gate to elsewhere, toward the gods outside who were so dear to Lovecraft.

American researchers have endeavored to discover the origin of a mythical book, the *Necronomicon,* which appears so frequently in H. P. Lovecraft's work. The fruits of this investigation appear in a work entitled *Necronomicon: The Book of the Mad Arab Abdul Al-Hazred,* in which the authors have reprinted certain magical texts they believe are associated with this mythical book. One of these texts reads: "To construct the porch through which will manifest those who come from the void, you must erect stones in certain configurations. First you will place the four cardinal stones that will define the direction of the four winds that blow according to the season. Toward the north, place the stone of the great chills that will be the gate of the winter wind, and you will carve there the emblem of the bull, sign of earth."

All of this is set up like a kind of cromlech, which cannot fail to bring to mind the Celtic cromlech of Rennes-les-Bains described by Father Boudet. The text continues: "These stones will be the gates by which you will invoke those who are outside the time and space of men. Pray on these stones at night when the light of the moon grows weak, turning your face in the direction from which they will come, by uttering the words and making the gestures that will bring the Old Ones and allow them once again to walk the Earth."

This gate-arch, which is found right next to the church of Mary Magdalene in Rennes-le-Château, this passage to elsewhere, is the one that the adepts of the *Hypnerotomachia Poliphilia* often mark on tombs and monuments with a steer's head—or steer's skull—and the famous *DM* writing dear to Nostradamus:

Quand l'escriture DM trouvée
En cave antique à lampe découverte
Loy Roy et Prince Ulpian éprouvée
Pavillon Royne et Duc sous la couverte.[5]

These were the words of Nostradamus, the mysterious sage of Provence. Analyzing these verses, Eric Muraise writes: "The quatrain says that from a sigil DM found in a cave and the Royne and the Duke (*duc* in the sense of *dux*, as head of the army), judicial proof of the legitimacy of a king (law of the king demonstrated by Ulpian, who was a famous Roman jurist) will be found." This brings us back to the region of Rennes-le-Château, where the legitimacy of the Merovingian kings is at stake. But the *DM* sigil has caused many authors to ramble, undoubtedly unaware of an extraordinary little book by Nostradamus, *The Interpretation of the Heiroglyphs of Orus Apollo*. There one may read that *DM* means *Diis Manibus*,[6] "dedicated to the manes gods," and that these two letters are regarded as making tombs inviolable. Furthermore, Nostradamus is perfectly explicit and, as if echoing the *Necronomicon*, entitles one strophe "How Do They Call the Infernal Gods They Call Manes *DM*?"

In addition, in a prose text Nostradamus explicitly states:

Several occult and secret things *in the hollow of the earth,* that is so close to rivers as to be one with them, will be displayed by floods and other secret perscrutations [excavations]. And for several great secrets of the laws and other divine institutions have been long concealed and will be delivered beneath the hollow of the Earth and others will be by Sun and Moon, openly displayed and found will be what has been hidden for so long *to the great satisfaction of the Christian religion.* . . . The continual torrents, thunder, hail, tempests, and impetuous rains will, by torrents, uncover antique sepulchres and treasures." (The italics are mine.)

---

5. [See chapter 12, note 12. —*Trans.*]
6. Something one might suspect if familiar with the *Hypnerotomachia Poliphilia*.

Now we may return to Jules Verne. Perhaps his despair before dying might be better understood in the context of his participation in a work whose ultimate purpose was the rehabilitation of these final gods. We should not scoff at such a theory and should refrain from cloaking ourselves too comfortably in the mantle of reason and positivism, for people with a reputation for good sense and rationalism, such as Anatole France, have believed in the possibility of such theories.

Moreover, we might raise once again the question that certain Nazi seekers thought to have resolved: Are there buried forces with ancient beliefs that are only waiting to be awakened, similar to Dracula who was called from the depths of his tomb? A future day will come when the valet of the vampire prince regenerates his master thanks to the blood of a victim. In ancient civilizations, human sacrifices offered the gods (or phantomlike forces that were considered as such and resembled what we call larva) the blood and vital forces they needed to manifest. In our day, sects—even in France and other countries of the West—practice vampirism in the purest tradition of these ancient religions. We could also see in the Holocaust perpetuated by the Thule Society and Nazism a reactualization of these sacrifices to what are customarily known as the dark powers.

It is in these conditions that we can ask what might have been the final thoughts of the author of *The Castle in the Carpathians*, this man whose tomb portrays him as emerging from his shroud and which depicts so well the principles of mysterious secret societies. Could he, too, have declared, *Et in Arcadia Ego?*

EPILOGUE

Throughout this book, I have demonstrated evidence of Jules Verne's membership in secret societies and I have emphasized the strange overlap that exists between his work and what has come to be known as the affair of Rennes-le-Château. I have also underscored that a number of other authors took an interest in this small town in the Razès region. There is legitimate cause for surprise in the effort, through the centuries, to leave encrypted messages concerning the treasure of Rennes. Why did "those who knew" not keep the secret to themselves? Why did they not make use of it themselves?

The sole coherent answer is connected to the return of the Merovingian dynasty in the person of the Great Monarch, which, it is alleged, will take place soon. Until that occurs, the time is not ripe for a complete revelation, but the message must continue to be passed down in order to increase the fraternity of people who are preparing for this advent. Tomorrow, perhaps, the banner of the Great Monarch will rise up the mob, but will this truly be the Great Monarch? What forces will he bring with him? Will he not be opening the doors of the underground world and unleashing the powers of shadow for a gigantic Walpurgis Night? Will he possess white powers or dark powers? Will the promised return to the Golden Age be the prerogative of Saturn-Satan? Will we see the rebirth of blood cults in the form of holocausts?

Perhaps this musing is all lunacy—but we have only to think of Jules Verne's terror as he faced death. There are forces that it is better not to disturb. This quote from Enel's *Gnomology* may say it best:

Ignoramuses! We foresaw life beyond the tomb like life on earth, with the same joys and pleasures. We did not realize that life is only a trial for the soul and that the physical body is its prison. By binding the soul to its mummy, we have imprisoned it eternally.

I was one of these vain imbeciles! I was a priest and a magician. I boasted of my knowledge and numerous were the victims I similarly bound for eternity. Thus I did in my turn and remain bound to the earth without hope, undergoing nameless sufferings. This is the true meaning of hell, and man created it himself by hobbling his destiny.

SELECTED
BIBLIOGRAPHY

Angebert, Jean-Michel. *The Occult and the Third Reich.* New York: The Macmillan Company, 1974.

———. *The Mystical Origin of Nazism and the Search for the Holy Grail.* New York: The Macmillan Company, 1974.

Barrès, Maurice. *The Sacred Hill.* New York: Macauley, 1929.

Barruel, Abbé. *Spartacus Weishaupt, fondateur des Illumines de Bavière.* Paris: Éditions du Prieuré, 1994.

Bergier, Jacques, and Louis Pauwels. *The Morning of the Magicians.* Chelsea, Mich.: Scarborough House Publishing, 1991.

Bonnefoy, Yves. *Dictionary of Mythologies.* Chicago: Chicago University Press, 1991.

Boudet, Henri. *Le vrai langue celtique et le Cromleck of Rennes-le-Bains.* Paris: Belfond, 1978.

———. *Origine du nom de Narbonne et exemples d'interprétation des mots gaulois par les racines saxonnes et l'Anglais* (hors commerce, a consulter à la bibliothèque de Carcassonne).

Brion, Marcel. *Leonardo da Vinci.* Barcelona: Ediciones B, 2005.

———. *L'Allemagne romantique: le voyage initiatique.* Paris: Albin Michel, 1977.

Bulwer-Lytton, Sir Edward. *The Coming Race.* Toronto: Magoria Books, 2007.

———. *Zanoni, a Rosicrucian Tale.* Whitefish, Mont.: Kessinger Publishing, 1942.

Chailley, Jacques. *The Magic Flute Unveiled: Esoteric Symbolism in Mozart's Masonic Opera*. Rochester, Vt.: Inner Traditions, 1992.

Charpentier, Louis. *Mysteries of Charters Cathedral*. New York: Avon, 1980.

———. *Les mystères Templiers*. Paris: Robert Laffont, 1967.

Cherisey, Philippe de. *Circuit* (hors commerce).

———. *L'énigme de Rennes* (hors commerce).

Colonna, Francesco. *The Strife of Love in a Dream*. London: Thames & Hudson, 1999.

Delacroix, Eugène. *Journal de 1822 à 1863*. Paris: Plon, 1980.

Dumas, Alexandre. *La route de Varennes*. Paris: Nouvelles Éditions Baudinière, 1978.

———. *Captain Pamphile*. London: Hesperus Press, 2006.

———. *Adventures of Lyderic*. London: Kay & Ward, 1981.

Eliade, Mircea. *The Forge and the Crucible*. Chicago: University of Chicago, 1978.

———. *Le Chamanisme*. Payot, 1978.

Evola, Julius. *The Mystery of the Grail*. Rochester, Vt.: Inner Traditions, 1995.

———. *The Hermetic Tradition*. Rochester, Vt.: Inner Traditions, 1994.

———. *Revolt Against the Modern World: Politics, Religion, and Social Order in the Kali Yuga*. Rochester, Vt.: Inner Traditions, 1995.

Farmer, Philip-José. *The Other Log of Phileas Fogg*. New York: Tor Books, 1993.

Flaubert, Gustave. *The Temptation of Saint Antony*. New York: Random House, 1992.

France, Anatole. *The Romance of the Queen Pédauque*. New York: Three Sirens Press, 1931.

———. *The Amethyst Ring*. New York: Dodd Mead and Co., 1926.

———. *Revolt of the Angels*. Rockville, Md.: Wildside Press, 2003.

Gadal, Antonin. *On the Path of the Holy Grail*. Haarlem, Neth.: Rozekruis Press, 2006.

Goethe, Johann Wolfgang. *The Green Snake and the Beautiful Lily*. New York: New American Library, 1962.

Grasset, Antonin. *Cryptographic Materials*. Paris: B. Allieu Éditions, 1983.

Graves, Robert. *The White Goddess*. New York: Farrar, Strauss, and Giroux, 1966.

———. *The Greek Myths*. New York: Penguin, 1993.

Guénon, René. *Fundamental Symbols: The Universal Language of Sacred Science.* Cambridge: Quinta Essentia, 1995.

———. *Symbolism of the Cross.* London: Luzac, 1958.

———. *The King of the World.* Hillsdale, N.Y.: Sophia Perennis, 2004.

———. *The Great Triad.* Cambridge: Quinta Essentia, 1991.

Hays, George. *Necronomicon, le livre de l'arabe dément Abdul-Al-Hazred.* Paris: Belfond, 1976.

Hugo, Victor. *Shakespeare.* Honolulu: University Press of the Pacific, 2001.

Hutin, Serge. *Aleister Crowley, le plus grand des mages modernes.* Verviers, Belgium: Marabout, 1973.

———. *Underground Worlds with the King of the World.* Paris: Albin Michel, 1976.

———. *Gouvernants invisibles et sociétés secretes.* Paris: J'ai Lu, 1972.

———. *L'immortalité magique.* Paris: Marabout, 1976.

———. *Tous les secrets sont en nous.* Paris: Dervy, 1975.

King, Francis. *Ritual Magic and Secret Societies.* London: Mayflower Books, 1976.

LeBlanc, Maurice. Complete Opus.

Le Forestier, Rene. *La Franc-Maconnerie templiere et occultiste.* Paris: Aubier-Montaigne, 1970.

Leroux, Gaston. Complete Opus.

Levi, Eliphas. *The Key of the Mysteries.* York Beach, Me.: Weiser Books, 1972.

Machen, Arthur. *The Great God Pan.* London: Creation Books, 1991.

———. *White People.* New York: Knopf, 1922.

Nerval, Gerard de. Complete Opus.

Nodier, Charles. *Francisco Colonna.* Chicago: Lakeside Press, 1929.

Nostradamus. *Centuries.* Parkland, Fla.: Universal Publishers, 2000.

Oldenbourg, Zoé. *Massacre at Montségur.* London: Phoenix Press, 2001.

Ovide. *Metamorphoses.* New York: Oxford University Press, 1998.

Plantard De Saint-Clair, Pierre. Preface of *Le vrai langue celtique et le cromleck de Rennes-le-Bains.* Paris: Belfond, 1978.

Poe, Edgar Allan. *The Narrative of Arthur Gordon Pym of Nantucket.* Mineola, N.Y.: Dover Publications, 2005.

Rabelais, Francois. Complete Opus.

Rahn, Otto. *Crusade Against the Grail.* Rochester, Vt.: Inner Traditions, 2006.

Ravenscroft, Trevor. *Spear of Destiny.* York Beach, Me.: Weiser Books, 1982.

Roussel, Raymond. *Locus Solus*. New York: Riverrun Press, 1984.

Sabbarthes. *Dictionnaire topographique du departement de l'Aude comprenant les noms de lieux anciens et modernes*. 1912, reedition Philippe Schrauben.

Sand, George. Complete Opus.

Scott, Walter. *Letters on Demonology and Witchcraft*. Whitefish, Mont.: Kessinger, 1997.

Serullaz, Maurice. *Delacroix*. Paris: Fayard, 1989.

Steiner, Rudolf. *The Secret Stream: Christian Rosenkreutz and Rosicrucianism: Selected Lectures and Writings*. Great Barrington, Mass.: Bell Pond Books, 1980.

Stoker, Bram. *Dracula*. Cambridge, Mass.: Candlewick Press, 2004.

———. *The Joy of Seven Stars*. New York: Tor Classics, 1999.

Vadim, Roger. *Histoire de vampires*. Paris: Robert Laffont, 1961.

Verne, Jules. Complete Opus.

Verne, Jean-Jules. *Jules Verne*. London: Macdonald and Jane's, 1976.

Voragine, Jacques de. *The Golden Legend*. Princeton, N.J.: Princeton University Press, 1995.

Wirth, O. *La Franc-Maconnerie rendue intelligible a ses adeptes*. Paris: Dervy, 1978.

THE NOVELS OF JULES VERNE

Joyeuses Misères de trois voyageurs en Scandinavie (1861)

Five Weeks in a Balloon (1863)

The English at the North Pole/The Field of Ice (1864)

Journey to the Center of the Earth (1864)

From the Earth to the Moon (1865)

In Search of the Castaways (1867–68)

Twenty Thousand Leagues under the Sea (1869–70)

Round the Moon (1870)

Uncle Robinson (1874–75)

A Floating City (1871)

Adventures de trois Russes et trois Anglais (1872)

The Fur Country (1873)

Around the World in Eighty days (1873)

The Mysterious Island (1874–75)

The Survivors of the Chancellor (1875)

Michael Strogoff (1876)

Off on a Comet (1877)

The Underground City or The Black Indies (1877)

Dick Sands and the Boy Captain (1878)

The Begum's Fortune (1879)

Tribulations of a Chinaman in China (1879)

The Steam House (1880)

Eight Hundred Leagues on the Amazon (1881)

L'École des Robinsons (1882)

Green Ray (1882)

Keraban the Terrible (1883)

L'Étoile du sud (1884)

L'Archipel en feu (1884)

Mathias Sandorf (1885)

Ticket No. "9672" (1885)

The Waif of the "Cynthia" (1885)

Clipper of the Clouds (1886)

Nord contre Sud (1887)

Le Chemin de France (1887)

Deus Ans de vacances (1888)

Famille-sans-nom (1889)

Topsy Turvy (1889)

César Cascabel (1890)

Mistress Branican (1891)

The Castle of the Carpathians (1892)

The Adventures of a Special Correspondent (1892)

Mirifiques Adventures de Maître Anifer (1893)

P'tit-Bonhomme (1893)

L'Île à hélice (1895)

Facing the Flag (1896)

Clovis Dardentor (1896)

An Antarctic Mystery (1897)

Le Superbe Orénoque (1898)

Le Testament d'un excentrique (1899)

Seconde patrie (1900)

Village in the Treetops (1901)

Les Histoires de Jean-Marie Cabidoulin (1901)

The Kip Brothers (1902)

Traveling Scholarships (1903)

Drama in Livonia (1904)

Master of the World (1904)

Volcano of Gold (1906)

Hunt for the Meteor (1908)

The Danube Pilot (1908)

The Secret of Wilhelm Storitz (1910)

INDEX